# Green Consumption in China



Based on theories discussion, policy analysis, and case studies, this title examines green consumption in China from both the macro level of policy evolution and the micro level of community participation and implementation.

Drawing on the theories of sustainable development, ecological philosophy, environmental economics, consumer psychology and behavior, and community participation, this book approaches the issues of green consumption in China from the legislative and administrative aspects and economic and information means. In looking into the cases of Shenzhen and Beijing, the book unravels the implementation and development of green consumption at the community level in terms of community participation and people's awareness of the issue. Combining global experiences and local empirical studies, it discusses the concepts, evolution, and influencing factors of green consumption. It focuses on China's policy and practice, as well as the institutional hindrance and policy suggestions for further progress.

This book will appeal to researchers, professionals, and policymakers interested in sustainable development, green economy, environmental economics, and sustainable consumption policy in China.

**Jin Min**, Professor at the School of Environment and Natural Resources, Renmin University of China and Member of the ISO Professional Committee of Waste Collection and Transportation Management (ISO/TC 297). Her research focuses on environment and resources policy, green economy, and sustainable production and consumption.

# Green Consumption in China

## Policy and Practice

**Jin Min**

Routledge
Taylor & Francis Group
LONDON AND NEW YORK

This book is funded by China Classics International.

First published in English 2024
by Routledge
4 Park Square, Milton Park, Abingdon, Oxon OX14 4RN

and by Routledge
605 Third Avenue, New York, NY 10158

*Routledge is an imprint of the Taylor & Francis Group, an informa business*



*British Library Cataloguing-in-Publication Data*
A catalogue record for this book is available from the British Library

*Library of Congress Cataloging-in-Publication Data*
Names: Jin, Min, 1967– author.
Title: Green consumption in China : policy and practice / Jin Min.
Other titles: Zhongguo lü se xiao fei zheng ce yan jiu. English
Description: Abingdon, Oxon ; New York, NY : Routledge, 2024. | Includes bibliographical references and index.
Identifiers: LCCN 2023014797 (print) | LCCN 2023014798 (ebook) | ISBN 9781032559476 (hardback) | ISBN 9781032559520 (paperback) | ISBN 9781003433040 (ebook)
Subjects: LCSH: Sustainable development—China. | Environmental economics—China. | Environmental policy—China. | Consumer behavior—China.
Classification: LCC HC430.E5 J5513 2024 (print) | LCC HC430.E5 (ebook) | DDC 333.70951—dc23/eng/20230424
LC record available at https://lccn.loc.gov/2023014797
LC ebook record available at https://lccn.loc.gov/2023014798

ISBN: 978-1-032-55947-6 (hbk)
ISBN: 978-1-032-55952-0 (pbk)
ISBN: 978-1-003-43304-0 (ebk)

DOI: 10.4324/9781003433040

Typeset in Times New Roman
by codeMantra

# Contents

# Figures

# Tables

# Preface to the Chinese Edition

As a new philosophy of consumption, green consumption is of great practical significance for optimizing and upgrading China's industrial structures, making Chinese products more internationally competitive, bringing an ecological perspective to consumption habits, promoting ecological progress in China, as well as achieving the sustainable economic development in China. In 2016, ten government ministries and commissions including the National Development and Reform Commission jointly issued the *Guiding Opinions on Promoting Green Consumption*, drawing up overall plans for promoting green consumption, which marks that green consumption is upgraded as a state-level issue.

Based on the theories of sustainable development, ecological philosophy, environmental economics, consumer psychology and consumer behavior, community engagement, etc., this book summarizes the advanced experience of international green consumption from four aspects: laws and regulations related to promoting green consumption, government green procurement, economic means, and information means. In conjunction with the practices of green consumption in China as well as specific policies, this book discusses China's policy on green consumption and its history, the improvement of green consumption policies as well as existing problems, and comes up with ways to solve problems, in order to offer refreshing ideas and perspectives for the sustainable development of China's economy and better living standards for the people. In light of the actual needs, this book uses the theory of community engagement to conduct an empirical study on the residents' awareness of green consumption, and explores the practices of green consumption at the community level in China. First of all, the book outlines the development status of green communities in China in the case of Shenzhen, and conducts case studies according to the corresponding assessment criteria. Second, a field survey was conducted on the current awareness of green consumption among community residents in Beijing through empirical research in light of Beijing policies on green consumption. Finally, from the perspective of the overall framework and community level regarding green consumption in China, the book explores how to effectively combine theory of green consumption with community engagement theory, and discusses how to initiate community sustainable consumption, so as to guide and facilitate the establishment and improvement of policy mechanism for community sustainable consumption.

The study and exploration of green consumption in this book is of theoretical and practical significance. At the theoretical level, the study of green consumption can bring diversity to ecological philosophical theory and help to explore the theory of ecological laws and sustainable development, which conforms to the view of ecological ethic consumption. In light of the actual needs, this book employs the theory of community engagement to conduct empirical research on the awareness of green consumption among community residents. Following the survey on the sustainable consumption and current policy among community residents, green consumption theory is combined with community engagement theory under the existing system of green consumption theory. In practice, on the basis of analyzing developed countries' experience in promoting green consumption and in light of China's reality, this book makes suggestions for promoting green consumption in terms of policy mechanisms, which acts as a basis for relevant government bodies to formulate the line, principles, and policies for promoting green consumption in China. Furthermore, based on the findings of the research *Survey on Sustainable Consumption Awareness among Community Households in Beijing and Policy Advocacy Project* jointly conducted by All-China Environment Federation and the United Nations Environment Programme (UNEP), the author conducted field research on the existing community management model, which exposes the weaknesses of the existing management model, seeks the areas for piloting sustainable consumption in communities, improves the management model of community sustainable consumption, and explores the effective ways for sustainable consumption for community residents.

The book's study on sustainable consumption in Beijing communities is based on the outcomes of a project by the UNEP. Our thanks go to Secretary General Xie Yuhong, Ms. Li Lei, and Ms. Gao Xiaoyi from All-China Environment Federation; Associate Professor Su Mingming from the School of Environment and Natural Resources of Renmin University of China; the members of the expert advisory team of the project, namely, Janet Salem (Project Officer, UNEP Regional Office for Asia and the Pacific), Ma Zhong (Former Dean of School of Environment and Natural Resources of Renmin University of China), Xia Kunbao (council member of All-China Environment Federation), Chen Shaofeng (Research Fellow, Institute of Science and Technology, Chinese Academy of Sciences), Shen Xiaoyue (Director of Environmental Economy and Management Policy Division, Policy Research Center for Environment and Economy, Ministry of Ecology and Environment of China), Du Huanzheng (Professor, Director of Yangtze River Delta Technology Institute for Circular Economy), Shi Lingling (a lecturer at Beijing Normal University), Wang Xiaohong (senior statistician, Urban Affairs Department, National Bureau of Statistics), Cui Dapeng (Special Research Fellow, Sustainable Development Research Center, Chinese Academy of Social Sciences), Lin Ling (President of Resources and Environment Branch of China National Institute of Standardization), Zhou Hongchun (Department of Social Development Research, Development Research Center of the State Council), as well as volunteers from Renmin University of China including Zhao Haoyang, Kong Lingxi, Guo Jiajia, Zhu Tingting, Cheng Bin, Cheng Yang, Gao Minghui, He Xin, Wunierbieke, and Zhou Yang. Our thanks also go to Dr. Guo Jiajia, of the School of Environment and Natural Resources of Renmin University of China, for the final compilation, editing, and proofreading.

# Acknowledgments

Dr. Guo Jiajia, lecturer at Xi'an University of Finance and Economics, China, assisted in the collection and collation of materials during the compilation of this book and completed the collation and collation of the whole book at the time of publication of the Chinese Version. Here I would like to express my gratitude.

# 1 Introduction

Since the dawn of the industrial society, the production capacity has been vastly improved, the global economy has been developing at a fast clip, and the ways people work, live, and make consumption have undergone revolutionary changes. While human beings enjoy the fruits of industrial civilization, they neglect to protect the earth's environment. Since the 1980s, the environmental problems with global implications have become increasingly conspicuous. The global environmental crises such as the greenhouse effect, ozone depletion, rapidly dwindling forests, land desertification, and acid rain have posed grave risks to the survival and development of mankind. In order to save the earth's environment, the international community has forged wide-ranging cooperative relationships in economic, political, scientific, and technological, trade, and other spheres, and has put in place a huge system of international environmental treaties to address the environmental issues. However, the environmental problems remain intractable principally because of the externality of market-oriented economic activities and the public nature of the natural environment.

In the face of the deteriorating ecological environment, many countries have begun to reflect on the strategies, policies, and actions they took. As the concept of full life-cycle gains recognition, consumption has become increasingly important for tackling environmental problems, and the green consumption emerges accordingly. Since the 1980s, the developed countries and regions have formulated a full range of policies to promote the green consumption and achieved good results. This concept attracted wide recognition and response at the United Nations Conference on Environment and Development (UNCED) held in Rio de Janeiro in 1992. *Agenda 21* adopted by the General Assembly stated that "All the countries should strive to promote sustainable consumption patterns."[1]

China's current situation of consumption has put enormous pressures on the ecological environment. In addition to promoting the green development of economy, the green consumption will also speed up the building of an ecological society and contribute to the building of a resource-conserving, environment-friendly society. The 18th and 19th National Congresses of the Communist Party of China (CPC) put forward the concept of green development, marking that the Chinese government regards the green consumption as a national strategy. The need to promote the green consumption, move faster to build a conservation culture, and promote the

DOI: 10.4324/9781003433040-1

green development of economy and society is put forward in the government documents such as *the Opinions of the CPC Central Committee and the State Council on Accelerating the Construction of Ecological Civilization, the Overall Plan for the Reform of the Ecological Civilization System*, and *the Guiding Opinions of the State Council on Actively Playing the Leading Role of New Consumption and Accelerating the Cultivation of New Supply and New Driving Power.*

To this end, ten government bodies including the National Development and Reform Commission jointly formulated and issued *the Guiding Opinions on Promoting Green Consumption*, whereby residents are guided to pursue a green way of life and consumption pattern. Therefore, it is of great significance to study and explore the concept of the green consumption, the emergence and development of green consumption at home and abroad, and analyze the factors that spur the green consumption.

## 1.1 The concept and connotations of green consumption

At present, there is no unified definition of green consumption. The concepts of sustainable consumption, ecological consumption, low-carbon consumption, etc., often come up as we criticize the consumerism and respond to the global ecological crises. It is, therefore, necessary to analyze the background and definition of these concepts, as well as their logical relationship, thereby gaining a better idea of the connotation of green consumption.

### *1.1.1 The concept of green consumption*

At present, there is no unified definition of green consumption in China.

The green consumption was first defined in *the Green Consumer Guide*, produced in 1987 by the British scholars Elkington and Hailes. According to the definition, the green consumption is a type of consumption that avoids the use of the following commodities: (1) the commodities that endanger the health of consumers and others; (2) the commodities that consume a large number of resources in the process of being produced, used and discarded; (3) the commodities that are unnecessarily consumed due to excessive packaging that exceeds commodity value or an excessively short life-cycle; (4) the commodities derived from rare animals or natural resources; (5) the commodities produced as a result of cruelty to or unnecessary deprivation of animals; and (6) the commodities that adversely affect other countries, particularly the developing countries.[2]

The Oslo Symposium on Sustainable Consumption, held in Oslo, Norway in 1994, gave the most authoritative definition of green consumption: The green consumption refers to the use of goods and services that respond to basic needs and bring a better quality of life while minimizing the use of natural resources, toxic materials, and emissions of waste and pollutants over the life-cycle, so as not to jeopardize the needs of future generations.

Some Chinese scholars and researchers have also preliminarily defined the green consumption from various dimensions. The concept of green consumption was first advanced by China Consumers Association, which covers three areas: In the process of consumption, the green consumption advocates that consumers choose the environmentally friendly products that are beneficial to their own health. In everyday life, the green consumption advocates that consumers save resources such as water and electricity, and rationally dispose of the domestic garbage. In terms of ideology, the green consumption guides consumers to adopt correct values, and respect nature as well as the environment. The Green Mile Studio, a non-governmental organization, defines the green consumption as a new idea of following the laws of ecology in order to accomplish the dual goals of developing the economy and protecting the environment. This definition shows the essence of green consumption: The green consumption is a guiding philosophy and idea. The most representative concept of green consumption is the "5R" principle, which stands for saving resources and reducing pollution (reduce); making green shopping (re-evaluate); reusing and multi-reusing (reuse); garbage sorting and recycling (recycle); protecting nature and all things coexisting (rescue).[3]

In summary, this book defines the green consumption as follows: consuming behaviors characterized by saving resources and protecting the environment, choosing efficient and environmentally friendly products and services, reducing resource consumption and emissions, and applying the concept of energy saving and environmental protection throughout the consumption.

The scope of research in this book focuses on three areas: green travel, garbage sorting, resource conservation, and green purchase. In terms of production, the book focuses on new energy and small-displacement vehicles, an area intimately related to the green consumption and green travel, and also the focus of government policy. In terms of disposal, the book focuses on the waste recycling and garbage sorting, which are closely related to the development of a circular economy. Resource conservation and green purchase are also key areas in the national policy.

### *1.1.2 Differentiation and analysis of relevant concepts*

In addition to the green consumption, terms such as sustainable consumption, low-carbon consumption, and ecological consumption are often seen in theoretical researches, media reports, and some other official documents. These concepts are somewhat related to the green consumption. The common denominators for the green consumption, sustainable consumption, low-carbon consumption, and ecological consumption are that the objects of consumption are low-pollution, low-energy-consuming green products and services, and these four patterns of consumption concern the relationship between man and nature.

#### *1.1.2.1 Sustainable consumption*

Internationally, there is no uniform definition of sustainable consumption. The most authoritative definition was given in the report of *the Policy Factors for Sustainable Consumption* published by the United Nations Environment Programme

(UNEP) in Nairobi in 1994. For the first time, the report defines the sustainable consumption as

> the use of goods and services that respond to basic needs and bring a better quality of life, while minimizing the use of natural resources, toxic materials and emissions of waste and pollutants over the life cycle, so as not to jeopardize the needs of future generations.[4]

The report notes that sustainable consumption is not a compromise between under-consumption due to poverty and over-consumption owing to affluence, but rather a new and rational pattern of consumption that applies to people at different income levels in the countries around the world.

The connotation of sustainable consumption is mainly manifested in the following three areas:

> From the perspective of goal, the sustainable consumption and sustainable development share the same goal of achieving the decoupling of economic growth and environmental degradation, improving the quality of life without leading to environmental degradation and competition for natural resources against the future generations, and promoting the social and economic development within the bearing capacity of the ecosystem.

The core of sustainable consumption is to reflect the concept of resource conservation and environmental protection, especially the concept of the full life-cycle, in production and consumption throughout, tighten the sustainable management of natural resources, and promote sustainable consumption and production in an all-round manner through various channels.[5] The sustainable consumption and production cover products and services throughout the full life-cycle of production and consumption, encompassing resource extraction, production input, distribution, sales, use, waste disposal, and reuse, so as to realize efficient use of resources and low pollutant discharge, and avoid the "zero transfer" of pollutants that lead to resource and energy consumption between different links of production and consumption in different regions.[6]

In terms of approaches, the sustainable consumption upholds "efficiency enhancement" and "pattern transformation." The sustainable consumption and production involve the improvement of resource, energy, and ecological efficiency in the production, marketing, use, and recycling of products. *The Johannesburg Plan of Implementation* adopted at the Earth Summit held in Johannesburg, South Africa, in 2002 emphasized the "more efficient consumption." Increasing efficiency will expand the aggregate scale. This is the "rebound effect." While improving efficiency, it is necessary to promote a shift in consumption pattern towards low-energy and low-material-intensity commodities and services[7] by changing the consumption behaviors and ways of life, so as to avoid the effect of efficiency enhancement being offset by the increased total consumption.[8]

The common denominators of the sustainable consumption and green consumption are that both pay attention to the impact of consumption on the natural environment and advocate the consumption of pollution-free commodities, pollution-free consumption, and conscious boycott and non-consumption of commodities and services that damage the environment or waste a lot of resources.

The differences between the sustainable consumption and green consumption are: (1) The origins of the two are different. From the perspective of their origins, the green consumption came before the sustainable consumption. After 30 years of development of the green consumption, people have advanced the concept of sustainable consumption on the basis of the theoretical exploration and practice. Therefore, the concept of green consumption is earlier and more mature.

(2) The scope of application is different. The sustainable consumption is an updated version of the green consumption and is more popular internationally. The concepts and connotations of the two are slightly different, but the green consumption is more in line with the reality of China. Therefore, this book focuses on the green consumption.

#### *1.1.2.2 The low-carbon consumption*

The common denominators between the green consumption and low-carbon consumption are that both consider the impact of consumption behaviors on the environment, pay attention to the relationship between man and nature, and pursue the goal of establishing a harmonious relationship between the economic society and the ecological environment. The low-carbon consumption is more targeted. It addresses the problem of unsustainable consumption from the perspective of carbon emissions, giving consideration to products, as well as the consumption behaviors and process, which has a stronger restraining effect on the consumption.[9]

The differences between the green consumption and low-carbon consumption are that (1) the starting points of the two are different. The low-carbon consumption focuses only on the impact of consumption on the environment, that is, the ecological dimension. In comparison, the green consumption pattern pays attention to the relationship between people as well as the relationship between man and nature, and its fundamental goal is to meet the people's growing demand for quality of life in the context of many constraints. The sustainable consumption is studied from many dimensions, including economy and society as well as ecology. (2) The goals of the two are different. Under the low-carbon consumption pattern, the carbon footprint of the targets of consumption and the consumption process is an important factor affecting consumers. The low-carbon consumption has the sole goal of reducing carbon emissions and slowing down the trend of climate warming. In comparison, the green consumption focuses on the overall impact on the environmental resources and requires consumers to ensure resource conservation and environmental friendliness when choosing the targets of consumption and consumption patterns, rather than paying attention to only the amount of carbon emitted. (3) The scope of the two is different. Despite a lack of accurate definition of low-carbon consumption, most scholars believe that low-carbon consumption involves both consumption of consumer services and consumption of producer services.[10] The green consumption requires that the products or services do not cause damage to the environment or other members of society in the process of use and will not generate excessive waste harmful to the environment after the use. In comparison, on the basis of green consumption, low-carbon consumption also requires that product production process and raw materials are environmentally friendly, cause waste in the production process as little as possible, can be recycled, and are harmless to the environment.

### *1.1.2.3 Ecological consumption*

The ecological consumption is a type of consumption that can continuously improve people's quality of life, with a moderate level of consumption, a reasonable consumption structure, and a healthy and green consumption pattern. It meets the needs of people of current generation without any prejudice to the consumption rights of other contemporaries and future generations. It is a type of consumption that balances economy, population, resources, and the environment and that promotes the all-round development of people.[11]

The common denominators between the green consumption and ecological consumption are as follows: Both emphasize that consumer goods will not cause harm to other members of society and the surrounding environment in the process of use and will not generate excessive residues that cause damages to the environment after use.

The differences between the green consumption and ecological consumption are: (1) The goals of the two are different. The goal of ecological consumption is to build a conservation culture, not to meet the consumption needs of human beings. The goal of green consumption is to meet the need for human development to the greatest extent under the premise of protecting environmental resources. (2) The targets of the two are different. Under the ecological consumption pattern, man is situated in the ecosystem as an integral part, rather than as an objective existence outside the ecosystem.[12] Although the green consumption places a high value on the balance between man and nature and pays attention to the improvement of the ecological environment, it emphasizes that the main subject in consumption is human beings, and the goal is to meet the consumption needs of human beings, reflecting the values of anthropocentrism. On the whole, compared with the low-carbon consumption and ecological consumption, the green consumption places a greater emphasis on the relationship between people, takes account of the economic and social dimensions, and argues that people are objective existence outside the ecosystem and have a higher status. The green consumption and sustainable consumption are of little difference in terms of concept and connotation, but the green consumption is more in line with the current reality of China and its future development, and enjoys historical, political, and mass support. Therefore, the theme of research in this book is China's policies on the green consumption. It specifically refers to the regulation and control policies implemented by the government through administrative means, economic means, and information means.

### *1.1.3 The extended connotation of green consumption*

From the perspective of the consumption process, the green consumption includes four links: concept, purchase, consumption, and disposal. First, the concept of green consumption is established. The green development is a necessary condition for the successful transformation of the economy. As a component of green development, the green consumption is an important path to building a resource-conserving, environment-friendly society. The green consumption should help consumers to develop a belief in the green consumption and guide consumers to pay attention to green information on their own initiative, purchase green products and services, and pursue a green way of life. Second, take the initiative to choose green products and services. Green products and services are the generic term for products and services that help protect the ecological environment and save resources and that are pollution-free, non-toxic, and beneficial to human health. Third, do not waste resources or pollute the environment as much as possible when making consumption. Consumers should have green consumption awareness and make green consumption, such as avoiding the use of disposable chopsticks and disposable meal boxes, using environmentally friendly shopping bags, and saying no to over-packaged products. Fourth, optimize the disposal of residues after consumption, reduce secondary pollution, and lessen the burden on the ecological environment. As the economy and overall purchasing power grow, the needs of consumers become increasingly diversified, and the quantity and variety of products as well as services are gradually increasing, but the resulting waste becomes a major burden on the ecological environment. Therefore, a reasonable treatment of waste is a key part of improving the process of green consumption by helping the operation of recycling and treatment enterprises, and reducing the secondary pollution to the environment.

From the perspective of consumption purpose, the green consumption can achieve the dual goals of protecting the environment and developing the economy. The green consumption emerges and develops in the context that human activities have inflicted great destruction on the ecological environment and interfered with the normal life and human health. Therefore, practicing the green consumption is somewhat passive. The limited natural resources and irreversible environmental damage compel the transformation of consumption pattern, and its passive purpose is to conserve the natural resources and improve the ecological environment. The relationship between the supply and demand is a key lever for regulating the market-oriented economy. The consumer demand can affect the production, supply, and modes of production to a certain extent. In the context of green development, the green consumption is advocated in order to transform the pattern of economic development at the consumption level. Therefore, the active purpose of green consumption is to promote the stable economic development and ensure the well-being of human beings.

## 1.2 The emergence and development of international green consumption

In the 17th century, the British scientist and philosopher Francis Bacon advanced the slogan that "knowledge itself is power." Transforming nature and acquiring material wealth from nature become the common value orientation of industrial civilization. In the 19th century, the thinker Friedrich Engels cautioned that the irrational use of and the transformation of nature by humanity will put human beings in a plight that is difficult to change. Despite this warning, many people still regard nature as a source of inexhaustible resources for humanity and believe that human beings face such a plight because of their limited capacity, and therefore, further efforts are needed to transform nature. As industrial civilization continuously advances, mankind faces tremendous challenges in resources and the environment while enjoying the glorious achievements and abundant material wealth created by industrial civilization. As the ecological crisis worsens, it has dawned on humanity that the current mode of consumption is irrational. As a result, green consumption, a mode of consumption that adapts to the requirements of nature and society, comes into being.

### *1.2.1 Proposal of green consumption*

In 1987, Mrs. Gro Harlem Brundtland, the then Norwegian Prime Minister, advanced the concept of sustainable development in *Our Common Future*. In 1992, the *Rio Declaration on Environment and Development* and *Agenda 21*, adopted at the United Nations Conference on Environment and Development, explicitly called for a reversal of unsustainable consumption modes. At the Organization for Economic Co-operation and Development (OECD) meeting held in 1994, the United Nations Commission on Sustainable Development (CSD) called for a viable plan for green consumption and production patterns.[13] As a result, governments and theoretical circles in many countries pay attention to and study green consumption as a strategic issue for pursuing sustainable development.

In December 2009, a United Nations climate conference was held in Copenhagen, Denmark. The concepts such as climate change, low-carbon economy, and low-carbon life have become household names thanks to the great importance attached by governments as well as widespread media coverage. The frequent occurrences of extreme climate events such as low temperature, droughts, and floods have made consumers in all countries aware of the necessity of pursuing green consumption.

The UNEP set the theme of the 41st World Environment Day in 2012 as "Green Economy: Does it include you?" Its purpose is to guide people to practice green economy in life, drive the sound transformation of society, and meet the growing needs of people for consumption. Western theoretical circles generally believe that green consumption, like sustainable consumption, eco-consumption, and low-carbon consumption, advocates moderate consumption, and draws attention to the impact of consumption behavior on the ecological environment. It is a new type of consumption. Western society has been fully aware of the weaknesses of traditional consumption patterns and opposed excessive consumption, stressing that consumer behavior and its impact on the environment are a concrete manifestation of the sustainable development strategy.

### *1.2.2 International development process of green consumption*

In the 1980s, Britain launched a green consumption campaign to encourage residents to opt for eco-friendly commodities and guide production enterprises to produce and manufacture goods under the premise of environmental protection. Thereafter, developed countries, particularly European Union (EU) member states, have advocated and promoted green consumption, so that green consumption is embraced around the world and becomes a more popular and practical new consumption mode.

According to a survey conducted by the European Community in 1992, the majority of Germans and Dutch people opt for commodities with less detrimental effects on the environment while shopping, and 66 percent of British consumers are willing to buy green goods at a premium. About two-fifths of Europeans tend to buy commodities that pass the standard certification, and most residents in the United States prefer organic fruit and vegetables. Since 1997, the international community has conducted a slew of activities with the theme of "sustainable development and green consumption." According to statistics from the OECD, by 1998, the world's total spending on green consumption reached US$200 billion. According to a survey conducted by the United Nations, by 1999, the world's total spending on green consumption reached US$300 billion; nearly 90 percent of consumers in Germany, the Netherlands, and the United States would consider the environmental impact when shopping for commodities; most Swedish residents would opt for highly priced eco-friendly commodities conducive to saving resources and energy; 80 percent of Canadians could accept eco-friendly products with a price 10 percent higher than that of ordinary commodities; and most Japanese people only preferred eco-friendly products.[14]

At the same time, green food is also favored in all countries. Back in the 1990s, the demand for green food in developed countries grew at a rate of over 20 percent per year. In 1994, Switzerland produced eco-friendly apparel that was immensely popular. An increasing variety of green goods are available in the international market. From the end of the 20th century and early 21st century, the craze for green roofs swept some countries. Trees and flowers grew on the rooftops in Paris. A wealth of green residential areas in London, bonsai gardens in Canada, and roof gardens in Japan and Germany had been built.

In developed countries, national policies play a huge role in promoting green consumption. Below is the example of green consumption of electronic and electrical products in the EU. The EU strategy for waste management adopted on February 24, 1997 called for the enactment of a special law on electronic waste as soon as possible. The EU promulgated the EU Directive on Waste of Electronic and Electrical Equipment (WEEE Directive) on October 11, 2002. The *On the Restriction of the Use of Certain Hazardous Substances in Electrical and Electronic Equipment* (RoHS Directive), also known as 2002/95/EC Directive, was adopted in January 2003. In 2005, the EU supplemented the 2002/95/EC in the form of Resolution 2005/618/EC, stipulating maximum limits for six hazardous substances. The WEEE Directive and the RoHS Directive were officially implemented on August

13, 2004 and July 1, 2006, respectively. Following the WEEE Directive and the RoHS Directive, the EU issued the EU Directive on Energy-using Products (EuP), requiring Member States to lay down specific requirements for related products at the latest before August 11, 2007, and adopt these as national laws, so as to ensure the effective operation of the EuP. By this time, the EU had released the WEEE, RoHS, and EuP directives for trade in household products. The EU released the amendment proposals for the WEEE Directive and RoHS Directive at the end of 2008 and upgraded the EuP Directive as the Energy-related Products (ErP Directive) in 2009, which further regulates and improves the circular economy development for household products.[15]

#### *1.2.2.1 The United States: from excessive consumption and huge emissions to moderate consumption and waste reduction*

The United States is a country with a vast territory, abundant resources, and developed science and technology. Due to the huge material wealth, Americans gradually developed the habit of making excessive consumption. In order to satisfy material interests, individuals and enterprises consumed natural resources immoderately, causing huge waste of resources and serious environmental pollution. Long-term over-consumption and wasteful practices caused an enormous discharge of waste. According to statistics, the United States produced 12 to 14 billion metric tons of solid waste, making it the world's biggest generator of waste,[16] and its $CO_2$ emissions accounted one-fourth of the global total. In view of this, the United States began to move towards moderate consumption and waste reduction since the 1970s. The *Solid Waste Disposal Act* (SWDA) of 1965 mandates nationwide control of land contamination by solid wastes in the United States, the protection of public health and the environment, and the rational recycling and reuse of waste. It also requires all states to formulate corresponding laws and plans to promote the recycling of wastes. The SWDA had been amended several times and was renamed the *Resource Conservation and Recovery Act*. The U.S. government promotes circular economy initiatives at the federal, state, and local levels to guide the public and businesses to develop the circular economy. For example, the U.S. Environmental Protection Agency launched the Resource Conservation Challenge program to conserve natural resources and energy through more effective management. The priorities of the program are: the recycling of municipal solid waste; reuse and recycling of industrial raw materials; the reduction of hazardous substances in products and wastes; the "greening" of products, particularly in the design and recycling of electronic products. The waste initiative is designed to cut municipal solid waste by preventing the generation of waste, recycling and purchasing recycled products, etc. The Coal Combustion Products Partnership aims to utilize the by-products such as coal ash and coal cinder as a result of coal combustion in coal-fired power plants.

The American circular economy practice was pioneered by large multinational corporations. DuPont can be said to be a leading enterprise in developing the circular economy in the United States. Founded in 1802 in Delaware, the United

States, as a global company based on scientific research, DuPont offers scientific solutions to improve the quality of life for people in areas such as food and nutrition, health care, apparel, home as well as construction, electronics, and transport. DuPont creatively upgraded the "3R" principle of the circular economy into the industry-oriented "3R manufacturing method" to achieve environmental protection goals of little or even zero emissions. For example, the company recovers chemicals from waste plastics through the circulation of materials among processes within the enterprise and develops multi-purpose ethylene products. Thanks to the methods such as no use of some environmentally harmful chemicals and the reduced use of chemical substances, the waste caused by production in 1994 decreased by 25 percent compared with that at the end of the 1980s, and air pollutant emissions were reduced by 70 percent. Through the use of approaches and technologies such as the whole-process production control, pyrolysis, and energy-saving efficiency method, greenhouse gases equivalent to 61 million metric tons of $CO_2$ had been reduced.[17]

In addition, with the support of the U.S. Environmental Protection Agency and other organizations, eco-industrial parks that cover the development and utilization of new energy, waste treatment and reuse, etc., emerged and then developed apace after 1993. The "Eco-Industrial Park Task Force" laid a better foundation for their development. In 1994, the U.S. Environmental Protection Agency and the Eco-Industrial Park Task Force designated four communities as demonstration sites for eco-industrial parks (2).[18] As a result of the popular idea of global sustainable development and the pressure on the ecological environment caused by huge wastes, the United States gradually realized the importance of moderate consumption. The prevailing environmentalist ideas in the United States have also prompted consumers to embrace green consumption.

#### *1.2.2.2 Germany: promote the guidance of green consumption by facilitating the establishment of environmental protection labeling system*

Germany launched the "Blue Angel" initiative in 1977, and its environmental label was introduced in 1978, making it the first country in the world to establish a national environmental protection labeling system. It made clear the goal of guiding consumers to make green consumption, encouraging green production by enterprises and guiding green markets through environmental policies. With the environmental protection labeling as the market orientation, Germany guides consumers to buy products with less detrimental impact on the environment, so as to encourage manufacturers to produce eco-friendly products and improve environmental quality. Germany enacted the *Electricity Transmission Act* in 1990, which mandated electricity operators to purchase renewable energy-based electricity produced by residents covered by their power supply services. In 2000, it enacted the *Renewable Energy Act*. At the same time, tightening the extended supervision and management of product responsibility is another approach for Germany to advocate green consumption. In accordance with Germany's *Closed Substance Cycle and Waste Management Act*, production enterprises are responsible for their products and must ensure that the entire production process of products meets the overall goal of the circular economy. Enterprises bear the costs incurred as a result of the development, production, and sale of products as well as waste recycling. Therefore, while organizing production and operations, producers should take the initiative to choose green materials and also reduce the amount of waste. The products produced and processed should be reused and also accompanied by recycling instructions that comply with relevant regulations. Any hazardous substances contained must be clearly marked. Germany also implements policies on the collection of garbage disposal fees and the return of collateral, which promote green consumption. According to Germany's packaging collateral system, customers are required to pay additional collateral when purchasing commodities with a packaging recovery rate of less than 72 percent. Moreover, where the amount of packaging or containers exceeds the preset standard, the customer is required to pay double collateral, which is returned only when the customer returns containers as required.[19] On August 8, 2007, the German government adopted the *Energy-using Products Act* (EBPG), translating the EuP Directive into German law as required by the EU, so as to ensure the implementation of the EU directive in Germany.[20] Germany is a leader in terms of the circular economy, and the concept of green consumption enjoys popular support thanks to the sound green consumption policy and the circular economy system.

#### *1.2.2.3 Japan: promote green consumption by enacting and implementing relevant laws and regulations*

Japan is an outstanding latecomer in industrialization, which was completed in Japan over a period of more than 100 years compared to nearly 300 years in Europe and the United States. At the same time, Japan was a victim of ecological damage and environmental pollution. In order to transform a way of life featuring mass consumption into a post-industrial lifestyle of optimal consumption, Japan has done a lot to promote green consumption.

Japan has established a sound legal system governing green consumption. The overall framework for building a circular economy consists of three levels: the basic level is a basic law – the *Basic Act for Establishing a Sound Material-Cycle Society*. The second level refers to the two comprehensive laws: *Waste Disposal Act* and the *Act on the Promotion of Effective Utilization of Resources*. The third level is special laws, including: (1) *Green Purchasing Law*, a comprehensive law for advocacy procurement at the material input end of the "closed-loop" economy for materials. (2) For the material output end of the circular economy, five pieces of laws and regulations were enacted according to the nature of products: the *Law for the Promotion of Sorted Collection and Recycling of Containers and Packaging*, *Home Appliance Recycling Act*, *Food Recycling Act*, *Construction Materials Recycling Law*, and *Automobile Recycling Law*.[21] Through these laws and regulations, Japan has established a complete and mutually supportive system at different levels, creating a favorable social environment for Japan to build a circular economy and promote green consumption.

The *Basic Act for Establishing a Sound Material-Cycle Society* stipulates responsibilities for the state, local governments, enterprises, and individuals. Encouraging the use of recycled products is the most basic component of Japan's system of regulations for a sustainable recycling-oriented society. At the same time, Japan enacted the *Green Consumption Law* and the *Green Purchasing Law* in 2001 and 2002 respectively, which require consumers to follow the principles of green consumption when making consumption or purchasing and to purchase commodities with less detrimental impact on the ecological environment. Governments at all levels should practice green purchasing and inform consumers of information about green products to promote a transformation in market supply and demand as well as people's consumption habits.

Over 60 percent of Japanese citizens often opt for products conducive to ecological environmental protection, according to a survey conducted by Japan on the implementation of green consumption in 2005. Nearly half of consumers tend to buy eco-friendly commodities when there is no difference in product price. At the same time, "ecological cabinets" and "ecological corners" that exclusively provide green commodities are set in shopping malls and supermarkets in Japan. Enterprises have also established a sound green purchasing network.

Developed countries regard the development of a circular economy as a starting point as well as an opportunity for raising public awareness of the environment, thereby promoting green consumption, so that the government, enterprises, and consumers are willing to bear corresponding responsibilities for green consumption.

## 1.3 Green consumption and transformation and upgrading of China's economy

The 21st century is a century of green economy and green consumption. A long-term and arduous task for humanity is to promote green consumption and sustainable development. China's fast-growing economy over the years has resulted in severe ecological environmental problems, and there is a grim resource and the environmental constraint on the further development of the economy. A good ecological environment is a necessary condition for sustainable development and a key manifestation of the people's pursuit of a better life. China initiated the green transformation and upgrading of the economy during the Twelfth Five-Year Plan period. Consumption, which accounts for one-third of the overall economic growth, will undoubtedly be a powerful driver for the green transformation of China's economy. Therefore, promoting green consumption is essential for China to achieve the green transformation of the economy as well as the long-term development of the country.

### *1.3.1 Pressure of China's current consumption on the ecological environment*

#### *1.3.1.1 The current situation of consumption in China*

Consumer spending refers to the total final consumption expenditure of permanent residents on goods and services and is the data that intuitively reflects the current situation of consumption. Since the beginning of reform and opening up, the concept of Chinese residents about consumption has changed several times, and individual consumption has gradually shifted from traditional consumption for meeting basic needs to consumption for further development and a better life.

Specifically, before 1978, residents mainly purchased bicycles, sewing machines, watches, and radios, which were used to meet basic needs. As household appliances gained popularity, color televisions, refrigerators, washing machines, and tape recorders became hot products. In the mid-1980s, China saw a boom in the sales of consumer durables represented by household appliances. In the 1990s, new-generation household appliances, including telephones, air conditioners, and personal computers, became popular among urban residents. As urban residents begin to make consumption to live a moderately prosperous life, we see irrational consumption such as showy, luxury, and excessive consumption. On the whole, the current structure of individual consumption in China is in the stage of transition from the subsistence consumption to consumption for a modern and moderately prosperous life.

Since the beginning of reform and opening up, the consumption level of Chinese residents, whether urban residents or rural residents, has shown an upward trend year by year. The per capita annual consumption expenditure made by rural residents in China soared from 116 yuan in 1978 to 9,630 yuan in 2015, an increase of 83 times. The per capita annual consumption expenditure made by urban residents soared from 456 yuan in 1981 to 27,088 yuan in 2015, an increase of 59 times (see Figure 1.1). However, in absolute numbers, the consumption level of urban residents is far higher than that of rural residents, and the difference is widening year by year.

Consumer demand is an important component of aggregate demand. In recent years, China has experienced inadequate aggregate demand, and a key reason for this is inadequate consumer demand. As Figure 1.2 shows, from 1981 to 2000,

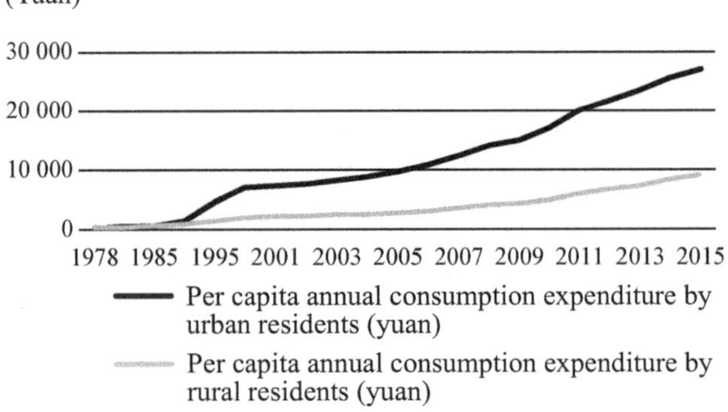


*Figure 1.1* Changes in per capita annual consumption expenditure by urban and rural residents in China.

*Source:* Based on the data from *China Statistical Yearbook*.

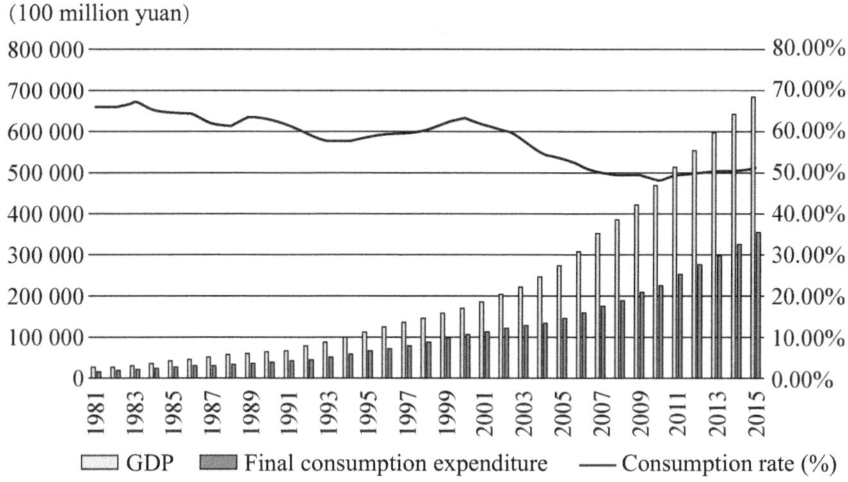


*Figure 1.2* GDP, final consumption expenditure and consumption rate.

*Source:* Based on data from *China Statistical Yearbook*.

China's consumption rate (consumption rate = final consumption expenditure/GDP) experienced a process of rise, decline, and then rise again. China's consumption rate began to decline in 2000 and plateaued from 2007 to 2015. It fell from 63.9 percent in 2000 to 51.6 percent in 2015 and maintained at about 50 percent.

In addition, the changes in the marginal propensity to consume (marginal propensity to consume = per capita consumption expenditure / per capita disposable income) of the residents reveal the situation of China's consumption level. In absolute terms, the consumption expenditure of residents has increased year by year alongside the increase of income. However, because the rate of increase in consumption expenditure is slower than that of income, the average propensity to consume of Chinese residents declined from 1981 to 2000. Moreover, the marginal propensity to consume of urban residents fell from 0.91 in 1981 to 0.70 in 2010, and the marginal propensity to consume of rural residents dropped from 0.85 in 1981 to 0.74 in 2010. The marginal propensity to consume of urban residents declined significantly (Table 1.1).

The problems in the current situation of consumption in China are as follows: (1) The level of individual consumption has been low for a long time. Unlike developed countries, the Chinese government primarily depends on investment to achieve a significant increase in the GDP. To transform the economy, it is necessary to stimulate domestic demand through consumption. (2) As China's economy rapid develops, the gap between the rich and the poor (urban-rural gap, regional gap) is widening. Influenced by the diversified Western cultures, Chinese residents blindly pursue a sense of satisfaction by making excessive consumption, and the consumption mode characterized by extravagance, waste, and extravagant consumption

*Table 1.1* Table of per capita disposable income, annual consumption expenditure, and marginal propensity to consume of urban and rural residents in China

| *Year* | *Per capita disposable income of urban residents* | *Per capita annual consumption expenditure of urban residents* | *Rural residents' marginal propensity to consume* | *Per capita disposable income of rural residents* | *Per capita annual consumption expenditure of rural residents* | *Rural residents' marginal propensity to consume* |
|---|---|---|---|---|---|---|
| 1981 | 500.4 | 456.84 | 0.91 | 223.44 | 190.81 | 0.85 |
| 1982 | 535.3 | 471 | 0.88 | 270.11 | 220.23 | 0.82 |
| 1983 | 564.6 | 505.92 | 0.90 | 309.77 | 248.29 | 0.80 |
| 1984 | 652.1 | 559.44 | 0.86 | 355.33 | 273.8 | 0.77 |
| 1985 | 739.1 | 673.2 | 0.91 | 397.6 | 317.42 | 0.80 |
| 1986 | 900.9 | 798.96 | 0.89 | 423.76 | 356.95 | 0.84 |
| 1987 | 1,002.2 | 884.4 | 0.88 | 462.55 | 398.29 | 0.86 |
| 1988 | 1,180.2 | 1,103.98 | 0.94 | 544.94 | 476.66 | 0.87 |
| 1989 | 1,373.9 | 1,211 | 0.88 | 601.51 | 535.37 | 0.89 |
| 1990 | 1,510.16 | 1,278.89 | 0.85 | 686.31 | 584.63 | 0.85 |
| 1991 | 1,700.6 | 1,453.81 | 0.85 | 708.6 | 619.79 | 0.87 |
| 1992 | 2,026.6 | 1,671.73 | 0.82 | 784 | 659.79 | 0.84 |
| 1993 | 2,577.4 | 2,110.81 | 0.82 | 921.62 | 769.65 | 0.84 |
| 1994 | 3,496.2 | 2,851.34 | 0.82 | 1,220.98 | 1,016.81 | 0.83 |
| 1995 | 4,282.95 | 3,537.57 | 0.83 | 1,577.74 | 1,310.36 | 0.83 |
| 1996 | 4,838.9 | 3,919.47 | 0.81 | 1,926.07 | 1,572.08 | 0.82 |
| 1997 | 5,160.3 | 4,186 | 0.81 | 2,090.13 | 1,617 | 0.77 |
| 1998 | 5,425.1 | 4,331.61 | 0.80 | 2,161.98 | 1,590.33 | 0.74 |
| 1999 | 5,854.02 | 4,615.91 | 0.79 | 2,210.34 | 1,577.42 | 0.71 |
| 2000 | 6,279.98 | 4,998 | 0.80 | 2,253.42 | 1,670.3 | 0.74 |
| 2001 | 6,859.6 | 5,309.01 | 0.77 | 2,366.4 | 1,741.09 | 0.74 |
| 2002 | 7,702.8 | 6,029.88 | 0.78 | 2,475.63 | 1,834.31 | 0.74 |
| 2003 | 8,472.2 | 6,510.94 | 0.77 | 2,622.24 | 1,943.3 | 0.74 |
| 2004 | 9,421.6 | 7,182 | 0.76 | 2,936.4 | 2,185 | 0.74 |
| 2205 | 10,493 | 7,942.88 | 0.76 | 3,254.93 | 2,555.4 | 0.79 |
| 2006 | 11,759.5 | 8,696.55 | 0.74 | 3,587.04 | 2,829.02 | 0.79 |
| 2007 | 13,785.8 | 9,997.47 | 0.73 | 4,140.36 | 3,223.85 | 0.78 |
| 2008 | 15,780.76 | 11,242.9 | 0.71 | 4,760.62 | 3,660.68 | 0.77 |
| 2009 | 17,174.65 | 12,264.6 | 0.71 | 5,153.17 | 3,993.45 | 0.77 |
| 2010 | 19,109.44 | 13,471.5 | 0.70 | 5,919.01 | 4,382 | 0.74 |
| 2011 | 21,809.8 | 15,161 | 0.70 | 6,977.3 | 5,221.1 | 0.75 |
| 2012 | 24,564.7 | 16,674 | 0.68 | 7,916.6 | 5,908 | 0.75 |
| 2013 | 26,955.1 | 18,022.6 | 0.67 | 8,895.9 | 6,625.5 | 0.74 |
| 2014 | 28,843.9 | 19,968.1 | 0.69 | 10,488.9 | 8,382.6 | 0.80 |
| 2015 | 31,194.8 | 21,392.4 | 0.69 | 11,421.7 | 9,222.6 | 0.81 |

*Source:* Based on data from *China Statistical Yearbook*.

prevails. (3) Material consumption is consistently dominant in the consumption structure. (4) As the average spending power of residents increases, people now make consumption for the enjoyment of a better life instead of merely subsistence. In China, changing consumption mode and the consumption structure is a profound reform.

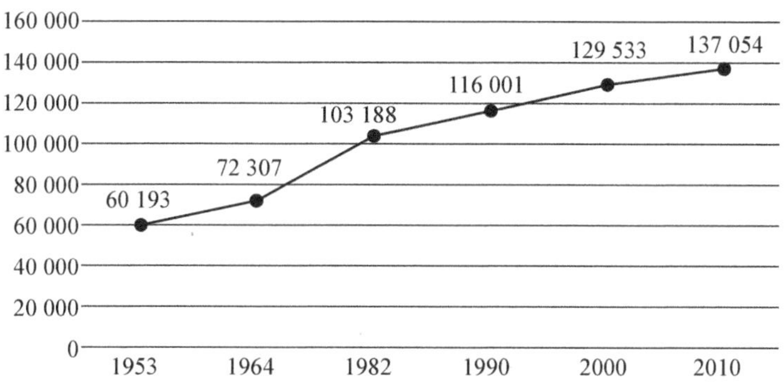


*Figure 1.3* Chart showing the trend of China's population.

*Source:* Based on census data.

*1.3.1.2 China's ecological environmental pressure caused by consumption*

China is facing a severe conflict in population, resources, and the environment, with a big population and fast population growth. The general picture of China's population growth since the 19th century is shown in Figure 1.3.

China is rich in aggregate resources and variety, but its per capita ownership is a case of absolute inadequacy. In addition, the coal-based energy mix leads to a sharp conflict between China's energy demand and ecological environment. China is now the world's largest consumer power and the second largest oil and electricity consumer, with cement and steel consumption accounting for nearly 50 percent and 35 percent of the world's total consumption, respectively, and alumina and copper consumption together accounting for 20 percent, but its GDP only accounting for 5 to 6 percent of the world's total.[22]

The demand for consumption increases the burden on the ecological environment. The basic situation of China's ecological environment is the deteriorating environment as a whole, an improving environment in some areas, the governance capacity lagging behind the speed of destruction, and a growing ecological deficit. These are mainly manifested as follows:

1 Serious air pollution. Air pollution, also known as atmospheric pollution, refers to the phenomenon in which certain substances enter the atmosphere due to anthropogenic activities or natural processes, reach sufficient concentrations for sufficient time, and then endanger human health. The air quality index (AQI) is a dimensionless index that quantitatively describes the condition of air quality. The larger the value, the higher the level and category, and the darker the color of characterization, the more serious the air pollution is, and the more harm it will cause to human health. The main pollutants for the air quality evaluation are fine particulate matter, inhalable particulate matter, sulfur dioxide, nitrogen dioxide, ozone, and carbon monoxide. Air pollution is caused by natural or human activities. Generally, industrial activities, burning of fossil fuels, and combustion in agriculture are the chief contributors to pollution.

The worsening air quality in North China and the supervision by public opinion are important for drawing public attention to air pollution, and the concept of "smog" gains popularity. According to the *China Climate Bulletin of 2015*, large-scale, persistent smog occurred in China 11 times in 2015 (mainly in November and December 2015). Frequent smog weather adversely affects traffic and human health. From November 6 to 8, 2015, smog weather struck Northeast China, with PM2.5 concentrations exceeding 250 μg/m$^3$ in some areas. The hourly peak concentration of PM2.5 in Harbin was close to 1,000 μg/m$^3$, and this figure even exceeded 1,000 μg/m$^3$ in cities such as Changchun and Shenyang. From November 29 to December 1, 2015, severe smog weather occurred in south and central areas of North China, the areas south of the Yellow River and north of the Huai River, the east of the region between the Yangtze River and the Huai River. It was accompanied by extensive fog with visibility of less than 1,000 m, and dense fog with visibility of less than 200 m in some areas. Due to the smog weather, many flights were grounded, and many expressways in North China were closed. This smog process, which was characterized by great intensity, wide-ranging impact, rapid development, dense fog mixed with severe smog, low visibility, etc., was the most severe smog weather process in 2015. In China, air pollution is caused by soot pollution, mainly stemming from industrial emissions. Its hazard falls into three categories: acute poisoning, chronic poisoning, and carcinogenic nature as a result of the different sources, nature, concentrations, and durations of the pollutants, differences in meteorological conditions, geographical environment, and other factors in polluted areas, as well as the difference in people's age and health status.

2 Serious soil erosion. Soil erosion occurs mainly as a consequence of serious damage to vegetation, coupled with the scouring of rainwater and surface water. It is caused by the interaction of unfavorable natural conditions and unreasonable economic activities by mankind. The unfavorable natural conditions refer to steep surface slope, soft soil prone to erosion, heavy rainstorm, and soil not protected by vegetation such as forest and grassland. Irrational economic activities refer to the activities of destroying forests and grasslands, cultivating steep slopes, overgrazing on grasslands, destroying ground vegetation through production and construction such as mining and road construction without providing timely remediation, dumping waste soil and rocks indiscriminately, and so on.

Soil erosion can wreak havoc on the local and downstream ecological environment, people's work and life as well as economic development. It is destructive in terms of reducing land fertility, silting up rivers, lakes, and reservoirs, polluting water, and upsetting ecological balance. According to the results of the second national remote sensing survey on soil erosion released by the Ministry of Water Resources in 2002, the area affected by soil erosion in China reached 3.56 million km$^2$, accounting for 37 percent of the total land area, including an area of 1.65 million km$^2$ caused by water erosion and the area of 1.91 million km$^2$ caused by wind erosion. Soil erosion mainly occurs Yunnan, Guiyang, Sichuan, Chongqing, and Hubei in the upper reaches of the Yangtze River as well as Shanxi, Shaanxi, Inner Mongolia, Gansu, and Ningxia in the middle reaches of the Yellow River. The area affected by soil erosion extends from the east to the west. In China, the northwest region is exposed to the most serious wind erosion.

3. The water body is heavily polluted. According to the data released by the Ministry of Environmental Protection (now the Ministry of Ecology and Environment), the survey on water quality in 968 surface water monitoring sections (points) under state control in 423 major rivers and 62 key lakes (reservoirs) across the country in 2014 shows that the cross section of rivers with water quality levels I, II, III, IV, V, and the level worse than level V accounted for 3.4 percent, 30.4 percent, 29.3 percent, 20.9 percent, 6.8 percent, and 9.2 percent, respectively. That is to say, the water quality of nearly 40 percent of water bodies in China does not meet the national level III standards for surface water environmental quality (level III water can be used for fish farming, and level II water can be used as drinking water sources). In June 2013, the Chinese Center for Disease Control and Prevention conducted a study of the causal association between the water environment in the Huai River Basin and deaths caused by digestive tract tumors, which verified for the first time the direct link between water pollution and a high incidence of cancer.

Moreover, the rapidly dwindling forest resources, desertification, reduction in biodiversity, etc., are all external manifestations of the damaged ecological environment. Pressure caused by population, industry, and market are the principal reasons for the deteriorating ecological environment. In modern times, China's population has burgeoned, becoming the biggest obstacle to China's modernization and imposing the biggest pressure on China's ecological environment. To survive, people destroy forests and develop wasteland, reclaim land from lakes, and engage in indiscriminate mining and digging, which wreak damage on vegetation. Many irrational human activities exceed the bearing capacity of the nature. China, which developed industry late and started from a low level as well as also bore the arduous task of catching up with and surpassing the developed countries, used to support fast economic growth by making heavy capital input, achieving economic prosperity at the expense of damage to the environment. It used to value short-term profits, but lacked long-term strategies and ignored the ecology. Short-term economic activities caused long-term and cumulative bad consequences to China's ecological environment.

Human beings play a main role in economic and social activities. Their behavior, particularly consumption, exerts a direct impact on the environment. Under the traditional extensive consumption mode, resources are extensively mined and utilized. In the traditional resource-depleted consumption mode, people only select natural resources useful to them for mining and processing, and transform them into products for reproduction and sales. Items that cannot be used temporarily in the production process are treated as waste. However, as the economy and society rapidly develop and the population burgeons, the scale of consumption expands as never before, and the amount of waste emitted into nature has surged, far exceeding the self-purification of the nature. Therefore, it is imperative to promote green consumption.

### *1.3.2 Green consumption contributes to transformation of the economy*

#### *1.3.2.1 Promoting ecological conservation in China*

Promoting ecological conservation is a major strategic plan made by China in view of the dwindling resources, serious environmental pollution, and the deteriorating ecosystem. It calls for a philosophy of ecological civilization for respecting nature, following its laws and protecting it, and for pursuing sustainable development.

In 2007, the report of the 17th Seventeenth CPC National Congress put forward the need to "promote ecological conservation and basically form an industrial structure, growth model, and consumption mode that conserves energy resources and protects the ecological environment." In November 2012, the 18th CPC National Congress, which keeps a foothold reality and innovation, made the decision to "vigorously promote ecological conservation," and required giving prominence to it and implementing an overall plan for promoting economic, political, cultural, social, and ecological progress. The Third Plenary Session of the 18th CPC Central Committee made top-level planning and stressed the necessity and importance of system building: To promote ecological conservation, it is necessary to establish a systematic and complete system for promoting ecological conservation and employ the system to safeguard the ecological environment. It is necessary to improve the property rights system of natural resource assets as well as regulation system for the use of natural resources, mark the ecological red lines, set up a sound system of compensation for use of resources and for damage caused to the ecological environment, and reform the administration system of ecological environmental protection.

To promote ecological conservation, we must keep to the basic national policy of conserving resources and protecting the environment; operate a policy that prioritizes conservation and protection and features natural restoration; focus on promoting green, circular, and low-carbon development; and shape spatial layouts, industrial structures, modes of production, and ways of life that are conducive to resource conservation and environmental protection, so as to reverse the deteriorating ecological environment at source. We mainly start with the following four areas: (1) Improve development of China's geographical space. It is in geographical space that ecological progress can be advanced, and we must cherish every bit of it. We should develop the marine economy, protect the marine ecological environment, resolutely safeguard China's maritime rights and interests, and build China into a maritime power. (2) Promote all-around resource conservation. Resource conservation is an important way to protect the ecological environment. We should conserve resources and use them efficiently, control the total amount of energy consumed, save energy and reduce its consumption, and promote water recycling. (3) Intensify protection of the ecosystem and the environment. A sound ecological environment is the fundamental basis for sustainable human and social development. We should expand the size of forests, lakes, and wetlands and protect biodiversity. We should accelerate construction of water conservancy projects and enhance our capacity for responding to floods, drought, and waterlogging in urban and rural areas. We should improve the system for preventing and mitigating natural disasters and become better able to respond to meteorological, geological, and seismic disasters. (4) Enhance system building to promote ecological progress. System building is crucial to protecting the ecological environment. We should carry out trials for trading energy savings, carbon emission rights, pollution discharge rights, and water rights.

Promoting ecological conservation helps to build a resource-conserving, environment-friendly society. Its goals are as follows:

> The establishment of functional zones should be basically completed, and a system for recycling resources should begin to take shape. Energy consumption and carbon dioxide emissions per unit of GDP as well as the discharge of major pollutants should decrease sharply. Forest coverage should increase, the ecosystem should become more stable, and the living environment should improve markedly.

Promoting ecological conservation shows that man and nature live in harmony. It means a fundamental change in the modes of production and consumption and is a long-term plan that concerns the well-being of the people and the future of the nation. Green consumption is an important component of green development, which is essential for promoting ecological conservation. To strike a balance between economic development and environmental protection, we must transform the mode of economic development, pursue green development, and practice green consumption.

#### *1.3.2.2 Green consumption and supply-side reform*

"Supply-side reform" refers boosting competitiveness and promoting economic development by releasing productive forces, starting with supply and production. The government raises total factor productivity and create new economic growth areas through policy means such as streamlining administration and delegating power, deregulation, financial reform, state-owned enterprise reform, land reform, and boosting innovation capabilities. Specifically, these include addressing the issue of "zombie enterprises," closing down outdated production facilities, and aiding the development of emerging fields.

The concept of "supply-side reform" was first advanced by General Secretary Xi Jinping at the 11th meeting of the Office of the Central Leading Group for Financial and Economic Affairs on November 10, 2015. At the subsequent executive meeting of the State Council, Premier Li Keqiang stressed the need to "cultivate and form new supply and new drivers of growth, thereby expanding domestic demand." At the APEC CEO Summit held on November 18, 2015, General Secretary Xi Jinping again mentioned the important role of "supply-side reform" in addressing economic problems. Monetary stimulus alone cannot effectively solve deep-seated economic problems of a global nature. It is necessary to carry out reforms at the structural level to make the supply system better adapt to changes in the demand structure. The Central Economic Work Conference held in December 2015 further pointed out the necessity and viability of supply-side reform and stressed that promoting supply-side structural reform is a major innovation to adapt to and guide the new normal in China's economic development, is an active choice to adapt to the new situation of competition in overall national strength after the international financial crisis, and is an essential requirement to adapt to a new normal for China's economic development.

In the 1970s and 1980s, Britain and the United States were mired in stagflation. In order to climb out of economic recession, the British and American governments employed the typical theories of the supply-side economics, namely "Reaganomics" and "Thatcherism," to reverse the economic downturn. Britain mainly adopted the methods of tax relief and tight monetary policy, while the United States focused on reform measures such as tight monetary policy and reform of state-owned enterprises. China's economic growth declined year by year since 2007, and the demand stimulus effect was small, which shows that insufficient demand is only a superficial illusion, and the mismatch between supply and demand is the crux essence of the problem. Therefore, we must place a high value on the supply side and set about conducting reform. Instead of simply copying the practice of the supply-side school, supply-side reform is intended to achieve economic restructuring and optimization, and to avoid a significant decline in potential growth. It is the continuation and focus of "comprehensively deepening reform" in the field of factors. The supply side corresponds to the demand side. The demand side focuses on investment, consumption, and export, while the supply side has four factors: labor, land, capital, and innovation. Therefore, the supply-side reform is intended to adjust the economic structure, so that the factors of production are allocated optimally. Investment, consumption, and export stimulate short-term economic growth, while the four factors boost the potential economic growth in the medium and long term. The two combine to spur stable economic development.

As the economic growth slows down, the growth trend of investment and exports also decreases significantly. Consumption becomes a key guarantee for economic growth. Therefore, promoting economic growth through consumption is a key means to ensure stable growth of economy and is also a basic element for cooperation with supply-side reform. In order to ensure the implementation of the strategy of expanding domestic demand and provide a powerful force driving consumption growth, we must innovate the consumption mechanism, protect the right to consume, and rationally distribute spending power. The mode of green consumption offers an important way to promote ecological conservation and build resource-conserving and environment-friendly society. It complies with the law of natural ecological evolution and the requirements for sustainable social development and can coordinate economic development with environmental protection. It minimizes the negative externalities of the environment while meeting people's consumption needs, thereby ensuring the important role of consumption in promoting economic development.

In a market economy, demand and supply influence each other. Green consumption affects the production side, changes the extensive mode of production, and promotes green products and services. This somewhat helps to promote supply-side reform and economic restructuring. According to the data from Ecological Finance Research Center of Renmin University of China, remarkable results were achieved in terms of green consumption during the Twelfth Five-Year Plan period. The consumption of coal, which is regarded as one of the major sources of environmental pollution, decreased for the first time in 2015. The proportion of consumption of clean energy such as hydropower, wind power, nuclear power, and natural gas in total energy consumption rose steadily, from 13.0 percent in 2011 to 17.9 percent in 2015. It can be seen that promoting green consumption conforms to the trend of consumption upgrading in China. Moreover, it promotes the effective matching of supply and demand by managing aggregate demand, moderately expanding aggregate demand and adjusting and reforming the composition of demand. This will create steady and long-term domestic demand to sustain economic development.

#### *1.3.2.3 Green consumption policies boost green economic development*

Green development is a model of economic growth and social development aimed at efficiency, harmony, and sustainability. In terms of connotations, green development is an innovative development model in line with the national conditions, which says no to extensive development and regards the ecological environment as an important basis and pillar of sustainable economic and social development, subject to the constraints of the capacity of the ecological environment as well as the carrying capacity of resources. From the perspective of short-term goals, green development is intended to transform the mode of economic development, with a view to building resource-conserving and environment-friendly society. From the standpoint of long-term goals, green development is a concrete action for achieving sustainable development, with the goal of effectively combining sustainable economic, social development, and environmental protection. In terms of content, green development covers a green approach to work, green consumption, green culture and education, green social management, green social trends, etc. These are different dimensions of green development, which have their respective characteristics and fields of application, but also depend on and influence each other. In essence, green development is a process of applying ecological culture to economic activity and results.

Since the Ninth Five-Year Plan issued in 1995, China has been exploring ways to transform the model of economic development. The outline of the 13th Five-Year Plan officially put forward pursuing green development and focusing on improving the ecological environment. The ecological environment is fundamental to economic and social development. Overall and comprehensive development must take into account environmental indicators and intergenerational equity. We should make overall plans to achieve sustainable development in terms of spatial and temporal dimensions. Green development is put forward as a result of the deterioration of the ecological environment, the government's strategic decisions, and the public awareness of environmental protection. It is also essential for China to boost its comprehensive strength and its international competitiveness. At the United Nations Climate Change Conference, the Chinese government expressed that it would work with the international community to address the grim challenges of climate change, shoulder its responsibilities as a big power, and honor its international obligations as a responsible major power. At the same time, it undertook to reduce carbon emission intensity by 40 to 45 percent by 2020 compared with 2005. Decisions on green development will go towards achieving this goal.

China boasts a vast territory and a large population, but its per capita share of resources is small. Therefore, in terms of consumption, we should comprehensively save and efficiently use resources, make clear the property rights of resources, improve the system for resource allocation, and create green consumption culture. We should launch campaign against excessive packaging, food waste, and excessive consumption and promote a social trend of frugal consumption.

China initiated green consumption in the 1990s. In 1999, China operated the green channel, began to vigorously advocate green consumption, and established and improved a green market with the support of the State Environmental Protection Administration, etc. The year 2001 was designated as the "Green Consumption Theme Year" by China Consumers Association. During the 12th Five-year Plan period, the number of green food enterprises and the scale of products increased at a rate of 8.4 percent and 6.9 percent, respectively. In 2016, the annual sales of green food was 458.8 billion yuan. AskCI forecast that by 2022, the market size would reach 635 billion yuan, and the future market size promises great potential. After more than 20 years of development, the achievements of China's green consumption can be summarized as follows:

1 Government departments attach great importance to green consumption by providing fiscal support directly or indirectly. In 1999, six government departments including the State Environmental Protection Administration (now the Ministry of Ecology and Environment) jointly launched the campaign to "open up green channels, develop green markets, and advocate green consumption." China Consumers Association designated "green consumption" as the consumption theme in 2001. As a result, the idea of green consumption is gaining acceptance and is respected in the 21st century. During the Eleventh Five-Year Plan period, a fiscal fund of 10 billion yuan was used for scientific research on energy conservation and emission reduction, and the non-governmental sector invested 50 billion yuan to launch the energy conservation and emission reduction project. During the Twelfth Five-Year Plan period, China vigorously promoted government procurement of energy-saving products, implemented projects to promote energy-efficient products for the benefit of the people, and promoted 7 million energy-saving vehicles, 220 million high-efficiency lighting products, 96 million high-efficiency and energy-saving household appliances, over 20 million kilowatts of high-efficiency motors, and 1.1 million remanufactured products. Investment from the central government budget and the central government

funding increased support for energy conservation and emission reduction. Comprehensive demonstration of fiscal fund policies for energy conservation and emission reduction was carried out in 18 cities. Green credit was promoted. By the end of 2013, the balance of green loans issued by 21 major banks reached 5.2 trillion yuan, and nearly 330 billion yuan in debt financing was provided for energy-saving and environmental protection enterprises. This actively promoted green consumption.

2 The Chinese people gradually embrace the concept of green consumption. In March 2001, a large-scale three-month survey organized by China Consumers Association with the theme of "10 million green consumer volunteers in action" officially kicked off. The survey results show that over 95 percent of consumers supported and made green consumption. According to the results of a survey conducted in 36 cities at the sub-provincial level and above in China, up to 98.9 percent of consumers are willing to participate in promoting green consumption. Environmental initiatives such as waste sorting and water saving are supported by over 97 percent of consumers. Up to 97.4 percent of consumers prefer eco-friendly homes and decoration, public transport, and resolutely resist wild animal products. Consumers who are willing to say no to plastic bags, disposable chopsticks, and tableware account for 95 percent of all consumers. In summary, a craze in green consumption is emerging in China.[23]

3 China has introduced many green standards. China's certification standards for environmental labeling products were officially released in 1993. In 1992, China Green Food Development Center and China Green Food Corporation were officially established, which were unprecedented in the food industry. *Administrative Measures for Green Food Labels* were also introduced at the same time. China Certification Committee for Environmental Labelling Products (CCCEL) was established in 1994. China's environmental labeling is implemented in accordance with the ISO14020 standards and the "Environmental management – Environmental labels and declarations for Type I Environmental labelling – Principles and procedures" in terms of certification methods and procedures, which are consistent with the practices of environmental labeling programs in foreign countries. While keeping abreast of international "ecological labeling" technology, it carries out mutual recognition work for environmental labeling. ISO14000 international environmental standard management system was first piloted in China in 1996. Although China does not have a systematic policy on green consumption, the role of promoting green development at the consumer level is obvious. Table 1.2 summarizes information on the types of environmental labels in China. China's environmental labeling falls into two categories: product certification and system certification, totaling more than ten types of certifications. While adding diversity to China's green product market, it also brings problems in green product management in China. Of course, the system certification of products and systems in line with international standards makes it possible for Chinese products and manufacturers to participate in global competition.

*Table 1.2* Types of environmental labels in China

| | *Type* | *Description* |
|---|---|---|
| Product certification | China's Type I Environmental Label | The highest level of environmental protection label for products in China |
| | China's Type II Environmental Label | Also known as "Self-declared environmental claims" |
| | China's Type III Environmental Label | Also known as "Environmental information announcement label" |
| | Organic products | All agricultural products produced and processed in accordance with international organic agricultural production requirements as well as corresponding standards, and certified by an independent, accredited certification body of organic food |
| | Green food label | Certification and marking for safe, high-quality edible agricultural products and related products produced in an ecologically excellent environment under comprehensive quality control in accordance with green food standards formulated and promulgated by the Ministry of Agriculture |
| | Environmental labeling products | The scope of certification covers environmental protection products as well as products for comprehensive utilization that are closely related to people's lives such as plates, paints, and furniture |
| | China Energy Label | It was jointly formulated and issued by the National Development and Reform Commission and the General Administration of Quality Supervision, Inspection and Quarantine in August 2004. It marked the implementation of energy efficiency labeling system in China |
| System certification | ISO14001 | International standard for environmental management system formulated by International Organization for Standardization (ISO) |
| | OHSMS18001-GB/T28001 | Occupational safety and health management system standards jointly developed by some European and Asian-pacific countries |
| | CDM | Clean Development Mechanism |
| | Food safety management system certification | Specify the requirements of a food safety management system |
| | ISO9001 | International standards for quality management system formulated by the ISO |

*Source:* Former Environmental Certification Center of the State Environmental Protection Administration.

4 During the Twelfth Five-Year Plan period, remarkable results were achieved in terms of green consumption. In 2015, China's total energy consumption reached 4.3 billion metric tons of standard coal, up by 19.2 percent over 2010, with an average growth rate of 3.6 percent over five years. It decreased by 18.8 percent and 3.1 percent compared to 2005 and 2010, respectively. The decline in growth

was 680 million metric tons of standard coal, equivalent to the total energy consumption of ten Beijing cities in 2014. The consumption of coal, which is regarded as one of the major sources of environmental pollution, decreased for the first time in 2015, down by 3.7 percent compared to 2014. The proportion of consumption of clean energy such as hydropower, wind power, nuclear power, and natural gas in total energy consumption steadily increased, from 13.00 percent in 2011 to 17.9 percent in 2015. Promoting green consumption conforms to the trend of consumption upgrading in China and improves people's living standards. Moreover, it promotes the effective matching of supply and demand by managing aggregate demand, moderately expanding aggregate demand and adjusting and reforming the composition of demand. This creates steady and long-term domestic demand to sustain economic development.[24]

5 China's market size for green consumption is expanding. According to the survey and analysis by AliResearch, by the end of 2015, the number of online green consumers in China reached 65 million. In 2015, Alibaba's online retail platform reduced $CO_2$ emissions by about 30 million metric tons. The total number of green consumers reached 65 million, an increase of 14 times in four years. The concept of "green consumers" was put forward for the first time. The emergence of huge green consumers is of great significance for the times. The Internet contributes to information transparency, and consumer sovereignty is emerging. The demand for green consumption released will better guide green supply and promote supply-side reform. AliResearch believes that green consumers refer to those consumers who have ecological awareness and have real willingness and spending power to purchase green products. They are green-conscious and have already or may translate the green awareness into green consumption behavior. AliResearch also found that in 2015, there were 200 million green basket products (green basket products refer to commodities with the green attributes of "resource saving, energy saving, environmental friendliness and health") in 50 categories on Alibaba's online retail platform. Consumption of green basket products accounts for 11.5 percent on Alibaba's retail platform, with a compound annual growth rate in the past five years of over 80 percent. An analysis of the frequency of consumption of green basket products shows that in the past five years, the number of high-level green consumers (over 20 purchases a year) significantly expanded, increasing from 19.4 percent in 2011 to 28.4 percent in 2015, a net increase of 9 percentage points. In addition to being a healthy way of life, green consumption minimizes the negative impact of economic activities on the environment and directly cuts the cost of treating environmental pollution. According to the calculations by China Research Center for Circular Economy and Environmental Assessment and Prediction under the Chinese Academy of Social Sciences and AliResearch, in 2015, Alibaba's online retail platform reduced emissions of 30 million metric tons of $CO_2$ as a result of reduced energy consumption and material consumption. The annual water savings by water-saving products sold on the platform is enough for use in Beijing for 13 days. The annual electricity saving from energy-saving products is enough for use in Beijing for 25 days. Eco-friendly packaging products sold on the platform reduce the quantity of plastic bags, and the oil converted from this reduction can be used for taxis in Beijing for 62 days.[25]

## Notes

1 Xu Shengguo, Chu Chunli, Ju Meiting, et al. A review of research on "green consumption". *Ecological Economics*, 2014, 30 (7): 65–69.
2 See Note 1.
3 Green Studio. *Green Consumption*. Beijing: The Ethnic Publishing House, 1999.
4 Jiang Hong. Green consumption: Green production driven by green demand. *Environmental Economics*, 2007 (Z1): 16–19.
5 Yu Haishan. A review of the definition of sustainable consumption. *Zhejiang Social Sciences*, 2001 (5): 88–92.
6 UNEP. SCP indicators for developing countries: A guidance framework, 2008.
7 Jin Yingjie. *On the Construction of a Sustainable Consumption Legal System in China: From the Perspective of Circular Economy*. Guangzhou: Jinan University, 2011: 1–20.
8 Li Ying, Liu Ben. A review of ecological consumption research in China. *Business Times*, 2010 (8): 23–24.
9 Liu Changsong. Scientific connotation and development path of low carbon consumption. *Journal of Poyang Lake*, 2015 (3): 37–51.
10 See Note 8.
11 Ni Lin. Evaluation index system and empirical evaluation of ecological consumption development in China. *Natural Resource Economics of China*, 2014 (5): 68–72.
12 European Commission (EC). Sustainable public procurement in EU member states: Overview of government initiatives and selected cases. Final Report to the EU High-level Group on CSR, 2007.
13 Cao Fengzhong. Sustainable production and sustainable consumption are the strategic foundations for promoting sustainable development. *Environmental Science Trends*, 1995 (4): 5–8.
14 Yin Shijie. On green consumption. *Jianghai Academic Journal*, 2001 (3): 23–26.
15 Liu Fuzhong. *Household Appliance Industry and Circular Economy*. Beijing: China Light Industry Press, 2010: 14
16 Wu Min. *Research on the Ecosystem of Industrial Structure in Wuhan Urban Circle*. Wuhan: Wuhan University of Technology, 2009.
17 Liu Fuzhong. *Household Appliance Industry and Circular Economy*. Beijing: China Light Industry Press, 2010: 28.
18 Research on the Development of Eco-Industrial Parks in the U.S. http://www.docin.com/p-657972015.html.
19 Yu Sulan, Sun Yuhong. Green consumption in Germany and Japan: Concept and practice. *Academics*, 2016 (3): 221–230.
20 Liu Fuzhong. *Household Appliance Industry and Circular Economy*. Beijing: China Light Industry Press, 2010: 24.
21 Liu Fuzhong. *Household Appliance Industry and Circular Economy*. Beijing: China Light Industry Press, 2010: 38.
22 Guo Dandan. *Research on Green Consumption Issues in the Context of Scientific Outlook on Development*. Jinan: Qilu University of Technology, 2013
23 Xiao Xie. Great potential of green consumption. *Popular Business*, 2001 (10).
24 Cao Mingdi. The 13th Five-Year Plan period: Let green development be a new driving force for economic growth. www.china.com.cn, March 11, 2016.
25 AliResearch, Alibaba Social Welfare Department. *China Green Consumer Report*, 2017.

# 2 Theoretical basics related to green consumption

Green consumption is a kind of high-level rational consumption, and is an environment-conscious consumption practice. It says no to traditional concepts, and reflects the new morality, new values, and a new outlook on life. The concept of green consumption guides consumers to make scientific and rational everyday consumption on the basis of coordinated development with nature, advocates healthy and moderate consumption, and upholds lofty consumer ethics and code of conduct. It brings about major changes in the mode of production by changing the mode of consumption, thereby adjusting the economic structure and promoting the development of ecological industries as well as consumption concepts. Analyzing and studying the theories of green consumption is important for improving the green consumption policy and guiding the practices of green consumption.

## 2.1 Theory of sustainable development

The theory of sustainable development was first advanced in *Our Common Future*, a report issued by the World Commission on Environment and Development in 1987. According to the report, sustainable development can be defined as "development that meets the needs of the present without compromising the ability of future generations to meet their own needs." The *Rio Declaration* adopted at the 1992 United Nations Conference on Environment and Development elaborated on the concept of sustainable development: "Human beings are entitled to a healthy and productive life in harmony with nature. The right to development must be fulfilled so as to equitably meet developmental and environmental needs of present and future generations."[1] The theory of sustainable development was extensively discussed among scholars at home and abroad as soon as it was put forward.

### *2.1.1 Overview of theory and its application at home and abroad*

The theory of sustainable development combines the two concepts of sustainability and development and stresses the sustainability of economic development, ecological progress, and social development: (1) The sustainability of economic development implies that economic growth must not exceed the carrying capacity of resources and the environment, and this is a necessary precondition for the

DOI: 10.4324/9781003433040-2

development of humanity. (2) The sustainability of ecological progress requires that the ecosystem can remain to be productive when it is impacted externally and can resist external damage through its own capacity. (3) The sustainability of social development implies the need to continuously improve the level of science and technology, productivity, and the living standards of mankind. This is an important way to achieve economic and ecological sustainability. In recent years, the academic circles have conducted in-depth study of the concept, theories, and ways to sustainable development and focused on three areas: the concept of the Earth system, the thought on ecological civilization, and the low-carbon economy.

According to the theory of sustainable development, the main challenge facing sustainable development is the unsustainable consumption pattern. Excessive and irrational consumption greatly depletes resources and damages the ecology, leading to a vicious circle of unsustainability. In a word, the basic idea of sustainable development is to strike a balance between intragenerational equity as well as intergenerational equity. Sustainable development encourages economic growth, but it is premised on the sustainable use of resources as well as the good conservation of the ecological environment. It has the ultimate goal of seeking all-round socialist advancement. Judging from the development strategies in the world, the paths to achieving sustainable development are mainly as follows: (1) Transform the traditional model of extensive economic growth and incorporate environmental protection and resource conservation into comprehensive decision-making. (2) Change the current concept of consumption and develop new-type private consumption model, that is, green consumption. (3) Use resource-saving and eco-friendly technologies in the production process to achieve cleaner production in an all-round way. (4) The legislative body issues legislation on environmental protection, and the government formulates relevant policies and conduct administrative intervention appropriately. In addition, it is to raise public awareness of the environment, so that the public engage in cleaner production and green consumption on their own initiative.

However, due to China's different national conditions, the ways and paths to achieve the goal of sustainable strategic development should be suited to China. China has successively studied and formulated the *Ten Major Countermeasures for the Environment and Development in China*, *Macro Strategic Research on China's Environment*, *China's Agenda 21*, etc. According to these research reports, China's sustainable development strategy can be divided into four areas: population, resources, environment, and social stability. The focus is on replacing China's traditional model of extensive development characterized by population expansion, resource waste, and environmental pollution with a new mode of balanced, stable, and sustainable economic development.

### *2.1.2 Relationship with green consumption*

Green consumption is essentially the manifestation of sustainable development theory in the field of consumption and is a key mechanism for realizing sustainable development. In addressing the relationship between man and nature, green consumption advocates that consumption by the present generations shall meet their needs without exceeding the carrying capacity of resources and the environment. In other words, mankind should maintain the balance of the ecological environment while exploiting nature to meet their needs. In dealing with the relationship between people, green consumption emphasizes and advocates intragenerational and intergenerational equity. Intragenerational equity means that consumption made by anyone should not endanger the survival and consumption of others. Intergenerational equity means that consumption made by the present generations should not endanger the survival and consumption of future generations. Green consumption raises requirements for people's view of consumption, consumption habits, consumption structure, mode of consumption, etc. We must not be overly frugal while overlooking our own consumption. At the same time, we oppose extravagant consumption and focus on sustainable consumption. This is consistent with the idea of sustainable development. It shows that green consumption is a component of the theory of sustainable development, a way of achieving sustainable development, and a concrete embodiment of sustainable development theory in consumption. Likewise, the basic principles of sustainable development theory can be used to develop and guide green consumption.

## 2.2 Theory of ecological philosophy

Ecological philosophy is the science of using the views and methodology of ecosystems to study the interrelationship between human society and the natural environment as well as its universal laws. It is the social-philosophical study of the interaction between human society and nature. The theory of ecological philosophy regards the relationship between man and nature as the basic philosophical issue. Pursing the goal of the harmonious development of man and nature is the philosophical foundation of sustainable development. Green consumption is a component of sustainable development, and the theory of ecological philosophical provides theoretical support for its development.

### *2.2.1 Overview of the theory and its application at home and abroad*

Two great philosophers, Martin Heidegger and Jin Yuelin, believed that anthropocentrism is the philosophical root and a fatal weakness of the traditional vision on development. They realize the negative aspects of technology and see that the catastrophic consequence of unrestricted use of technology is the loss of human existence, as well as the complete alienation of man. For a long time, people's thoughts work within the framework of anthropocentrism, as well as subject-object polarization. Therefore, mankind regard themselves as the center of the world and the masters of nature, the world as the object, and everything in nature as raw materials for technological production. Man can exploit nature as they like. This unethical vision on development invisibly causes intergenerational inequality as well as inequality among present generations.

Ecological philosophy is a philosophy of human action. Ecological philosophy refers to the transition of philosophy to ecology and the environment and is the paradigm shift of philosophy. It has the theme of the relationship between human action and the environment. When philosophy focuses its attention on the world and people's thinking, it inevitably pays attention to people's actions. As a result, ecological philosophy is the complete development of philosophical logic. Paying attention to the world, people's thinking, and human action is the process of philosophy. Focusing attention on human action is to focus on ethics and morality. Environmental ethics and ecological morality are the norms of human behavior. As a result, ecological philosophy is the first to develop in the field of environmental ethics. Environmental ethics extends the people's moral concern to the ecological environment. Morality is the code of conduct, the general rule that people should observe in their social activities, and the value symbol that guides people to make choices and act. Therefore, value is the basis of moral philosophy. Due to rights derived from value, natural values and natural rights become the content of basic theoretical research for ecological ethics.

China's ecological philosophy originated from the study of environmental ethics and developed as a result of the dialectics of nature. The relationship between man and nature extends to the field of ethical research, and ecological philosophy developed from environmental ethics.[2] Thinking about issues such as the value of nature and the relationship between man and nature leads to debates over "anthropocentrism" and "non-anthropocentrism" in environmental ethics. The issues of natural values and natural rights are the focus of debate regarding environmental ethics. The ecological view of nature originates from the analysis of problems arising from science and technology as well as technological alienation. The association of the conception of nature with values is determined by the whole thinking of ecological philosophy.

Ecological conservation aims to achieve ecological sustainability, which is a major part of sustainable development. As a result, the thinking on the principal role for promoting ecological conservation must be established within the basic framework of sustainable development strategy and follow the laws of sustainable development strategy. The strategy of ecological conservation is formulated and realized based on this premise. It is necessary to alter the traditional vision on development, say no to the traditional mindset, act according to a new way of thinking, and promote ecological conservation for the sake of the coexistence of man and nature. In essence, man is part of the natural world. From the standpoint of human survival and development, nature provides the objects of labor and means of labor for production. The material exchange between man and nature is the foundation of society. From the standpoint of the interaction between man and nature, human activity must not exceed the bearing capacity of nature and must not violate the laws of nature. Therefore, for nature to survive normally, mankind must work to coordinate "humanized nature" with "natural nature," so as to promote sustainable economic development on the basis of maintaining the quality of natural resources and sustained supply and promote the healthy development of humanity without exceeding the carrying capacity of environmental system as well as its renewal capacity.

### 2.2.2 *Relationship with green consumption*

Green consumption is a kind of philosophical reflection on traditional mode of consumption, and the result of rational choices and moral self-discipline. It is a mode of consumption in line with the principles of ecological ethics. It abides by ecological laws, advocates reasonable consumption, resources saving, and environmental protection, and promotes the harmony between man and nature. It meets the objective requirements of the ecological ethical conception of consumption and shows the profound significance of ecological ethics. It is recognized that the increase in absolute and relative amount of consumer demand caused by excessive population growth and luxury consumption has a huge impact on the ecosystem. Some countries are taking necessary steps to check excessive population growth, but people do not recognize the huge negative effects caused by the increase in the relative amount of consumer demand, especially luxury consumption. That is to say, there is a lack of necessary restrictions and effective norms regarding relative consumer demand. As a concept of consumption promoting ecological conservation, green consumption requires mankind to pursue a healthy and fruitful life in coordination with nature, rather than leveraging their technology and funds to pursue development in a way that exhausts resources, destroys the ecology, and pollutes the environment. At the same time, it is necessary to replace linear consumption with rational consumption, make moderate consumption, guard against inordinate consumer demand, be more ecology-conscious, and prevent waste and the destruction of the ecological environment. The theory of demand and restrictions in ecological philosophy is a key theoretical basis for green consumption and also the chief theoretical support for the concept and connotations of green consumption. Furthermore, green consumerism advocates the unity and harmony between man and nature, as well as a frugal and fulfilling life.[3] After people's basic needs in material terms have been satisfied, a rich intellectual and cultural life can truly reflect the quality of life. It shows the viewpoint of the dialectical unity in ecological philosophy.

## 2.3 Theory of environmental economics

Environmental economics is a branch of economics. It mainly uses the principles of economics and environmental science to find ways and means to solve the conflict between economic growth and environmental protection. The consumer behavior studied under environmental economics refers to the demand of consumers, namely what they want, what factors guide them to make purchases, consumers' willingness to make green consumption as well as determinants, ecological environmental performance of such behavior, and so on. These studies will provide key support for formulating green consumer economic policies.

### 2.3.1 *Overview of the theory and its application at home and abroad*

As the economy developed rapidly in the late 1960s and early 1970s, resource and environmental issues became more prominent. Some scholars began to study environmental economic issues, with a focus on the relationship between environmental pollution and economic activities. In 1981, the United Nations Environment Program used "environmental economy" the theme of the *Report on Environmental Status*,[4] marking that environmental economics becomes an independent discipline. In China, environmental economics emerged in the mid-1970s. The first paper on environmental economics – "Research on Environmental Economics Should Be Conducted Quickly" – was published in October 1978, marking the emergence of environmental economics in China. As reform and opening up deepened in the 1980s, the theoretical basis of research on environmental economics also shifted from socialist political economy to market economy, and environmental economics was extensively studied. At present, research on environmental economics covers many disciplines and fields such as environmental policy economics, international environmental economics and policies, spatial environmental economics, macro-environmental economics, and environmental evaluation and accounting. The study of environmental economics is a key theoretical basis for formulating policies on environmental economics, including ecological environmental taxes, resource pricing, and market dealings.

Environmental economics is mainly to coordinate environmental protection with economic development, with a focus on the environment's relationship with economic development and technological progress, as well as equity and efficiency. Environmental economics mainly employs method of comparative analysis, cost-benefit analysis, environmental value measurement, shadow project, input-output method, as well as system engineering method.

### *2.3.2 Relationship with green consumption*

Environmental economics provides strong support for policies on green consumption. After studying the economic value of green consumption, the influencing factors of green consumption, etc., we can formulate supporting policies on environmental economics that promote green consumption. We can also promote green consumption by innovating the environmental economic system for green consumption, spreading the concept of green consumption, strengthening information-based management, etc. The principal means of promoting green consumption at home and abroad include fiscal support, tax guidance, and environmental certification. Consumers should intend to buy certified green products in theory, but because green products are expensive than ordinary products, their sales are lower in the market. In view of this, supporting policies on environmental economics are needed. On the one hand, the production of eco-friendly products enjoys fiscal support, including green subsidies, tax relief, and green credit. For example, subsidies are given to farmers to reduce the use of pesticides and chemical fertilizers, and preferential tax rates are provided for leading agricultural product enterprises that obtain green certification, so as to reduce the production and operation costs of producers and then reduce product prices. On the other hand, environmental taxes and fees are levied on production enterprises (or farmers) that waste resources or pollute the environment in the production process, so that the cost of their products reflects the scarcity level of resources and environmental damage costs, thereby achieving the purpose of raising product prices.

## 2.4 Consumer psychology and consumer behavior theory

Consumer psychology and consumer behavior theory studies the characteristics of consumer psychology and behavioral rules as consumers purchase products and services. The content of study for the two disciplines is similar. However, the study of consumer psychology is more in-depth, while the study of consumer behavior covers the psychological factors affecting consumer behavior, and also other influencing factors such as culture, society, and individuals. For studying consumer psychology and customer behavior, the academic circles adopt the methods such as observation, experiment, questionnaire, interview, and models. Their use has aided macroeconomic decision-making and improved the effect of macro-regulation. It not only helps enterprises make marketing activities more effective and boost their competitiveness but also help consumers improve quality and make healthy consumption.

### *2.4.1 Overview of theory and its application at home and abroad*

Consumer psychology refers to the psychological features and activities exhibited by consumers when making consumption. Consumers usually experience four types of consumer psychology: crowd psychology, psychology of seeking difference, mind of rivalry, and psychology of seeking realistic benefits. Consumer psychology activities are divided into seven stages: emergence of needs, formation of motivations, collection of commodity information, preparation for making purchases, selection of goods, use of goods, and evaluation of and feedback on goods. Consumer psychology is influenced by a host of factors, such as the consumption environment, consumption guide, and shopping places. Companies usually influence consumer psychology by devising appropriate marketing strategies. Most of the research on consumer behavior is based on the paradigm of "values-attitude-behavior," and it is believed that the existing dominant values are the fundamental reason for the formation of consumption mode. The factors affecting consumer behavior can be divided into internal drive and external stimuli. Internal drive includes the personality characteristics of consumers, psychological activities, etc. External stimuli include social environment, consumption trends, commodity factors, marketing, etc.

Therefore, consumer psychology and behavior science is of important guiding significance for the design of questionnaire for this book, as well as for the identification of external stimuli and internal drivers for consumers' cognition and practice of green consumption.

The theory of consumer psychology and consumer behavior emerged and develops as a result of the Industrial Revolution. In the context of a significant increase in production capacity and intensifying competition among manufacturers, some scholars began to study the relationship between consumer behavior and the sales of products by manufacturers. American sociologist Thorstein Veblen is one of the first scholars to study consumer behavior, who published *The Theory of Leisure Class* in 1899. He analyzed social phenomena by combing sociology with economics. From a sociological viewpoint, Thorstein Veblen analyzed the characteristics of the leisure class in the process of social and cultural development as well as their influence on the social system and other classes. Psychologist Scott noted in his report that psychological knowledge can be employed in sales and advertising to spur consumer demand. In the 1940s, research on consumer behavior focused on the research into motivation. Maslow's Hierarchy of Needs was also put forward at this stage. Based on people's needs, Maslow explored people's motivation and the study of human behavior, pointing out that people's needs progress from a low to high level. When the needs of a certain level are met, higher needs will emerge. Seeking higher needs will become the force driving consumer behavior. After 1960, consumer psychology and consumer behavior theory became an independent discipline, which has been fully studied and extensively used.

### *2.4.2 Relationship with green consumption*

Consumers play a main role in green consumption, and their behavior will affect the development and promotion of green consumption. Studying the factors that affect consumer behavior and psychology is of crucial significance for promoting green consumption in China. Factors that affect consumer behavior and psychology include disposable income, product prices, age, gender, schooling, alternatives, as well as consumption concept and awareness. From the perspective of green consumption, the findings of research by experts and scholars reveal the relationship between green consumption and the aforesaid factors. High-income consumers pay more attention to and make green consumption. Compared to ordinary products, green products require higher production costs, and their prices will be higher accordingly. Older consumers and younger consumers make green consumption for different purposes: health consideration for the former and a respect for green consumption concepts and quality of life for the latter. Women are more conscious of green consumption than men. Consumers with a higher level of education pay more attention to and make green consumption. Consumers' concept and awareness of green consumption is also a critically important influencing factor. The theory of consumer psychology and consumer behavior provides key theoretical support for green consumption and is one of important theories that enterprises shall know and refer to for green marketing. In promoting green consumption, the government must also observe the objective laws revealed by the theory of consumer behavior. Green consumption is a new type of consumption model. To promote green consumption, it is necessary to follow the laws of economics, especially the theory of consumer behavior. Therefore, consumer psychology and consumer behavior theory is of great significance for studying green consumption.

## 2.5 Community engagement theory

The theory of community engagement originated in the 1950s from the theory of community development. Everyone should champion and promote ecological conservation as it is closely related to everyone. We can promote a moderate, green, low-carbon, healthy way of life and consumption model by building green communities, strengthening publicity and education on ecological conservation, and raising citizens' environmental awareness.

### *2.5.1 Overview of theory and its application at home and abroad*

The concept of community engagement originated from *Community Development – Making the Small Town a Better Place to Live in and a Better Place in Which to Do Business*,[5] a book published by American sociologist Frank Farrington in 1915. It is a process in which residents within a community participate and give full play to their creativity in order to promote community economic development and social progress.

Community engagement is a kind of behavior and action to actively express and realize the rights and interests and is a key manifestation of public engagement. The theory of community engagement requires extensive and good interaction between communities and the public. On the one hand, it influences and manages the everyday behavior of residents through the community. On the other hand, it reflects residents' demands for the city and community administration through the community. At present, the academic circles apply the community engagement theory mainly to tourism development, environmental protection, poverty alleviation and development, etc. In terms of engagement methods, the community engagement theory draws on five engagement methods in the theory of public engagement: (1) information exchange; (2) consulting; (3) engagement; (4) collaboration; (5) authorized feedback. The theory of community engagement analyzes the implementation methods of public engagement and reflects the important role of communities in public engagement. It has important guiding significance for promoting green consumption at the community level.

### *2.5.2 Green community and green consumption*

A green community refers to a community that independently establishes and maintains a community environmental management system and a mechanism for public participation in environmental protection in the long term. Guided by the idea of sustainable development, it mainly advocates that residents choose a green and fashionable way of life. It is one of the basic functional units of green city building. Green communities serve the four functions of supervising environmental law enforcement, offering policy advice, providing education on environmental protection, and advocating eco-friendly lifestyle. Specifically, it refers to the following six areas: (1) a joint meeting involving the government and all walks of life; (2) a garbage sorting and transport system; (3) green space; (4) a team of volunteers; (5)

a venue for spreading environmental protection knowledge; (6) a certain number of families that promote ecological conservation.

Green community is a key practice to promote green consumption at the community level. Since the community is a basic unit of social administration and directly deals with residents, building green communities helps residents establish the concept of green consumption, and promotes green consumption in a subtle manner.

## Notes

1 Zhang Kunmin. Sustainable development and its implementation in China. *Journal of Tsinghua University (Philosophy and Social Sciences)*, 1999 (4): 1–8 + 44.
2 Li Shiyan, Lu Jiayin. The history of Chinese ecological philosophy theory. *Journal of Nanjing Forestry University (Humanities and Social Sciences Edition)*, 2016 (1): 32–42.
3 Bao Qingde, Zhang Yan. Ecological philosophical thoughts on green consumption. *Studies in Dialectics of Nature*, 2004 (2): 4–7 + 28.
4 Dong Xiaolin. *Environmental Economics*. Beijing: China Communications Press, 2005.
5 Basic situation of community building and development overseas. http://www.cucc.org.cn, October 4, 2005.

# 3 International policies on green consumption and their practices

As green consumption emerges and develops worldwide, governments have released policies to advocate and promote green consumption. This chapter primarily discusses and summarizes the foreign policies and practices of green consumption, with a view to providing reference and guidance for improving China's policy on green consumption as well as related practical activities.

## 3.1 Administrative measures to promote green consumption

To promote green consumption, the state needs to use administrative means for regulation at the macro level, establish a comprehensive and multi-tiered system of laws and regulations, and put green consumption under the framework in the form of command control. Developed countries incorporate the top-level planning for green consumption into the administrative means, mainly legal norms, in order to ensure the promotion and implementation of policies.

### *3.1.1 The United States*

The United States is a key participant in the modern environmental protection movement. From Rachel Carson's *Silent Spring* that initiated the environmental protection movement to the emergence and development of the concept of environmental protection, the United States has a mature legal and regulatory system for green consumption. A salient feature of this system is the combination of green consumption and pollution prevention and control. In the 1970s, the United States enacted a number of laws and regulations to protect the ecological environment to promote green consumption.

The *Pollution Prevention Act* promotes green consumption while preventing pollution. Instead of making end-of-pipe treatment of pollution, this act prevents and reduces the generation of pollutants at source. Green consumption is mentioned as one of the means to prevent pollution.

Green consumption, together with resource reduction and enhancement of energy efficiency, constitutes a legal and policy to prevent pollution. The *Executive Order Federal Acquisition, Recycling and Waste Prevention*, the *Solid Waste Disposal Act*, and the *Regulations for the Administration of Hazardous Waste* share

DOI: 10.4324/9781003433040-3

similar characteristics. The upper level of the U.S. environmental law system is the *National Environmental Policy Act* (NEPA), and the lower level includes *Resource Conservation and Recovery Act* (RCRA),[1] the *Comprehensive Environmental Response, Compensation and Liability Act*, etc. In order to encourage the establishment of green consumption model, the U.S. government promotes green procurement through federal decrees and presidential executive orders. The U.S. Government has successively formulated a slew of green procurement plans, such as the "Plan for Procurement of Circular Products," "Energy Star" program, "Ecological Agricultural Products Act" and the Environmentally Preferable Purchasing (EPP) program. The *Comprehensive Procurement Guideline* (CPG) is the main criterion for the U.S. federal government to establish a green procurement system. The United States divides green procurement products into seven categories: products containing recyclable components, products that protect the ozone layer, energy-saving and water-saving products, alternative fuel vehicles, and bio-based products, more eco-friendly products, and substitutes for toxic chemicals. The U.S. government has set green procurement standards for each type of products, which are amended according to social progress and environmental development. In January 2007, the U.S. Federal Government issued Executive Order 13423, which calls for the wider use of environmental management system in government procurement in order to better manage and promote green procurement. In October 2009, the U.S. federal government issued Executive Order 13514, which, on the basis of Executive Order 13423, expands the demand and scope of procurement of green products in government procurement plans and emphasizes that 95 percent of future procurement contracts (except for military field such as weapons) should meet the goal of prioritizing the procurement of eco-friendly products. Moreover, the Order emphasizes that purchasers of electronic products should prioritize products and equipment registered in the Electronic Product Environmental Assessment Tool (EPEAT), in that EPEAT helps identify desktops, laptops, and displays that have a low environmental impact.

In terms of resource recycling, the U.S. Resource Conservation and Recovery Act (RCRA) offers guidance on the whole process of waste collection, distribution, recycling or disposal otherwise. It is exhaustive compared to resource recycling laws enacted in various countries. As the principal parties that bear legal obligations, governments and enterprises are required to carry out friendly cooperation on resource recycling and jointly promote the model of green consumption. California's *Beverage Container Recycling and Litter Reduction Act*[2] is a typical example of this law at the state level. *Beverage Container Recycling and Litter Reduction Act*, which was adopted in 1987, stipulates that a few cents of recycling fees are imposed on plastic beverages, so as to encourage consumers to send waste bottles to recycling stations in exchange for recycling fees consumers paid. In Los Angeles, every mineral water bottle is labeled with a 5-cent recycling fee. In 1989, California passed the *Integrated Waste Management Act*, which requires that 50 percent of waste should be disposed of through source reduction and recycling by 2000, and that cities that fail to meet the requirements are fined US$10,000 per day. It is also stipulated that glass containers must use 10 to 25 percent of recycled materials, and plastic waste must use 30 percent of recycled materials. In 2003, California was also the first to pass the *Electronic Waste Recycling Act of 2003*, which provides for the management and recycling of waste from all video display devices sold in California, which officially entered into force on January 1, 2005. The fee is paid in advance at the time of purchasing electrical appliances. Electronic waste subject to the Act includes: used cathode ray tube (CRT) televisions and computer monitors, laptops, liquid crystal displays, plasma televisions, and liquid crystal displays televisions. Before the implementation of the act, manufacturers should inform all retailers of their products by October 1, 2004 which electronic equipment products are subject to electronic waste charges.[3]

At the same time, the United States also enacted economic laws and regulates consumption through market mechanisms to promote green consumption. The *Executive Order Federal Acquisition, Recycling and Waste Prevention* and the *Comprehensive Environmental Response, Compensation and Liability Act* are representative of these laws. The latter on environmental infringement liability and compensation helps to adjust the legal relationship of green consumption and clarifies the legal liability for green consumption.

Furthermore, the United States promulgated macro-strategic administration laws such as the *National Environmental Policy Act* and the *Energy Policy Act*, which confirm the status of green consumption in the national environmental policy in the form of law and promote the development of the legal mechanism for green consumption.

### *3.1.2 Europe*

Europe is the region where the industrial revolution occurred early and is also one of the key birthplaces of the modern environmental protection movement. Member states of the European Union have jointly planned for green consumption and made tremendous progress in this regard. The *Green Consumer Guide* published in Britain in 1987 marked the emergence of green consumption ideas in developed countries, triggering the "green consumption movement." The movement calls on consumers to buy eco-friendly products, thereby prompting producers to manufacture eco-friendly products. It is an environmental protection movement that affects production through green consumption. Thereafter, this movement swept across Europe. The EU has introduced a slew of policies and measures to promote green consumption.

The Council of the European Union has successively promulgated or updated guiding legislative documents such as the Restructuring the Community framework for the taxation of energy products and electricity, the Packaging and Packaging Waste Directive (PPWD) and the Water Framework Directive. The institutional design focuses on the provision of green consumption products and services, with the aim of promoting the development of green consumer products such as clean energy, green packaging products and water-saving products, and developing consumers' habit of making green consumption. This design facilitates industrial innovation while promoting green consumption and transforms and upgrades the

European economy. At the same time, the Energy Labelling Directive formulated by the EU stipulates standards for energy consumption and requires that product energy levels must be specified in product advertisements and technical publicity materials to guide consumers to buy eco-friendly products. In 2004, the EU promulgated the Buying Green – A Handbook on green public procurement, established an information database on procurement products, and designated over 100 kinds of commodities for green procurement. Government procurement in developed countries such as the EU member states accounts for 15 to 25 percent of GDP. Green government procurement becomes the preferred means to lead green consumption. The procurement power of government bodies affects the market share of eco-friendly goods and consumer orientation. The EU directives are specific for promoting renewable energy development. EU directives governing the development of renewable energy mainly include: Directive 2001/77/EC on the promotion of electricity produced from renewable energy sources in the internal electricity market; Council Directive 2003/96/EC for restructuring the Community framework for the taxation of energy products and electricity; 2003/54/EC concerning common rules for the internal market in electricity; 2005/32/EC establishing a framework for the setting of eco-design requirements for energy-using products. The green paper on energy policy entitled A European Strategy for Sustainable, Competitive and Secure Energy published in 2006 identifies priority areas for development in the energy sector to ensure sustainable energy development. In the same year, the EU published the Action Plan for Energy Efficiency, which sets the goal of achieving energy savings of 20 percent by 2020 as well as the concrete steps taken to achieve the goal. In 2008, the Directive of the European Parliament and of the Council on the promotion of the use of energy from renewable sources was issued, and policy documents such as the White Paper on Energy Policy, the White Paper on Renewable Energy, the Green Paper on Energy Supply, and EU directives were issued, which promote the development of renewable energy. Regulation on persistent organic pollutants and amending Directive 79/117/EEC in 2004, Regulation for Registration, Evaluation, Authorization and Restriction of Chemicals (REACH) of 2006, Regulation concerning the export and import of dangerous chemicals of 2008, and other important technical trade measures have far-reaching and long-term impact. These involve not only equipment itself but also the upstream and downstream supply chains for parts and raw material industries. In 2009, the EU published the Energy Related Products (ErP) Directive, which replaces the Eco-Design of Energy Using Products (EuP) Directive issued in 2005. It extends energy-using products in the EuP Directive to energy-related products and improves the energy efficiency of products related to energy use. The ErP Directive sets minimum performance and energy consumption requirements for products and requires manufacturers and importers to evaluate the environmental impact factors of products throughout their life cycle and then to optimize designs based on the evaluation results in order to minimize the environmental impact of products. This directive will affect the life cycle of energy-related products, ranging from design to production to retirement. As a directive under CE marking, the ErP Directive is mandatorily enforced along with EMC, safety regulations, radio communications, and other requirements. In 2013, the EU formulated a new energy strategy called Outline for Environmental and Energy Financing to improve energy efficiency, develop renewable energy, and achieve energy connectivity within the EU. European countries have developed green consumption programs. In particular, Germany and the United Kingdom have achieved remarkable results.

To promote sustainable consumption and production, the European Commission issued in 2008 the *Sustainable Consumption and Production and Sustainable Industrial Policy (SCP/SIP) Action Plan*, which focuses on improving the environmental performance of products and increasing consumer demand for sustainable products. The action plan includes eight areas: (1) raise eco-design requirements for more products; (2) strengthen the energy and environmental labeling system; (3) operate incentives and government procurement for energy-efficient products; (4) implement green public procurement; (5) consistency between product data and methods; (6) cooperate with retailers and consumers; (7) improve energy efficiency, promote industrial innovation and provide environment capacity for industry; (8) promote sustainable consumption and production on a global scale.

The laws of European countries on green consumption include domestic legislative documents based on binding legislative documents such as EU directives on green consumption, and the provisions of domestic laws of European countries governing green consumption. The former refers to the implementation of the EU's legal mechanism on green consumption at the specific level and is not elaborated here. Discussion here focuses on the latter.

Germany is one of the earliest countries to promulgate the most comprehensive legislation on the circular economy. Germany is a representation of advanced ideas in terms of both the overall structure of the *Circular Economy Act* and the practical significance of its promulgation. At the same time, Germany is also a model for the establishment of the EU's legal system for green consumption. In 1996, Germany enacted the *Closed Substance Cycle and Waste Management Act*, which mainly includes: requiring all social actors, including consumers, to reduce the use of resources as much as possible; and requiring residents to sort garbage caused by consumption of by-products in order to restrain their behavior. The legal system is implemented to guide citizens' consumption, reduce consumption activities harmful to the environment, and encourage people to make green consumption. A dedicated government management and supervision organization is established to ensure the rational use and safe disposal of waste. Economic value is created in the process of green consumption, and a transition to green consumption is promoted. Germany is also the first country to formulate and implement environmental labeling. As an innovative policy tool for green consumption, the "Blue Angel" label has been recognized and supported by the public and has led to the rise of environmental labeling certification. Furthermore, Germany places a premium on the government-driven effect by stipulating that the government shall prioritize the purchase of green products.

The United Kingdom adopts integrated management legislation. In September 2002, the UK Department for Environment and the Department of Trade and Industry (DTI) published the *Changing Patterns: UK Government Framework for*

*Sustainable Consumption and Production* on sustainable production and consumption, which is a long-term policy. Under this long term policy, the British government puts forward a path to economic development that does not pollute the environment, efficient use of resources, product life cycle assessment, measures to help consumers gain more information about products and services, measures to invest in technologies that reduce environmental burden and promote technological innovation, and other schemes. The UK's *Action Plan on Green Consumption* employs a slew of policies to guide group consumption and purchasing patterns, starting with energy efficiency, waste recycling, water, personal transport, and catering. Moreover, the UK National Consumer Council and the UK Sustainable Development Commission jointly held a roundtable meeting on promoting green consumption. In 1995, Britain enacted the *Home Energy Conservation Act.* In 2003, the British government also issued a white paper entitled *Our energy future – creating a low carbon economy*, which notes that the United Kingdom has been fully aware of the threat posed by energy security and climate change, and that under the guidance of the sustainable development concept, Britain should reduce the consumption of high-carbon energy sources such as coal and petroleum as much as possible, cut greenhouse gas emissions, and achieve a win-win situation of social and economic development as well as environmental protection through a slew of means such as technological innovation, institutional innovation, industrial transformation, and development of new energy. The United Kingdom is one of the earliest countries to introduce standardization and has a good foundation in this regard. In the United Kingdom, standardization has played a key role in terms of technical support, support, and leadership for sustainable consumption, ensuring the effective implementation of laws, policies, and plans relating to sustainable consumption. The British Standards Institute (BSI) published BS8900 sustainability standards, including *BS8900-1 Basic Framework and Detailed Rules, BS8900-2 Evaluation of Sustainability Management Organizations, BS8900-3 Principles and Frameworks for Sustainable Procurement – Guide.* In the areas of environmental sustainability management and sustainable use of resources, BSI published *BS42020 Biodiversity – Code of Practice for Planning and Development, BSEN16001 Energy Management System, BS ISO 14046 Environmental management – water footprint – principles, requirements and guidelines*, etc. In terms of promoting the development and application of new energy, the BSI pays attention to smart telecommunications (application of big data, Internet, cloud platform, blockchain, etc., in the field of energy-saving telecommunications), alternative energy, and other fields, such as battery electric vehicles, hot engines using gaseous energy, biogas, LPG, or hydrogen. It includes energy consumption and recycling; grid connection, development of electrical energy reserves, and mutual conversion between electrical energy and thermal energy, potential energy and batteries; bioreactors and biofuels for power generation. In April 2006, Britain introduced a new standard for building energy conservation, which stipulates that new buildings must be installed with energy- and water-saving facilities. The United Kingdom plans to equip all buildings with energy-saving lamps over eight years, thereby reducing greenhouse gas emissions in the lighting field by 70 percent.

On July 15, 1975, France adopted the first *Waste Disposal Act*, under which governments at all levels are required to collect and transport domestic and industrial waste in a unified manner within 15 years, classify these into daily and dangerous categories, and transport these to designated places for separate disposal. The first *Waste Disposal Act*, which is mainly targeted at hygiene and health, obliges properly disposing of garbage and waste products to minimize pollution to the environment. This is a type of passive environmental protection. By the 1990s, certain progress was made in the management and technology of waste disposal. On July 13, 1992, France adopted the second *Waste Disposal Act*, which requires all regions to sort and recycle waste within ten years. The second law reflects the new philosophy of environmental protection, requiring garbage recycling as much as possible, and clarifying the responsibilities and obligations of all citizens to promote environmental protection. Based on these two laws, the French environmental authorities developed a full variety of regulations on garbage disposal. These guide the collection, transport, and final disposal of many types of waste, ranging from household garbage, expired medicines, used batteries, obsolete batteries, used tires to scrapped automobiles. France formulated the *Decree on the Prevention and Management of Waste Electrical and Electronic Equipment* in accordance with the EU Waste Electrical and Electronic Equipment (WEEE) Directive, designating four waste collection and recycling companies to dispose of e-waste. The latest version of the decree, which became effective on November 15, 2006, stipulates that in accordance with the principle of "whoever produces, sells, or uses it is responsible for recycling, and bears relevant environmental protection costs," manufacturers bear the costs of recycling electronic and electrical waste, retailers are responsible for transport, and newly sold electronic and electrical equipment will be marked with recycling costs to remind consumers that it is costly to recycle and dispose of these products. For example, it costs an average of 8 euros to dispose of a TV set and about 13 euros to dispose of a refrigerator. At the same time, the decree demands that all sellers of electronic and electrical equipment should not refuse to accept the same kind of waste electronic and electrical products returned by customers when selling new products; manufacturers must be responsible for properly disposing of such e-waste and help local governments establish e-waste recycling stations. Moreover, local governments should formulate policies to facilitate sorting and disposal of e-waste by residents and aid environmental protection companies in waste collection and disposal.

The Icelandic government has innovated the taxation law system. In addition to mainstream environmental taxes such as carbon tax, the Icelandic government imposes an environmental tax of up to 15 pence per disposable plastic bag, which effectively controls the use of disposable plastic bags. Income tax is used to subsidize other links of green consumption, such as waste management.

### *3.1.3 Japan*

Due to Japan's large population, small territory, resources scarcity, and heavy reliance on foreign countries in addition to the legacy burden of environmental hazards, green consumption is of important significance to Japan, because it directly concerns its national security.

In 2001, Japan promulgated the *Green Consumption Law*, which advocates a green purchasing model for residents. A salient feature of this law is its focus on the recycling of resources. The *Law for Promotion of Effective Utilization of Resources* is a basic law in this field and is an important legal norm for "promoting circulation of materials, lessening the burden on the environment, achieving healthy economic development, and building a sustainable society" under the *Basic Act on Establishing a Sound Material-Cycle Society*. On this basis, Japan has also successively promulgated special laws such as *Waste Management and Public Cleansing Law*, *Containers and Packaging Recycling Act*, *Home Appliance Recycling Law*, *Food Recycling Law*, and *Building and Materials Recycling Act*, incorporating all aspects of waste generation within the scope of resource recovery law.

Japan is also concerned about energy conservation. The *Specification Plan for Environmental Tax* is another key law promulgated in Japan in 2004 to cut energy consumption, enhance energy efficiency, and protect resources as well as the environment. This law controls emissions by imposing tax on fuel collectors at the upward, midstream, and downstream level. Income tax is used to support the development and promotion of new energy sources. For example, subsidies are provided for new energy sources development projects and tax preference is given to enterprises or individuals that use new energy sources. Furthermore, this law supports the introduction of energy-saving equipment and the improvement of energy-saving technologies, and various support policies are implemented for relevant enterprises and individuals.

Japan values the government's demonstration role in driving green consumption and ensures the dominance of green consumer products and services in government procurement by means of the *Green Purchasing Law*. In 2002, Japan enacted the *Green Purchasing Law*, which stipulates the green procurement obligations that the government, enterprises, and individuals should discharge when the government provides information on eco-friendly goods and services. The law is primarily based on the strong purchasing power of the government. It then supports environmental protection enterprises and eco-friendly products by signing priority purchase contracts with eco-friendly product producers in order to promote green consumption. At present, the Japanese government's government vehicles and office supplies are all green products, and green procurement in society accounts for over 80 percent.

Japan introduced the "frontrunner" energy efficiency benchmark system in 1999, which is the main basis for the energy-saving standards for products in various fields. The Frontrunner Program reviews the energy efficiency of products every year after setting the frontrunner energy efficiency standard values. When the energy efficiency standard value of a certain product increases by 30 percent compared with the standard, the energy efficiency standard value will be reset. The dynamic adjustment of the energy efficiency standards promotes the dynamic upgrading of the product mix. The Frontrunner Program provides R&D, financial and financial support to leading manufacturers, benefitting leading enterprises.

Moreover, it rewards and subsidizes retailers and consumers to ensure good promotion results.[4] The Frontrunner Standard consists of six parts: product range, target year, target benchmark value (energy efficiency limit value), measurement methods, methods, and mark for judging the completion rate of benchmark value. The product range and types are determined according to factors such as energy consumption, amount of energy used, relevant testing standards, and testing capability. The target year is determined on the basis of full consideration to energy consumption, energy level, social demand, product development period, facility and equipment investment as well as construction cycle, and development prospects of highly efficient and energy-saving technologies. The target year is different for different types of products, and is generally set at four to eight years. The target benchmark or limit value is determined based on the product classification according to the maximum energy efficiency value and the potential for energy efficiency enhancement. It can be a numeric or non-numeric computational formula. The measurement method is mainly based on the Japanese Industrial Standards (JIS). Participation in the frontrunner system operates on a voluntary basis, but intervention measures will be taken if the manufacturer's product or imported product falls far short of the frontrunner program's criteria.

At the same time, Japan has also passed laws governing the obligations and responsibilities of consumers. The *Basic Act on Establishing a Sound Material-Cycle Society* stipulates: (1) The nationals must be clear about their responsibilities and observe the basic principles, extend the service period of products regarding special commodities, prioritize the use of reproduced products, aid in the sorting and recycling of resources, reduce the generation of waste after consumption, promote the rational recycling of products, and assist national and local public environmental protection groups in launching relevant countermeasures. (2) The nationals are obliged to properly send recyclable products and containers to the relevant authorities and to assist the managers in recycling. (3) The nationals are obliged to raise circular consumption awareness on their own initiative.

### 3.2 Economic means to stimulate green consumption

The economic means to stimulate green consumption mainly include three types: positive incentives featuring fiscal subsidies, comprehensive incentives featuring deposit returns, and negative incentives featuring taxation. For positive incentives, the government subsidizes green products to reduce prices and make them more attractive to consumers. Its principal purpose is to motivate consumers to buy green products and stimulate consumer demand for green products. As one of economic means for government regulation, fiscal subsidy plays an important role in encouraging and promoting green consumption. In developed countries, many policies have been put in place in this regard. On the one hand, fiscal subsidies and tax preference are given to green products to encourage the production of green products. On the other hand, fiscal subsidies are used to encourage consumers to make green consumption, such as subsidies for energy-saving products, green buildings, and new energy vehicles.

For comprehensive incentives, an additional fee called deposit is added when a product is sold. When a consumer puts the waste product into the designated recycling equipment, such deposit is immediately returned. The practice of deposit return can be regarded as a combination of taxes and subsidies. It is earmarked for a fixed purpose and has a low degree of fiscal dependence. While avoiding the unregulated disposal of hazardous waste, the deposit return system also promotes the recycling of some waste. It saves resources while cutting costs. The deposit return system is intended to rationally dispose of product waste and is a continuation of consumers' responsibility to make green consumption and is also an essential part of green consumption.

For the negative incentives, the government internalizes the cost of environmental damage caused by enterprises through taxation, thereby achieving environmental protection in the process of consumption. From an economic viewpoint, the root cause of environmental problems is that the prices of environmental resources do not properly reflect the scarcity of environmental resources. The best way to tackle environmental problems is to achieve the effective allocation of environmental resources by means of rational pricing and paid use of environmental resources.

Ecological tax (environmental tax), which is a tax levied by the state on pollution-causing units or individuals in accordance with the law, aims to regulate environmental pollution, raise funds for environmental protection, and protect resources and the environment. It is an economic means of internalizing the social costs of environmental pollution and ecological damage into production costs through taxation. Ecological taxes in Western countries mainly fall into three categories: (1) Tax levied on pollutants discharged by enterprises; (2) Tax levied on acts that require high energy consumption and materials; (3) Tax levied on acts that pollute the urban environment and the living environment. Developed countries value the use of ecological tax means in the process of promoting green consumption.

### *3.2.1 The United States*

#### *3.2.1.1 Ecological tax*

The United States has the most comprehensive ecological tax system, which covers gasoline taxes, mining taxes, solid waste disposal taxes, etc. The ecological tax system is mainly divided into four areas: (1) Taxes on fuel, such as gasoline and diesel, can effectively regulate drivers' driving behavior and change their mode of travel; (2) Taxes on energy, such as coal tax and mining tax, can slow down the exploitation of resources and promote the effective use of resources; (3) Taxes on acts that pollute the urban environment and the living environment, such as taxing household garbage, advocating garbage sorting, and guiding residents to make green consumption; (4) Tax incentives and relief, such as direct tax reductions, investment tax credits, and accelerated depreciation, adopting tax incentives and reductions for energy-saving and eco-friendly products, and influencing consumer behavior through prices. Under the *Energy Policy Act* of 2005, the United States introduced a US$1.3 billion budget bill to encourage residents to choose energy-saving equipment such as zero-pollution solar energy, starting in 2011. The use of energy-efficient equipment in house decoration is entitled to a federal individual income tax credit of up to US$500 under the condition of 50 percent less energy consumption than a typical household.[5]

#### *3.2.1.2 Fiscal subsidies*

In 2009, the U.S. Department of Energy invested US$2 billion in the research and development of electric vehicles in support of the promotion of new-generation electric vehicles and also offered a US$7,500 tax credit to consumers who buy new-generation hybrid vehicles. The U.S. government also invested US$400 million in building infrastructure related to electric vehicles. New energy vehicles are also blossoming under the favorable economic policies.

In addition, the United States values the responsibility of enterprises in promoting green consumption, requiring enterprises to control pollution at source, to vigorously promote cleaner production, and placing a high value on the reduction of environmental risks and ecological effects in the process of product R&D as well as production and services. From 2006 to 2015, the U.S. government provided US$5 billion in subsidies to related enterprises, US$2 billion in subsidies for clean coal utilization technologies, as well as loan security and other subsidies for energy conservation and the R&D of new nuclear energy technologies.

### *3.2.2 Europe*

#### *3.2.2.1 Ecological tax*

Denmark's ecological tax is the most representative. The Danish government operates a policy under which household waste is disposed of according to the combined methods of category and quantity. On the one hand, sorted and unsorted waste is priced separately, with a lower fee for sorted waste. At the same time, different tax rates apply according to different waste disposal methods. On the other hand, the government requires urban residents to put garbage in containers of a uniform standard, and prices garbage in full containers. This practice can control the quantity of waste discharged, urge residents to sort garbage on their own initiative while increasing the recycling of garbage, and promote green consumption.

Germany's ecological tax includes fuel tax, vehicle tax, renewable energy tax, etc., and its fuel tax rate is the highest in the EU. At the same time, Germany curbs water pollution by imposing a water pollution tax. The tax rate is based on the pollution units of wastewater. The tax rate is uniform and continuously raised, and the tax revenues are earmarked for fixed purposes. Since 2002, fuel and electric power have also been included in the scope of ecological tax.

Since 1998, Italy has reduced the use of plastic bags by imposing an ecological tax on the production and use of plastic bags. Beginning in 2005, France has imposed separate domestic taxes on 95 and 98 unleaded gasoline as well as diesel oil. The rate of internal tax on petroleum products varies according to the fuel types. In

*Table 3.1* Ecological taxes in OECD member states as a proportion of their respective GDP in 2000

| *Country* | *Proportion (%)* | *Country* | *Proportion (%)* |
|---|---|---|---|
| Denmark | 4 | Norway | 3 |
| Sweden | 3.8 | Portugal | 2.7 |
| Greece | 3.5 | Mexico | 2.1 |
| The Netherlands | 3.2 | The United States | 2 |

Source: Based on OECD statistics.

the case of tax rate for refined oil products announced in March 2010, an internal tax of €0.606 per liter of 95 unleaded petrol and a value-added tax of €0.119 per liter was levied. Consumers must pay a punitive purchase tax of up to €2,600 when buying a new large-displacement automobile.

The ecological taxes in developed countries are highly mature, and the ecological tax revenue is significant in the total tax revenue in most countries. Table 3.1 shows the Organization for Economic Co-operation and Development (OECD) Survey in 2000 regarding the share of ecological tax revenues in their member states in their respective GDP for the current year. Denmark tops the ranking with 4 percent, followed by Sweden, Greece, the Netherlands, Norway, Portugal, etc. In Mexico and the United States, the ecological tax also accounts for 2 percent of their respective GDP.

#### *3.2.2.2 Fiscal subsidies*

Back in 1994, France's "old car scrapping program" gave a subsidy of 5,000 francs per new car (equivalent to 6 percent of the cost of a new car) to encourage the replacement of old cars that were used for over ten years old with new cars. A total of 1.56 million old vehicles were recycled, resulting in a significant reduction in exhaust gas emissions.

At the same time, the French government also offers fiscal subsidies to enterprises that buy energy-saving equipment or technologies. Subsidy for demonstration projects can account for 20 to 30 percent of the total project investment. In order to encourage the development and promotion of new energy vehicles, European countries provide subsidies for green products such as hybrid vehicles and electric vehicles. The amount of subsidies is significant. For example, an electric car in France can be subsidized by up to 7,000 euros, and the United Kingdom has been giving a car purchase allowance of 5,000 pounds for each low-speed plug-in eco-friendly automobile since 2014. In 2010, France launched the "New Car Replacement Bonus" program, which stipulates that consumers receive a bonus of 100 to 5,000 euros if they buy an eco-friendlier car with a small displacement.

#### *3.2.2.3 Deposit return*

The deposit return system is widely applied to the disposal of municipal solid waste. OECD member states have been advocating or mandatorily enforcing the deposit return system. The European countries that operate the deposit return system for metal cans are mainly Portugal and Sweden, and the return rate is 50 to 90 percent for beer cans and soft drink cans. More than ten countries operate the deposit return system for plastic beverage containers, with a return rate of over 60 percent. The return rate for wine bottles and alcohol bottles reaches 60 to 80 percent. Germany and Austria also operate a deposit return system for fluorescent tubes, detergent packaging, paint packaging, and automobile batteries, with a return rate of 60 to 80 percent.

In 1991, Germany implemented the *Waste Sorting and Packaging Ordinance* to reduce the generation of package waste and to reuse or recycle unavoidable disposable package waste. This ordinance puts responsibility on all links involved in the packaging from production to recycling, such as package manufacturers, product manufacturers, package ingredient suppliers, so as to achieve the reuse or recycling of all available packages. The German government has established a system for collecting and sorting commercial packages and provided funding with licensing fees such as "green dots." The German government stipulates that when the total number of reusable beverage containers on the market is less than 72 percent, a mandatory deposit is required and the deposit is refunded when the container is returned. German retailers must prioritize selling products with reusable containers. The law requires all producers assume responsibility not only for products but also for the collection of their packaging, and orders enterprises engaged in transport, agency, and sales, as well as packaging enterprises and wholesalers to recycle used packaging. At the same time, they can transfer recycling responsibilities to specialized recycling companies. The Duales System Deutschland (DSD) (a social organization), founded in 1990, plays a key role in packaging recycling. As a non-governmental organization that comprises nearly 100 production and sales enterprises, DSD enjoys tax exemption under the packaging ordinance. By 2000, the company had 1.79 million members, who pay to the DSD according to the type and weight of packaging materials used, and have the right to use the "Green Dot" packaging recycling mark. Non-member companies must abide by the relevant provisions of packaging ordinance and recycle packaging materials independently, which is more costly.

### 3.2.3 Japan

#### 3.2.3.1 Carbon tax

From 1991 to 2001, Japan promulgated many laws on waste, chemicals, renewable energy, climate warming, etc. For example, in 1998, the Japanese government established the Countermeasures Promotion Center to study global warming and formulated the corresponding *Act on Promotion of Global Warming Countermeasures*. In July 2008, the Japanese cabinet issued the *Action plan for achieving a low carbon society*, which elaborates on the goals and efforts required for building a low-carbon society in Japan, specifies the national low-carbon strategy, and proposes concrete measures, including the government's fiscal and taxation policies, government oversight and management, etc.[6] Japan's carbon tax scheme was put forward by the Ministry of the Environment in 2004, finalized in October 2005, and officially entered into force in January 2007. From the perspective of objects, carbon tax is mainly targeted at units that use fossil fuels, including major consumers of energy such as coal, oil, and gas, as well as enterprises that use fossil energy for power generation, including homes and offices. Therefore, carbon tax is imposed on both upstream production and downstream consumption. From the perspective of the tax rate, a tax of 2,400 yen per metric ton of carbon has a certain impact on the national economy and people's living standards. Carbon tax revenue is a steady source of funding that helps to implement the environmental protection policy. The carbon tax is principally used to prevent climate warming. It is also used for forest conservation, improving energy efficiency of buildings, developing new energy vehicles, promoting the development of low-emission motor vehicles, building low-carbon cities, etc. When the Ministry of the Environment was formulating its carbon tax scheme, it performed calculation and found that if all the carbon tax revenue was used for energy subsidies, it could significantly reduce $CO_2$ emissions, a reduction of about 5.1 million metric tons per year.[7] Since Japan introduced a carbon tax in 2007, it has achieved significant results in reducing greenhouse gas emissions, inhibiting excessive energy consumption, promoting progress in energy-saving technologies, and raising the recognition of carbon tax among the nationals. Japan's greenhouse gas emissions fell from 1.365 billion metric tons in 2007 to 1.207 billion metric tons in 2009, or a decrease of 11.58 percent. Thereafter, Japan further refined the carbon tax scheme in 2011 and 2012, so that the carbon tax rate has a low starting point and gradually increases.

#### *3.2.3.2 Fiscal subsidies*

The production of green products by enterprises is the basis and precondition for promoting green consumption. Government subsidies for producers of green products are also an important economic means to promote green consumption. Since the 1990s, the Japanese government has been subsidizing companies that use eco-friendly technologies in the production of products. In terms of the fiscal budget, the Japanese government subsidizes the R&D of green technologies by small and medium-sized enterprises (SMEs) in order to support them in producing green products, with a subsidy accounting for over 50 percent of technology development expenses. The Japanese government generously subsidizes emerging industries that produce green products. The subsidy for new green enterprises with a technology development period of less than two years can account for up to 70 percent of the total expenses. In order to promote eco-friendly vehicles with lower emissions, the government issues subsidies to individuals and enterprises that purchase clean energy vehicles. The Ministry of Economy, Trade and Industry (METI) allocates 38 billion yen per year to subsidize household high-efficiency water heaters and new energy management systems for buildings. For families and SMEs that purchase solar power generation equipment, the Japanese government also provides certain subsidies. In addition to the above, the Japanese government also subsidizes manufacturers of equipment that turns waste into resources, with the subsidies accounting for about half of the production and experimental expenses. An enterprise that purchases advanced energy equipment can be subsidized by one-third. Such direct subsidy greatly reduces the cost of emission reduction for consumers and enterprises and also motivates them to reduce emissions on their own initiative.[8]

#### *3.2.3.3 Tax reduction policy*

In order to encourage consumers and businesses to purchase and use energy-saving products and technologies, the Japanese government has promulgated a slew of tax reduction policies. While fuel engines made in Japan are highly advanced in terms of emission and fuel saving, the Japanese government made further requirements in the "Action Plan for the Development and Popularization of Vehicles with Little Public Hazards" released in July 2001. By 2010, the number of vehicles with little public hazards in use will reach 10 million, of which 3.5 million will be clean energy vehicles. To this end, the Japanese government has issued many supporting policies to encourage the public: reduce the purchase tax for some new vehicle types, and reduce the vehicle use tax in the first two to three years for such new cars; consumers who purchase eco-friendly vehicles, including natural gas-fueled vehicles and electric vehicles, will be exempt from vehicle purchase tax and other taxes (such as automobile weight tax). Japan implemented "green tax system" on April 1, 2009 on a large scale. In terms of corporate tax reduction, enterprises buying recycling equipment are exempt from part of fixed asset tax and income tax; enterprises purchasing waste plastic recycling treatment equipment are entitled to a special tax rebate equal to 14 percent of the equipment price in addition to the general tax rebate; enterprises purchasing deinking, glass fragment, and debris removal equipment and other equipment are entitled to the refund of fixed asset tax for a period of three years. In addition to the aforesaid tax reduction policies, the Japanese government also imposes a corporation tax on SMEs at the rate of 18 percent, which is four percent lower than the original tax rate, with the purpose of promoting energy conservation and emission reduction in SMEs.[9]

In terms of financing, the Japanese Government stipulates that Development Bank of Japan (DBJ), Japan Finance Corporation for Small and Medium Enterprises, and National Life Finance Corporation must provide low-interest financing to producers of green products to fully ensure that they have adequate funds for development. Since 2000, Japan's annual budget for fiscal subsidies related to environmental protection has approached US$13 billion.[10] In order to encourage more consumers to buy eco-friendly cars, the Japanese government has developed a slew of policies on preferential tax reductions and subsidies and divided vehicles into pure electric vehicles, hybrid vehicles, clean diesel vehicles, natural gas-fueled vehicles, and other low-emission vehicles with low fuel consumption. Consumers who buy pure electric vehicles, hybrid vehicles, and clean diesel vehicles are entitled to being exempt from various taxes.

## 3.3 Information-based means to encourage green consumption

Information means are one of the internationally popular measures for promoting green consumption. Information means include the use of green label, publicity, education, etc. Increasing the use of green labels in the market and strengthening publicity and education are important guarantees for promoting green consumption.

### *3.3.1 German "Blue Angel" ecolabel*

The Blue Angel is the world's first labeling system relating to environmental and consumer protection. It was put forward in 1978 by the Federal Ministry of the Interior. In 1986, the Blue Angel system was transferred to the German Federal Ministry for the Environment. Since the Blue Angel logo originates from the logo of the United Nations Environment Programme, it is a blue logo. Blue Angel is a voluntary tool to promote product innovation and provide guide for green government procurement. It is a standard for product performance, environmental performance, etc. Standards have been set for environmental protection, health protection, workplace safety, product safety, and use efficiency. The Blue Angel is also a public brand, which is a great confidence booster. At the same time, supported by the German government, it enjoys a high degree of transparency and recognition. It works with multiple stakeholders, becoming a milestone in promoting sustainable consumption.

#### *3.3.1.1 The setting of environmental labeling agencies*

Four institutions in Germany are involved in the formulation and management of the environmental labeling system, viz. Environmental Label Jury (ELJ), RAL-German Institute for Quality Assurance and Certification (RAL), Federal Environment Agency (FEA), and the Federal Ministry for the Environment, Nature Conservation and Nuclear Safety (BMU).

The Environmental Label Jury (ELJ) is an 11-member independent decision-making group under the Blue Angel body. Members are appointed by the President of the Ministerial Conference on the Environment for a term of three years without remuneration. They have voting rights and not subject to the BMU. This group is primarily responsible for the review and revision, including the selection of product types, the drafting of evaluation criteria, and the finalization of product standards. The ELJ is staffed mainly by the Church of Jesus in Germany, nature conservation groups, consumer associations, the Deutscher Werkbund, environmental organizations, the German Federation of Trade Unions, as well as journalists, environmental experts from the Bundestag, presidents, and former presidents of the federal states attending the Ministerial Conference on the Environment.

Founded in 1925 as the body for issuing the "Blue Angel" label, the RAL-German Institute for Quality Assurance and Certification (RAL) is a non-governmental and non-profit organization with over 140 member associations. Guided by RAL, these associations formulate standards for the quality of industrial and trade products and services, organize expert hearings on technical reports and draft standards, sign contracts with those who pass certification, and ensure the implementation and quality of standards by managing the use of contracts. For the sake of neutrality, RAL assessors come from industry and trade associations, consumer organizations, trade federations, and governments. RAL's activities are primarily funded by government appropriations, certification fees and private sponsorships, and 22 percent of its annual budget comes from certification income.

The German Federal Environment Agency (FEA), an environmental protection agency, represents the German government and is a key part of the Federal Ministry for the Environment, Nature Conservation and Nuclear Safety. It is responsible for reviewing the Blue Angel product types, drafting technical reports and standards, and participating in the approval of such green label.

The Federal Ministry for the Environment, Nature Conservation and Nuclear Safety (BMU) is a government agency responsible for nuclear safety and the development of green energy sources. It is the owner of the Blue Angel label and publishes the decisions made by the ELJ on a regular basis.[11]

#### *3.3.1.2 Introduction to Blue Angel*

In 1978, Germany officially launched the Blue Angel program and established rigorous standards and approval procedures for products awarded the ecolabel. The Blue Angel ecolabel is a model for the ISO14024 standard. Under the Blue Angel program, 80 standard documents for product groups in use have been formulated, and upwards of 10,000 products and services carry the Blue Angel label, of which 17 percent are from the international market and have high market recognition.

Blue Angel is a "soft market means." The Blue Angel program is a voluntary program, under which businesses voluntarily apply for ecolabel. Consumers voluntarily purchase products bearing the ecolabel, and there is no requirement for mandatory government procurement, but the government refers to the standard of this label when formulating the policy on green procurement. The Blue Angel provides or spreads information to consumers and producers keen on environmental protection, guiding them to purchase or produce eco-friendly products. This actually affects changes in product demand and the industrial structure.

The Blue Angel program adopts a phased incentive strategy. When most manufacturers meet the set standards, higher-level specifications will be formulated to lead the industry to make breakthroughs in the existing product design. The declaration documents submitted by manufacturers shall be trusted to an appropriate extent during the audit process. Hailed as the world's most stringent environmental label, it exercises prudence to speed up the applications.

The government's strong publicity, guidance, and consumer support are essential for the success of the Blue Angel system. The German eco-labeling system values public engagement and the government's good policy guidance. Local pilot and publicity activities such as "Blue Angel" action day are carried out.

#### 3.3.1.2.1 MANAGEMENT MECHANISM

The Blue Angel program is implemented according to four procedures: (1) Product category proposal; (2) The German Environment Agency prepares technical literature and draft standards, and the RAL organizes expert hearings and makes recommendations; (3) The ELJ decides whether to accept the draft standards; (4) The manufacturer applies to the RAL, a certificate is issued, and a contract for use is signed.

Product selection. The selection of Blue Angel products is a process in which multiple stakeholders are involved in the product selection process and is different from government-led programs. Anyone can make a proposal on product category. Then, it is checked and recommended by the Federal Environment Agency. Then, the ELJ selects the product category for further investigation. The final selection of product category is submitted to the Federal Environment Agency for confirmation. For product category assessment, the product life cycle assessment method is used to identify key environmental impact. It will evaluate the damage caused by a product to different environmental factors (such as harmful substances, and exhaust gases or waste discharged into air, water, and soil). The label should be awarded to products that protect the environment at a higher level than other like products. The products selected should also take account of factors such as quality, safety, and health protection.

Setting of standards. The German Federal Environment Agency prepares technical literature and draft standards, and the RAL organizes expert hearings and makes recommendations. The draft standard shall exactly define the scope of product categories, include specific criteria for obtaining the label, and detail the test results necessary to meet these criteria. Background research is wide-ranging, including market survey, product research, discussions with producers and consumers, and expert opinions. However, such standards and the categories of products that can be awarded the label are not invariable. Any individual or group can recommend or apply to the German Federal Ministry for the Environment for increasing the product categories. Upon receipt of the application, the German Environment Agency shall immediately perform a review and, if it is deemed viable, make a categorization proposal and conduct further review. Then, an expert hearing will be held. The experts participating in the hearings came from the German Industry Federation, representative producers and suppliers, consumer associations, commodity testing foundation, environmental federations, the trade circles, etc. All issues related to environmental labeling of products are discussed at such hearings. The basis of discussions is the proposed award criteria, with a focus on the product category. With the consent of the experts, standard products under application for additional product categories will also be reviewed before it is decided whether to accept application.

Certification implementation. For Blue Angel label, a third-party organization is responsible for reviewing and certifying all applications. The certification examination is stringent, with a wide scope of participation. The label certification process is democratic and flexible. Producers must first confirm whether their products belong to the scope of certification. If yes, they submit a written application. The body of the application should be based on the standards and requirements of such labeling. Then, the appraisal body reviews the applicant's production management quality system as well as environmental management and testing system and performs a sampling survey on the relevant products on site. After the sampled products are assessed by experts, the RAL signs a contract with eligible producers. Thereafter, eligible manufacturer have the right to use the Blue Angel label.

##### 3.3.1.2.2 IMPLEMENTATION EFFECT

The Blue Angel program has gained universal recognition among the nationals since its implementation, and the label carries unquestionable authority, with remarkable results. Nowadays, consumers in Germany will first check if a product carries the Blue Angel label before buying. They have complete trust in products with the Blue Angel label. A survey by the German magazine *Environmental Awareness* in 2004 showed that 83 percent of German consumers were aware of the Blue Angel, 100 percent of them thought it was wise to choose products with such label, and 49 percent of consumers were willing to buy products with the "Blue Angel" label at a premium. From January 1, 1999 to December 31, 2008, about 500 to 700 manufacturers in Germany and the rest of the world used "Blue Angel," and over 3,000 products and services carried "Blue Angel" label. This shows that the German "Blue Angel" program has been recognized all over the world.[12]

### *3.3.2 Nordic Swan Ecolabel*

The environmental labeling of products have rapidly developed in Nordic countries, North America, Japan, Germany, Australia, and other regions and countries since 1989 after Germany. The Nordic Swan Ecolabel, based on the Nordic Commission logo, depicts a white swan soaring against a green background.

#### *3.3.2.1 Development process*

In 1989, the Nordic Council of Ministers adopted a resolution to use the Nordic Swan Ecolabel and developed an independent and impartial labeling system. The Nordic Swan Ecolabel is the world's first transnational environmental labeling system and is currently recognized as a top environmental label in Europe. It is an environmental labeling system for products with a positive encouraging nature and manufacturers voluntarily apply for such label. The participating countries are Norway, Sweden, Iceland, Finland, and Denmark, and the Nordic Environmental Standards Collaborative Committee has been established to organize national management committees to carry out joint management.

After several years of consultation and preparations, the five Nordic countries officially began to use the environmental labeling for products since 1989 in accordance with the principles of harmonization, relative independence, complete voluntariness, etc. The principle of harmonization refers to the use of a unified product environmental labeling plan and system in the five Nordic countries to facilitate mutual recognition worldwide in the future. The principle of relative independence means that the environmental labeling system for products in the five Nordic countries is independent as far as other countries in the world are concerned. The principle of complete voluntariness means that manufacturers in the five Nordic countries apply for environmental label on a purely voluntary basis.

The Nordic Swan Ecolabel now covers 69 categories of products (see Table 3.2), and 2,023 labels have been issued. The Nordic Environmental Standards Collaborative Committee determines whether a product can be awarded the Nordic Swan Ecolabel and makes a final certification for each product group. The Nordic Environmental Labelling Program serves three purposes: first, to inform consumers and help them choose products less harmful to the environment; second, to encourage producers to incorporate environmental factors into product design and production; and third, to regard market forces as a supplement to environmental regulations.

#### *3.3.2.2 Management of the ecolabel*

The Nordic Swan Ecolabel is usually valid for three years. Should new requirements be made, companies are required to reapply. If a product does not meet these requirements at that time, the certification label will be withdrawn. The validity period of the certification is subject to the relevant standards documents. If the validity period of a standards document is extended without modifications, there is no need to reapply. This ensures that products can be improved according to technological progress and new research findings, reducing the negative impact on the environment.

Each of the member states has a National Management Committee responsible for their respective work related to Nordic Swan Ecolabel. The National Management Committee is the representative of environmental management agencies, non-governmental organizations, trade and industry, and research institutions in each member state. The representatives of each committee compose the Nordic Swan Ecolabel coordination organization, which is responsible for finalizing product categories and formulating product specification standards. The Nordic Environmental Labelling Collaborative Committee determines whether a product can be awarded the ecolabel and makes the final certification for product groups. With the consent of the Nordic Environmental Labelling Collaborative Committee, each member state can develop environmental label specifications and standards for products in light of domestic conditions. Nordic environmental label is financed by government subsidies and fees paid by companies producing ecolabel products (0.4 percent of annual product sales).

The Nordic Swan Ecolabel assesses the ecological environmental impact of products in the whole life cycle – from selection of raw materials to end-of-life

*Table 3.2* 69 product categories covered by the Nordic Swan Ecolabel

| Product category | | | | | | | | | |
|---|---|---|---|---|---|---|---|---|---|
| 1 | Acceleration controller | 15 | Chemical products for building | 29 | Copy and printing paper | 43 | Floor care products | 57 | Textiles and leatherware |
| 2 | Adhesives | 16 | Chemicals list | 30 | Copiers | 44 | Floors | 58 | Laundry |
| 3 | Cleaners for dry cleaning | 17 | Cleaning products | 31 | Printers | 45 | Furniture | 59 | Tissues |
| 4 | Audiovisual equipment | 18 | Cleaning services | 32 | Fax machines and multi-functional office equipment | 46 | Oilproof paper | 60 | Toys |
| 5 | Paper and pulp products | 19 | Cleaning agents for food industry | 33 | Cosmetics | 47 | Reusable towel services | 61 | Washing machines |
| 6 | Primary battery (chemical battery) | 20 | Enclosed fireplaces using biofuels | 34 | Antifreeze | 48 | Hotels and youth hostels | 62 | Car tires |
| 7 | Biofuel pellets | 21 | Enclosed toilet system | 35 | Detergent for dish-washing machines | 49 | Heat pumps | 63 | Windows |
| 8 | Oil- and gas-fired boiler burners | 22 | Coffee filters | 36 | Dish-washing machine detergent used by professionals | 50 | Detergent for hand washing of dinnerware | 64 | Writing instruments |
| 9 | Candles | 23 | Manure loading box | 37 | Durables | 51 | Printing houses | 65 | Sanitary products |
| 10 | Care products used on automobiles or ships | 24 | Compressors | 38 | Dishwasher | 52 | Personal computers | 66 | Supermarkets and grocery stores |
| 11 | Paper envelopes | 25 | Rechargeable battery and charger | 39 | Refrigerators and freezers | 53 | Restaurants | 67 | Lubricants |
| 12 | Toner cartridges | 26 | Horticultural machinery | 40 | Solid biofuel pellets | 54 | Shampoo | 68 | Hair conditioners |
| 13 | Shower gel | 27 | Liquid and solid soaps | 41 | Outdoor playground equipment | 55 | Indoor paints | 69 | Buildings |
| 14 | Decoration | 28 | Boards for furniture industry | 42 | Superfine fiber cleaning cloths and mops | 56 | Small dwellings | | |

disposal, with a focus on energy and resource consumption, the discharge of waste water, waste gas, and solid waste generated in the production process, and components inherent in products that are harmful to the environment. Moreover, it has requirements for the quality and functions of products. Relevant standard requirements are set for each group of products based on environmental factors in the whole life cycle, and products with the ecolabel are subject to stringent supervision. If the standards are improved and amended during the period of label use, the application, approval, and issuance of a new label must be carried out in accordance with the new standard.

In terms of selection of product items, countries investigate the environmental impact of products, the potential for environmental improvement, the level of market acceptance, etc., through market survey on the types and quantities of products on the market, the countries of manufacture, consumer demand, product competition, and so on. The environmental labels for the service sector such as hotels, catering, photo studios, and dry cleaning shops are being launched.

### *3.3.3 Ecolabels in Japan*

Since the 1980s, Japan's economy developed, and its people became more affluent and began to make luxurious consumption. The significantly increased consumption of energy and resources resulted in a serious pollution of the living environment. In view of this, the Japanese environmental protection body formulated in December 1986 the "Long-term Plan for Environmental Protection – How to Protect the Environment in the 21st Century." The plan is designated to evaluate eco-friendly production methods and encourage the adoption of various measures to reduce the environmental impact of products and maximize the recycling and utilization of products, so as to advocate an advanced and clean way of life and raise the public awareness of environmental protection. In 1989, Japan Environment Association (JEA) began to officially implement the ecolabel program under the leadership of the environmental authorities. The objective of the project is to spread knowledge of the environmental impact of products and encourage consumers to choose environmentally sound products. This is achieved by authorizing certain products to use ecolabels. The use of eco-labeled products can reduce the environmental impact of everyday activities and contribute to environmental protection.

The pattern of the Japanese ecolabel shows hands embracing the earth, symbolizing "protecting the Earth and the environment with our hands." Two arms are in the shape of English letter "e," representing "environment," "Earth," and "ecology." In principle, the color of the label should be blue monochrome, but other colors in monochrome can be used according to the different color systems of packaging. The words "Protect the Earth" in Japanese are written on the upper part of the label, and the environmental protection effect is indicated on the lower part.

### *3.3.3.1 Institutional setting and management process*

#### 3.3.3.1.1 INSTITUTIONAL SETTING

In order to ensure the effective running of the ecolabel program, the Ecolabel Secretariat of Japan Environment Association is responsible for the implementation and management of the program. The Japan Environment Association has established the ECO Mark Steering Committee, the ECO Mark Committee for Establishing Category and Criteria, and the ECO Mark Committee for Product Certification. A working group (WG) is established under the ECO Mark Committee for Establishing Category and Criteria to draft product standards as required. The composition and responsibilities of each division are as follows:

The ECO Mark Steering Committee is composed of experts in environmental protection and personnel from administration bodies, consumer groups, and relevant enterprises. It is primarily responsible for financial budget, project plans, and other important policy issues.

The ECO Mark Committee for Establishing Category and Criteria is composed of experts and personnel from enterprises, consumers, and third-party organizations relating to product categories. It is primarily responsible for selecting the categories of ecolabel products, formulating draft standards for certification of eco-labeled products, and reviewing the life cycle of products from an environmental perspective.

#### 3.3.3.1.2 MANAGEMENT PROCESSES

When awarding ecolabels, Japan Environment Association will comprehensively consider a product's social impact and environmental impact, manufacturer behavior, consumer behavior, etc. It includes the following standards: Appropriate environmental pollution prevention measures are put in place in the production stage; a product can be easily disposed of when it is discarded after use; the product can save energy and resources when used; the quality and safety of the product must conform to relevant laws, specifications, standards, etc. The product price should not be excessively high compared with similar products.

Despite the stringent requirements, Japanese companies still actively apply for the ecolabel in order to improve corporate image, follow the trend of consumption, and boost sales. In terms of certification and implementation, the applicant submits materials reviewed by a third party. The processes are as follows:

1 Select a product category.

Submit a proposal for a new category of eco-labeled products – ECO Mark Committee for Establishing Category and Criteria reviews the new category – Select product categories – Working Group prepares the draft standards – Public comments on draft standard (60 days) – ECO Mark Committee for Establishing Category and Criteria deliberates the draft – Decide to establish new product category and certification standard and issue an announcement.

2 Certification procedures.
   Apply for eco-labeling certification – certification committee appraises the product – pass eco-labeling certification – sign a licensing contract – indicate the ecolabel on the product.
3 Selection and requirements concerning eco-labeled products.
   In accordance with the "Guidelines for Ecolabel Organization and Implementation" and "Essentials of Ecolabel Specifications," the Japanese administration authorities re-established in 1995 the procedures for the formulation of ecolabel specifications and standards as well as application methods to bring them into line with ISO14024. Product items are selected in the following ways:
4 Accept proposals from the general public in accordance with the "Essentials of Ecolabel Product Project Proposal";
5 Product items that the Administration Bureau deems necessary to be open according to the results of the investigation, or "product items that need to be open" approved by the Ecolabel Promotion Committee;
6 Newly selected product items need to be publicly announced.

The principle of selecting eco-label products is that a product in use causes a small environmental load, the use of such product helps to improve the environment, its disposal has a minimal environmental impact, and it has a significant contribution to environmental protection in other areas.

Products awarded the ecolabel must comply with the following:

1 Take appropriate environmental pollution prevention and treatment measures at the production stage;
2 The product must be easily disposed of after use;
3 The use of the product can save energy and resources;
4 The quality and safety of the product must conform to relevant laws, specifications, and standards;
5 The price of the product should not be excessively high compared with similar goods.

By the end of 2008, the Association had identified 47 product categories and 4,617 eco-labeled products.

#### *3.3.3.2 Implementation status*

In 1989, the Japanese ecolabel program covers seven categories of products, such as CFC-free aerosol products. By March 2003, Japan Environment Association had expanded the ecolabel product category to 5,476 products in over 50 categories, such as solar hot water supply system, waste tire products, and rainwater collectors, as shown in Table 3.3.

Moreover, Japan has issued a slew of policies to support the eco-labeling system. The "environmental points system" is also an economic stimulus policy formulated by the Japanese government to spread the concept of green consumption.

*Table 3.3* Ecolabel product categories in Japan

| Product category | | | | | |
|---|---|---|---|---|---|
| 1 | Wrapping paper | 18 | Personal computers | 35 | Fire extinguishers |
| 2 | Glassware | 19 | Refined powdered slag of blast furnace and blower connector | 36 | Panels made of wood or similar materials |
| 3 | Ozone-friendly gas systems and equipment | 20 | Offset print ink | 37 | Drainage devices |
| 4 | Cloth shopping bags | 21 | Energy-saving leakage detectors | 38 | Filter bags for cooking treatment |
| 5 | Filters for kitchen sinks | 22 | Water-saving devices | 39 | Filters for cooking oil |
| 6 | Triangle filter for kitchen sinks | 23 | Biodegradable lubricating oil | 40 | Lacquers, paints containing aromatic hydrocarbons and waterproofing coatings |
| 7 | Printers | 24 | Refillable containers | 41 | Easy-to-repair school chairs |
| 8 | Printer paper | 25 | Recyclable containers/packaging | 42 | Wood products made from waste wood, tinned-out wood and small-diameter logs |
| 9 | Recyclable suitcase with post-use collection system | 26 | Recyclable road construction materials | 43 | Burning equipment using waste cooking oil |
| 10 | Soundproof and shock-resistant mats | 27 | Replaceable ink cartridges and cassettes | 44 | Plastic products made from recycled substances |
| 11 | Collectors for waste cans | 28 | CFC recovery systems in air conditioners | 45 | Construction materials using recycled materials |
| 12 | Copiers | 29 | Garbage disposal | 46 | Hot water supply system using solar energy |
| 13 | Solar cell-powered products | 30 | Unbleached coffee filter | 47 | Garments made from recycled PET resin |
| 14 | Solar-powered clocks and watches | 31 | Cellulose sponge | 48 | Home textiles made from recycled PET resin |
| 15 | Household gloves made of natural rubber | 32 | Building materials made from waste materials | 49 | Industrial textiles made from recycled PET resin |
| 16 | Paper for correspondence | 33 | Products made from waste tires | 50 | Toilet paper |
| 17 | Unbleached apparel, towels, sheets, and pillowcases | 34 | Soap made from waste cooking oil | | |

The so-called "environmental points system" refers to a system in which Japan supports consumers in buying eco-friendly household appliances through state fiscal subsidies (294.6 billion yen). Citizens who buy household appliances that meet the energy-saving standards can obtain "environmental points," which can be used in exchange for designated goods or services related to environmental protection. The "environmental points system" is designed to leverage market forces to integrate strengthening environmental protection, stimulating consumption, and encouraging energy conservation, so as to achieve the goals of curbing climate warming, revitalizing the economy, and popularizing microwave digital radio and television.

### *3.3.4 The "Energy Star" label in the United States*

#### *3.3.4.1 Development process*

Standards are used as a management tool. Formulating energy efficiency standards for energy-using products is a key component of the energy conservation and consumption reduction program in all countries. As the world's largest energy consumer, the United States faces a severe imbalance between energy supply and demand. In the 1970s, the United States legislated to determine the legal status of energy efficiency standards and label. Energy Star is a U.S. government-led energy conservation program targeted at consumer electronics. The Energy Star program was launched in 1992 by the U.S. Environmental Protection Agency and the Department of Energy to reduce energy consumption and greenhouse gas emissions. The program was then adopted by Australia, Canada, Japan, Taiwan of China, New Zealand, the European Union, and other countries and regions. The Energy Star is a voluntary energy-saving certification system. Manufacturers obtain the Energy Star label through self-declaration. Products generally outperform the minimum energy efficiency standards for corresponding categories. Manufacturers are required to test every basic model of all products with the label, ascertain the energy efficiency value, and report the energy efficiency characteristics of their products to the Department of Energy. The Energy Star standard generally saves 20 to 30 percent more energy than U.S. federal standards. The first products covered by this program were generally electrical appliances such as computers. It was gradually extended to cover motors, office equipment, lighting, household appliances, and then to buildings. The U.S. Environmental Protection Agency (EPA) launched the Energy Star program for buildings in 1996. The EPA assists voluntary participants in assessing the energy use of their buildings (including lighting, air conditioning, office equipment, etc.), and planning energy efficiency improvement action plan for such buildings as well as follow-up operations. Therefore, "Energy Star" label can also be seen in homes or commercial buildings that introduce new environmental concept.

#### *3.3.4.2 Product range*

The Energy Star program originally targeted at computer products and then covered various products. It now covers 60 kinds of terminal energy-using products in five categories[13]: commercial equipment, household appliances, office equipment, lighting products, and building materials, mainly including:

1 Computers and office equipment, such as displays, printers, fax machines, copiers, all-in-one, etc.;
2 Household appliances and similar products, such as refrigerators, air conditioners, washing machines, TV sets, and video recorders;
3 Heating and refrigeration equipment, such as heat pumps, boilers, and central air conditioning;
4 Large commercial buildings as well as newly built housing, doors and windows, etc.;
5 Industrial and commercial products, such as transformers and power devices;
6 Lighting products, such as household lamps;
7 Commercial food equipment, such as commercial ice cream makers, commercial dishwashers, etc.;
8 Other commercial products, such as vending machines and channel signs.

Currently, the products covered include fluorescent lamps, ornamental string lights, LED lamps, power adapters, switching power supply, ceiling-mounted fan lamps, audio-visual products, battery charging equipment, printers, household appliances, and other types of products.

#### *3.3.4.3 Application status*

A total of seven countries and regions have participated in the Energy Star program promoted by the U.S. EPA, viz. the United States, Canada, Japan, Taiwan of China, Australia, New Zealand, and the EU. An international Energy Star program meeting has been held annually since 2001. More than 30 categories of products have been included in the certification scope, such as household appliances, heating/refrigerating equipment, electronic products, and lighting products. The most common products in the Chinese market are lighting products, including lamps, such as traffic lights and exit indicators.

On April 14, 2010, the EPA and the Department of Energy jointly announced the adjustment of the certification process for Energy Star labeling to ensure that only eligible products are awarded the label. After this adjustment, the clauses with immediate effect are as follows: In order to obtain the Energy Star label, manufacturers must submit a complete test report and evaluation results, which must be certified by the EPA; manufacturers can only obtain the Energy Star label after the EPA has examined and approved such product as an Energy Star qualified product. At the same time, for the review of Energy Star qualifications, the EPA has upgraded the approval system. Instead of relying on the automatic approval process, it examines all new qualification applications for approval. The EPA and the Department of Energy further strengthened the Energy Star certification procedures at the end of 2010. It is stipulated that all manufacturers are required to submit test results issued by accredited, approved laboratories to ensure that products meet Energy Star requirements. The products covered include windows, doors, skylights, fluorescent bulbs, etc. Under the new testing procedures, the Energy Star program covers more than 60 product categories, including freezers, refrigerator-freezers, washing machines, dishwashers, water heaters, room air conditioners, etc.

In the United States, over 28,000 models of products and 1,000 manufacturers participate in the Energy Star program, and over 13,000 stores sell products with Energy Star label. In 1993, Bill Clinton signed a presidential decree stipulating that all federal government procurement must choose products with the Energy Star label, making it somewhat a mandatory standard.

For different types of products, the EPA and the Department of Energy have detailed standard requirements. It generally includes two parts: the Partner Commitment and the Technical Requirements of Products. Technical requirements generally include (but are not limited to) the following: (1) Definition. It includes definitions of products related to Energy Star certification. (2) Scope of product certification. It stipulates the range of Energy Star labeled products (e.g., models, specifications, etc., similar to the concept of "covered products" in U.S. federal laws). (3) Energy efficiency specifications for certified products. It specifically stipulates energy efficiency specifications for Energy Star certified products (e.g., limit value. Limits for current and future times are specified for many products).

Facts have proved that this Energy Star program adopted by the U.S. government has changed consumers' spending habits, raised the energy efficiency awareness among consumers and manufacturers, and ensured the market guidance. The Energy Star program is a key component of the U.S.'s energy-saving management measures for energy-using products, with a significant impact on the regulations and standards on energy saving in the world. The Energy Star certification has somewhat become a permit for products to enter markets in developed countries. Energy Star certification is processed in three steps: it determines whether a product has met or can meet Energy Star standards, and the manufacturer becomes an Energy Star partner and fulfills its obligations as an Energy Star partner.

Compared with China's energy efficiency standards and the EU's EuP/ErP directives, the American Energy Star program has more stringent requirements and more technical items. In contrast, China's energy efficiency standards are low, with much room for improvement. At the same time, practical obstacles such as inadequate laws and regulations, lack of industry self-regulation, and low public awareness of energy efficiency exist in the implementation process.

## 3.4 Experience of developed countries in promoting green consumption

Developed countries start with the building of a circular economy in their efforts to protect the environment and promote green consumption. China can draw on the rich experiences of developed countries in promoting green consumption, so as to improve China's green consumption economy, strengthen policies on green consumption, and promote the better development of the green consumption economy. Specifically:

1 Sound legal mechanism and system.

   Developed countries have enacted sound laws and regulations on environmental protection involving green consumption made by the government, enterprises, and individuals in the entire process from production to consumption. Japan adopts the legal system divided into three levels. The United States has enacted a series of laws *Resource Conservation and Recovery Act*. Germany is the first to implement the *Circular Economy Law*. Formulating legal systems for environmental protection governing green consumption at different levels or tiers has become a key step for various countries to promote green consumption. It has also become an important legal guarantee for promoting green consumption. A sound legal mechanism and system includes a slew of laws and regulations, covering both the overall plan and details, the guidance of policies as well as detailed rules for implementation, the determination of rights and obligations as well as the policy of rewards and punishment. Japan's laws related to green consumption cover the main players, targets, and process of consumption as well as production, providing the necessary legal support for promoting green consumption.

2 Improve policies on green government procurement.

   The government is the administrator of a country and a special consumer in green consumption. Developed countries place a high value on the role of the government in promoting green consumption. Promoting green consumption through government consumption has become a key part of green consumption. Supported by the strong national finances, the government can procure green products and services in a planned and targeted manner, guiding the consumption tendency of enterprises and individuals. Government procurement in EU member states accounts for 15 to 25 percent of their GDP, bringing into play the potential of government procurement in green consumption.[14] Developed countries including the United States and Japan have formulated policies as well as laws and regulations on green government procurement and have begun to guide the procurement of green products in a planned manner, providing a staunch support for green consumption.

3 Strengthen economic regulation means for green consumption.

   Green government procurement requires the cooperation of enterprises, and the means of economic regulation require the guidance of the government. Therefore, green government procurement and economic regulation policies are mutually reinforcing. In essence, consumption is an economic activity. Leveraging economic means to guide green consumption can yield great results. The production of green products is the precondition for promoting green consumption, but it is more costly to produce green products. To promote enterprises to produce more green products, it is necessary to bring into play the key role of economic regulation policies. Since the 1990s, the Japanese government has been subsidizing enterprises that use eco-friendly technologies to produce green products. In terms of fiscal budget, the Japanese government subsidizes SMEs in the R&D of green technologies, with a subsidy accounting for over 50 percent. For emerging industries that produce green products, the Japanese government provides generous subsidies. The subsidy for new-type green enterprises with a technology development period of less than two years is up to 70 percent of the total costs. In terms of financing, the Japanese Government stipulates that Development Bank of Japan (DBJ), Japan Finance Corporation for Small and Medium Enterprises, and National Life Finance Corporation must provide low-interest financing to producers of green products to fully ensure that they have adequate funds for development. A series of subsidy policies issued by the Japanese government have effectively promoted the development of green products producers as well as green consumption.

4 Increasing information-based publicity and education is an important guarantee for promoting green consumption.

The people of developed countries have a high level of environmental awareness. These countries can promote the implementation of laws on green consumption because various media means are used to educate the general public about green consumption and raise their environmental awareness. Environmental labeling systems put in place in these countries demonstrate the necessity of guiding green consumption by means of environmental labeling. The UK's *Action Plan for Green Consumption* advocates a transition to green consumption by guiding people to develop eco-friendly consumption habits such as saving water and electricity and recycling waste. The Japanese government organizes mass public welfare activities under the theme of "3R" to advocate the use of green packaging and waste recycling.

Some developed countries employ educational means by incorporating environmental protection concepts such as green consumption and sustainable development into textbooks for primary and secondary school students. In the United Kingdom and Italy, for example, "sustainable schools" activities are held at schools to encourage students to develop green consumption habits. Back in the 1960s, non-governmental organizations in Japan provided environmental education in schools. In the 1970s, the Japanese Ministry of Education, Culture, Sports, Science and Technology (MEXT) began to provide environmental education in schools (including education on sustainable consumption). In 1990, the Japanese Society of Environmental Education was officially established. In order to promote environmental education in schools, the MEXT compiled and published the *Guidance Materials on Environmental Education* for teachers.[15] In 1993, the MEXT began to designate typical cities, towns, and villages for the promotion of environmental education, with a view to promoting integrated environmental education in schools, families, and regions. The research findings are included in the special issue (published annually) of "Materials on Secondary Education" compiled by the MEXT. After 1994, the MEXT held an annual meeting for environmental education presentation and exhibition, when research findings on resolving environmental problems were presented, and the future orientation of environmental education was discussed for further popularization and development. In 2003, the Japanese government enacted and promulgated the *Law for Enhancing Motivation on Environmental Protection and Promoting Environmental Education*, which points out that environmental education in schools and society are the main links in advancing environmental education. These publicity and education activities have influenced people's ways of life, raised public awareness of environmental protection, and created the necessary culture for promoting green consumption.

## Notes

1 The *Resource Conservation and Recovery Act* is an amended version of the *Solid Waste Disposal Act*, which was revised in 1968, 1970, 1973, 1976, 1980, and 1984. It was renamed *Resource Conservation and Recovery Act*.
2 http://www.bottlebill.org.
3 Liu Fuzhong. *Household Appliance Industry and Circular Economy*. Beijing: China Light Industry Press, 2010: 13.
4 The new energy efficiency leader system will promote the upgrading of China's household appliance industry. www.cheaa.com, August 05, 2013.
5 Chen Yajun. Energy conservation and environmental protection: A realistic and eternal topic: Interpretation of the U.S. Energy Policy Act of 2005. *China Inspection and Quarantine*, 2006 (10): 39.
6 Li Guozhi. Japan's fiscal policy for developing low-carbon economy and reference value. *Contemporary Economy & Management*, 2014 (1): 94–97.
7 Su Hang, Sun Jian. The role of fiscal policy in Japan's low-carbon economic development. *Journal of Dongbei University of Finance and Economics*, 2010 (6): 61–65.
8 See Note 7.
9 See Note 7.
10 See Note 7.
11 Beijing Energy Conservation and Environmental Protection Center, China Household Electric Appliance Research Institute. 2016 Beijing Green Consumption Development Report.
12 Hu Ye. *Research on the German Environmental Labeling System*. Changsha: Hunan Normal University, 2010.
13 Zhu Peiwu, Jiang Jianping. Analysis of the latest developments in the U.S. Energy Star program. *Sino-Global Energy*, 2010 (8): 89–92.
14 Wu Yuping. Conform to international trends and promote sustainable government procurement in China. *Environmental Protection*, 2007 (15): 68–70.
15 Japan's *Environmental Education Guidance Materials* stipulate the objectives and requirements for environmental education for students of elementary schools, junior high schools, and senior high schools, respectively.

# 4 China's policies on green consumption and its evolution

## 4.1 China's macro policy framework for green consumption

China got off to a late start compared to developed countries in terms of green consumption, but the policy system in this regard is also gradually improving. In 1999, six departments including State Environmental Protection Administration (now the Ministry of Ecology and Environment) jointly launched a program to "open up green channels, cultivate green markets, and advocate green consumption." In October 2006, the Ministry of Finance and the State Environmental Protection Administration jointly issued the "Implementation Opinions on the Government Procurement of Environmental Label Products" and the "List of Environmental Label Products for Government Procurement," which is China's first list for green government procurement. This is a breakthrough in China's policy of promoting sustainable consumption and building an environment-friendly society. In June 2009, the National Development and Reform Commission and the Ministry of Finance organized the implementation of the "project to promote energy-efficient products for the benefit of the people," which subsidizes manufacturers of highly energy-efficient products through the central government funding. Then, manufacturers sell them at the subsidized prices. This policy has significantly stimulated the market sales of energy-saving products and spurred industrial upgrading. From June 1, 2012 to May 31, 2013, the total market size for color TV sets, refrigerators, washing machines, air conditioners, and water heaters reached 497 billion yuan thanks to the policy of promoting energy-saving household appliances for the benefit of the people. This represents an increase of 11.7 percent compared to the period from June 2011 to May 2012. The *Circular Economy Development Strategy and Short-term Action Plan* issued by the State Council on January 23, 2013 regards green consumption as a key measure to promote the development of circular economy at the social level and sets specific requirements for promoting green consumption. On February 17, 2016, ten departments including the National Development and Reform Commission jointly issued the *Guiding Opinions on Promoting Green Consumption,* which made plans for green product consumption, green service provision, financial support, etc. It mentions supporting the development of the sharing economy, encouraging the effective utilization of individuals' idle resources, and developing car-hailing service in an orderly manner. All these

DOI: 10.4324/9781003433040-4

are significant for China's practice of promoting green consumption and advancing ecological conservation.

#### *4.1.1 Administrative means of promoting green consumption*

Under the international trend of environmental protection, the Chinese government has continuously prepared policies to guide and promote the practice of green consumption. In 2005, the State Council issued the *Decision on Applying the Scientific Outlook on Development and Strengthening Environmental Protection.* According to the decision, the government should advocate eco-friendly consumption models and implement environmental labeling, environmental certification, and green government procurement systems in terms of consumption. The report of the 18th CPC National Congress issued in 2012 proposed a way of life that saves resources and protects the environment. The 12th Five-Year Plan states that green consumption is a way to promote green development. In 2016, ten departments including the National Development and Reform Commission jointly issued the *Guiding Opinions on Promoting Green Consumption.* After more than ten years of development, China has basically put in place a policy system for green consumption.

This chapter divides the administrative means for green consumption into four parts: overall guidance, resource conservation and green purchase, garbage sorting, and green travel. It is summarized into the policy system framework as shown in Table 4.1.

##### *4.1.1.1 Guiding outline*

In order to fully implement the guiding principles of the 18th CPC National Congress and the 3rd, 4th, and 5th Plenary Sessions of the 18th CPC Central Committee, put into practice the guiding principles from General Secretary Xi Jinping's major speeches, apply the vision of green development, promote green consumption, advance ecological conservation, and promote green economic and social development, ten government bodies including the National Development and Reform Commission jointly issued the *Guiding Opinions on Promoting Green Consumption* on February 17, 2016, which is China's first master document governing green consumption. The purpose is to fully implement the green consumption model by 2020 and advance all-round green development in political, economic, and educational terms.

The *Guiding Opinions* put forward the orientation of development and overall measures for spreading the concept of green development, guiding residents to practice eco-friendly lifestyles and consumption models, promoting public institutions to take the lead in making green consumption, promoting enterprises to increase the provision of green products and services, launching campaign against waste in society, and establishing a sound long-term mechanism for green consumption. The promulgation of the *Guiding Opinions* means that top-level planning is being made for China's policy on green consumption, and the abstract concept of green development is applied in concrete terms to the fields such as

*Table 4.1* Current framework of China's policy system on green consumption

| | *Policies and regulations* | *Promulgated by* | *Promulgation date* |
|---|---|---|---|
| Overall guidance | *Guiding Opinions on Promoting Green Consumption* | Ten ministries and commissions including the National Development and Reform Commission | February 17, 2016 |
| Conservation of resources and green purchase | *Circular on Promoting Water Pricing Reform, Promoting Water Conservation, and Protecting Water Resources* | General Office of the State Council | April 19, 2004 |
| | *Opinions on the Implementation of Government Procurement of Environmental Label Products* | Ministry of Finance and State Environmental Protection Administration | October 2006 |
| | *Circular on Establishing a System for the Compulsory Government Procurement of Energy-Saving Products* | General Office of the State Council | July 30, 2007 |
| | *Circular on the Guiding Opinions on the Trial Tiered Pricing for Household Electricity Consumption* | National Development and Reform Commission | November 29, 2011 |
| | *Guiding Opinions on Accelerating the Establishment and Improvement of the Tiered Pricing System for Urban Household Water Consumption* | National Development and Reform Commission and Ministry of Housing and Urban-Rural Development | December 31, 2013 |
| Resources conservation and green purchase | Catalog of Energy Efficiency Star Products (2014) | Ministry of Industry and Information Technology | November 17, 2014 |
| | *Circular on Doing a Good Job in the Work of Water Conservation Publicity Week in Cities in China in 2015* | General Office of the Ministry of Housing and Urban-Rural Development | April 7, 2015 |
| | Order No. 244 of the Beijing Municipal People's Government on *Beijing Municipal Measures on Water Conservation* in 2012 | Beijing Municipal People's Government | April 12, 2012 |
| | *Guide to Corporate Green Procurement (Trial)* | Ministry of Commerce, Ministry of Environmental Protection, Ministry of Industry and Information Technology | December 22, 2014 |
| | *Regulations for the Implementation of the Government Procurement Law of the People's Republic of China* | State Council | January 30, 2015 |
| | *Decision of the Standing Committee of the National People's Congress on Amending Six Laws Including the 'Law of the People's Republic of China on Energy Conservation'* | National People's Congress | July 2, 2016 |
| | *Measures for the Administration of Water Efficiency Labeling* | National Development and Reform Commission, Ministry of Water Resources, General Administration of Quality Supervision, Inspection and Quarantine | September 13, 2017 |

| | | | |
|---|---|---|---|
| Garbage sorting | *Measures for the Administration of Municipal Household Waste* | Ministry of Construction | April 28, 2007 |
| | *Circular on Strengthening the Work of Municipal Solid Waste Disposal* | The State Council approved and forwarded it to the Ministry of Housing and Urban-Rural Development and other departments | April 19, 2011 |
| | *Law of the People's Republic of China on the Prevention and Control of Environmental Pollution by Solid Waste* | National People's Congress | October 30, 1995 |
| | *Circular on the Work of Demonstration Cities (Districts) on Household Waste Sorting* | The Ministry of Housing and Urban-Rural Construction, the National Development and Reform Commission, the Ministry of Finance, the Ministry of Environmental Protection, the Ministry of Commerce, etc. | March 14, 2014 |
| | *Scheme for a Compulsory Waste Sorting System (Draft for Comments)* | National Development and Reform Commission, Ministry of Housing and Urban-Rural Development | June 15, 2016 |
| | *Implementation Plan for the Household Waste Sorting System* | National Development and Reform Commission, Ministry of Housing and Urban-Rural Development | June 18, 2017 |
| Green travel | *Circular on Encouraging the Development of Energy-Saving and Eco-friendly Small-Displacement Vehicles* | Forwarded by the General Office of the State Council to the National Development and Reform Commission and other departments | December 25, 2005 |
| | *Circular on Reducing Vehicle Purchase Tax on Passenger Vehicles with Displacement of 1.6 Liters or Below* | Ministry of Finance and State Taxation Administration | December 23, 2009 |
| | *Circular on Launching Pilot Work on Demonstration and Promotion of Energy-saving and New Energy Vehicles* | Ministry of Finance and Ministry of Science and Technology | January 23, 2009 |
| | *Circular on the Work of Expanding the Demonstration and Promotion of Energy-saving and New Energy Vehicles in the Field of Public Services* | Ministry of Finance, Ministry of Science and Technology, Ministry of Industry and Information Technology, National Development and Reform Commission | May 31, 2010 |
| | *Circular on Implementing the Pilot Program of Subsidies for Purchase of New Energy Vehicles by Individuals* | Ministry of Finance, the Ministry of Science and Technology, Ministry of Industry and Information Technology, National Development and Reform Commission | May 31, 2010 |
| | *Circular on Applying for New Energy Demonstration Cities and Industrial Parks* | National Energy Administration | May 25, 2012 |

*Table 4.1* (Continued)

| | *Policies and regulations* | *Promulgated by* | *Promulgation date* |
|---|---|---|---|
| | *Circular on Issuing the Plan for the Development of the Energy-saving and New Energy Vehicle Industry (2012-2020)* | State Council | June 28, 2012 |
| | *Guiding Opinions on Accelerating the Development of Green, Circular and Low-Carbon Transport* | Ministry of Transport | May 22, 2013 |
| | *Guiding Opinions on Accelerating the Promotion and Application of New Energy Vehicles* | General Office of the State Council | July 14, 2014 |
| | *Circular on Issuing the Implementation Plan for the Purchase of New Energy Vehicles by Government Organs and Public Institutions* | The National Government Affairs Administration, the Ministry of Finance, the Ministry of Science and Technology, the Ministry of Industry and Information, and the National Development and Reform Commission | June 11, 2014 |
| | *Catalogue of New Energy Vehicle Models Exempted from Vehicle Purchase Tax (Three Batches)* | Ministry of Industry and Information, State Taxation Administration | December 19, 2014 |
| | *Circular on Incentives for the Construction of New Energy Vehicle Charging Facilities* | Ministry of Finance, Ministry of Science and Technology, Ministry of Industry and Information, National Development and Reform Commission | November 18, 2014 |
| | *Policy on Fiscal Support for Promotion and Application of New Energy Vehicles in 2016-2020* | Ministry of Finance, Ministry of Science and Technology, Ministry of Industry and Information, National Development and Reform Commission | April 22, 2015 |
| | *Catalogue of Recommended Models for Promotion and Application of New Energy Vehicles (12th Batch in 2018)* | Ministry of Industry and Information Technology | December 4, 2013 |

green concept, green lifestyle and consumption model, public green consumption, supply of green products and services as well as opposing waste. At the same time, administrative means such as laws and regulations, economic means such as taxation and finance, and information means such as label certification are employed to establish a sound long-term mechanism, thereby promoting green consumption through multiple measures. According to the *Guiding Opinions*, it is required to strictly implement the government's system of priority procurement and compulsory procurement for energy-saving and eco-friendly products, expand the scope of green government procurement, improve the standards system and execution mechanism, and scale up green government procurement. In terms of establishing a sound long-term mechanism for green consumption, tax incentives are provided for projects or products that meet the conditions for energy and water conservation, environmental protection, and comprehensive use of resources in accordance with regulations. Energy-intensive, high-polluting products and some high-end consumer goods are subject to consumption tax. The financial industry will actively provide credit business for green consumption and study the establishment of a points system for green consumption.

Although the *Guiding Opinions* were released later relative to the trend of green consumption in China and the world, *Guiding Opinions* cover all key areas and measures for promoting green consumption, and is a policy to guide China's green consumption practice. However, due to a lack of practice and experience, the *Guiding Opinions* need to be improved by policies in terms of details and performance.

#### *4.1.1.2 Policy on resource conservation and green purchase*

In terms of resource conservation, there are comprehensive policies governing water and electricity saving. In order to leverage the role of market mechanisms and price levers in the allocation of water resources, the regulation of water demand, and the prevention and control of water pollution, the General Office of the State Council issued the *Circular on Promoting Water Pricing Reform, Promoting Water Conservation, and Protecting Water Resources* in 2004. Since 2008, the Ministry of Housing and Urban-Rural Development has launched the event of Water Conservation Publicity Week in Cities in China for eight consecutive years. The tiered electricity and water pricing policies, which were issued by the National Development and Reform Commission, have achieved good results in guiding residents to conserve water and electricity, but there are weaknesses in terms of operating rules and detailed guidance.

Guided by the Catalog of Energy Efficiency Star Products, green purchase is mainly in the form of mandatory green government procurement and guidance of residents to make green purchase. The *Government Procurement Law of the People's Republic of China*, which became effective on January 1, 2003, regards the protection of the environment as an important part of procurement policy. In 2005, the State Council issued the *Decision on Applying the Scientific Outlook on Development and Strengthening Environmental Protection*, which states that in terms of consumption, we shall vigorously advocate eco-friendly consumption methods and put into practice environmental labeling, environmental certification, and green government procurement systems. In order to leverage the exemplary role of government bodies in energy and water conservation, and environmental protection, and promote the development of circular economy and sustainable development, the Ministry of Finance and the State Environmental Protection Administration jointly issued the *Opinions on the Implementation of Government Procurement of Environmental Label Products* and the *List of Environmental Label Products for Government Procurement* in accordance with the *Government Procurement Law* and *Environmental Protection Law* on October 24, 2006. The Implementation Opinions were fully implemented on January 1, 2008, blazing a trail in green procurement by public institutions in China. The procurement list covers automobiles, office supplies, building and decoration materials, electrical appliances, etc. The promulgation of the Implementation Opinions and the Procurement List facilitates green government procurement, providing institutional and policy support for making green government procurement. In 2007, the General Office of the State Council issued the *Circular on Establishing a System for Compulsory Government Procurement of Energy-Saving Products*, which put forward mandatory requirements for green government procurement. Since the system for of government procurement energy-saving products was implemented, 19 *Lists of Environmental Label Products for Government Procurement* have been issued. The products on the list cover many fields such as household appliances, lighting appliances, office equipment, mechanical and electrical products, electrical equipment, automobiles, building materials, and new energy products. It is also required to strictly implement the system of priority procurement and compulsory procurement of energy-saving products by public institutions in practice and build a framework for the green government procurement system.

In order to promote the building of a resource-conserving and environment-friendly society, guide and promote enterprises to fulfill their environmental responsibilities, create a green supply chain, and achieve green, low-carbon, and circular development, the Ministry of Commerce, the Ministry of Environmental Protection and the Ministry of Industry and Information Technology jointly issued the *Guide to Corporate Green Procurement (Trial)* (hereinafter the Guide) in 2014 to promote the establishment of a green supply chain between enterprises and guide enterprises to highlight their main responsibility for environmental protection. The Guide contains explicit provisions on the environmental responsibility of enterprises in conjunction with the *Environmental Protection Law*. It is intended to guide and promote enterprises to make green procurement in order to force suppliers of raw materials, products, and services to improve environmental management level, promote eco-friendly production, stimulate green consumption in society, and gradually create a green procurement chain. The Guide recommends that enterprises avoid purchasing products on the "blacklist," including products "causing high pollution and bringing high environmental risks" listed in the *Comprehensive List for Environmental Protection* formulated by the Ministry of Environmental Protection. At the same time, it is recommended that enterprises make green provisions in procurement contracts, reduce the procurement quota, and suspend procurement or terminate procurement contracts for suppliers and buyers that violate environmental laws. If a supplier conceals violations of environmental protection law and causes losses to the buyer, the buyer has the right to safeguard its legitimate rights and interests according to the law. Moreover, it is stressed that buyers can offer incentives to suppliers that meet the requirements by appropriately increasing the procurement price, raising the purchase quantity, shortening the payment period, etc. The incentive and restraining role of the market mechanism can drive suppliers to better protect the environment, and reduce environmental pollution and environmental risks.

The 75th executive meeting of the State Council held on January 30, 2015 adopted the *Regulations for the Implementation of the Government Procurement Law of the People's Republic of China*. The *Regulations* came into effect on March 1, 2015. The *Regulations* refine and clarify the relevant provisions of the *Government Procurement Law* and play an important guiding role in enhancing the quality and efficiency of government procurement and promoting its scientific management. The *Regulations* have made explicit provisions on the application scope and operation procedures of electronic procurement and non-tendered procurement, the time limit for confirmation of the appraisal report, the time limit for responding to inquiries, etc. These have promoted the standardized and law-based government procurement, as well as the establishment of a standardized and transparent government procurement work mechanism that allows fair competition, supervision, and accountability.

General Secretary Xi Jinping stressed again at the 12th meeting of the Central Leading Group for Financial and Economic Affairs in January 2016 that the fundamental purpose of supply-side structural reform is to improve China's overall productive forces and implement the people-centered philosophy of development. While working to achieve an appropriate expansion of aggregate demand, it is necessary to cut overcapacity, reduce excess inventory, deleverage, lower costs, strengthen areas of weakness, increase high-quality supply in the production field, reduce inefficient supply, expand effective supply, make the supply structure more responsive and flexible, raise total factor productivity, and make the supply system better adapt to changes in the demand structure. As the largest owner of information, the government should guide the rational development of the market through its decisions and conduct. As the scale of procurement expands, the "bellwether" role of the government's huge procurement has increased accordingly. As a kind of macro-regulation behavior, government procurement not only serves a role of regulating but also has the functions of promoting economic development and improving social governance. As the share of green procurement and innovative procurement in government procurement increases, it will have a greater role in leading non-governmental production enterprises, especially high-tech industries in the knowledge economy. At the same time, given the long-term and complex nature of government procurement of services, the requirements and standards the government puts forward will promote the upgrading and innovation of enterprises and at the same time optimize the industrial structure. Therefore, government procurement is an important driver for supply-side reform. In 2015, the scale of government procurement nationwide was 2,107.05 billion yuan, a year-on-year increase of 21.8 percent, accounting for 12 percent and 3.1 percent of national government expenditure and GDP, respectively. It can be seen that China's government procurement promises huge potential, and green government procurement is significant for the development of green consumption.

#### *4.1.1.3 Policies for promoting waste sorting*

As the economy and society develop and the level of material consumption increases sharply, the amount of household waste generated in China has increased significantly. According to the analysis performed by Cai Jianguo, a professor at Tongji University, the amount of household waste collected and transported in large and medium-sized cities in China reached 185 million metric tons in 2015. If trucks with a loading capacity of 2.5 metric tons are used to transport them, the bumper-to-bumper length would reach nearly 500,000 kilometers, equivalent to circling the equator 12 times.[1] Moreover, the environmental hazards from improper disposal of waste become increasingly prominent, becoming an obstacle to new-type urbanization. Waste sorting is a complex systems project and a revolution in everyday life and social management. It involves raising public environmental awareness, changing residents' conduct in everyday life, improving public governance capabilities at the community level, upgrading urban and rural garbage removal systems and disposal models, tightening the management of fiscal and public utility funds, adjusting and innovating industrial policies, and improving the administrative capability of government bodies. Therefore, promoting waste sorting is essentially part of the ongoing economic reform, social reform, and environmental management reform in China. Household waste sorting can effectively improve the urban and rural environment, promote resource recycling, accelerate the building of a resource-conserving and environment-friendly society, and improve the quality of new-type urbanization and ecological conservation. The absence of institutional constraint is a key reason for the slow progress in waste sorting. The current laws and regulations only encourage the sorting of household waste, and there is a lack of explicit rigid constraints and institutional norms for the functions of governments at all levels, the rights and obligations of citizens, and the waste sorting behavior.

China has long ago launched a policy of advocating waste sorting, but the effect leaves a lot to be desired. The *Law of the People's Republic of China on the Prevention and Control of Environmental Pollution by Solid Waste* stipulates that urban household waste should be gradually sorted and transported and should be rationally utilized or made harmless. The *Measures for the Administration of Municipal Household Waste*, which were promulgated on April 28, 2007, are applicable to the cleaning, collection, transport, and disposal of municipal household waste as well as related management activities. Thereafter, policies on the disposal of municipal household waste have been introduced. The *Circular on the Work of Demonstration Cities (Districts) on Household Waste Sorting* issued in 2014 has had an impact on the sorting of household waste in cities.

In December 2016, General Secretary Xi Jinping stressed at the 14th meeting of the Central Leading Group for Financial and Economic Affairs that the universal implementation of the waste sorting system concerns the living environment of more than 1.3 billion Chinese people and is related to whether waste can be reduced, recycled, and made harmless. It is necessary to accelerate the establishment of a waste disposal system featuring sorted delivery, collection, transport, and disposal to establish a law-based waste sorting system that is promoted by the government, involves all the people, coordinates urban and rural areas, and adapts to local conditions, and to increase the application of the waste sorting system. As a matter of fact, there is a clear road map for the garbage issue under the framework of promoting ecological conservation. The *Integrated Reform Plan for Promoting Ecological Progress* released in September 2015 clearly calls for "accelerating the establishment of a compulsory waste sorting system." On June 15, 2016, the National Development and Reform Commission and the Ministry of Housing and Urban-Rural Development jointly issued the *Scheme for a Compulsory Waste Sorting System (Draft for Comments)* in accordance with a central plan. It states that by the end of 2020, municipalities directly under the Central Government, provincial capitals, cities with independent planning status, and other cities in the first group of demonstration cities pilot compulsory waste sorting in urban areas. After solicitation of opinions, the General Office of the State Council forwarded on March 18, 2017 the *Implementation Plan for the Household Waste Sorting System* (hereinafter referred to as the "Plan") issued by the National Development and Reform Commission and the Ministry of Housing and Urban-Rural Development, which makes plans to promote household waste sorting, improve urban management and services, and build an excellent living environment.

According to the *Plan*, in order to promote the sorting of household waste, it is necessary to follow the principles of reduction, recycling, and harmless treatment, accelerate the establishment of a waste disposal system featuring sorted delivery, collection, transport, and disposal, and establish a law-based waste sorting system that is promoted by the government, involves all the people, coordinates urban and rural areas, and adapts to local conditions. By the end of 2020, China had basically established a system of laws, regulations, and standards for waste sorting and developed a household waste sorting model that can be replicated in other areas. The recycling rate of household waste reaches more than 35 percent in cities that implement mandatory sorting of household waste. According to the *Plan*, all provinces (regions) are encouraged to select cities where conditions permit to implement compulsory sorting of household waste. National ecological conservation pilot zones and new cities and new districts take the lead in implementing compulsory sorting of household waste. Public institutions and enterprises within the scope of compulsory sorting of household waste play a main role in implementing compulsory sorting. Existing local regulations that require mandatory sorting of household waste should prevail. Cities that require compulsory sorting of household waste should formulate and issue measures before the end of 2017 to detail the requirements for waste sorting. On the basis of sorting hazardous waste, other categories are reasonably selected for sorting. Cities that implement compulsory sorting should select different types of communities for the pilot demonstration of compulsory sorting of household waste. The *Plan* emphasizes that it is necessary to strengthen the establishment of a supporting system for household waste sorting, establish a collection and transport system that matches sorted categories, promote the establishment of a recycling system that coordinates the garbage collection and transport system with the use of renewable resources, improve terminal treatment facilities linked to waste sorting, and explore the establishment of a base for waste co-processing and utilization, ensuring that facilities for sorting, recycling, utilization, and disposal are connected. The *Plan* requires that all local governments should strengthen organization and leadership, make clear the principal responsibilities of people's governments of cities, improve laws and regulations, improve supporting policies, and innovate systems and mechanisms. All people are mobilized to sort garbage through publicity and education in all shapes and forms to ensure effective progress.

By this point, China has had an explicit overall idea for household waste sorting: (1) Clarify the leading role of the government. From the perspective of waste sorting and treatment in China, the government must play a leading role in advancing the household waste sorting system. Provincial people's governments and competent departments of the State Council should increase guidance on the sorting of household waste. The people's governments of cities should assume the primary responsibility, improve relevant laws and regulations, step up financial support, and tighten supervision and inspection. Public institutions and enterprises with clear responsibilities should play a leading and demonstration role and promote public participation in household waste sorting. (2) Promote the sorting of household waste in a step-by-step manner. The sorting of household waste involves all aspects of social life and cannot be achieved overnight. In practice, we should implement the methods of household waste sorting featuring compulsory sorting and guided sorting. In some areas where conditions permit, compulsory sorting should be piloted at public institutions and enterprises. As for urban residents, the guided sorting method is still the primary method on account of the imperfect laws and regulations. (3) Determine the sorting methods in light of local conditions. In China, climatic characteristics, development levels, and living habits vary from region to region, and the composition of household waste varies considerably. In order to avoid "one-size-fits-all" approaches, all local governments should formulate sorting methods in light of the reality, reasonably determine the categories for compulsory sorting, and detail the requirements for sorting, collection, transport, and disposal. Local governments should have great flexibility in this regard. (4) Pay attention to systematic support. Household waste sorting is a complex systems project. Collection, recycling, disposal, and other links directly determine the success or failure of waste sorting. The *Plan* calls for the establishment of the collection and transport system, the recycling system, and the construction of terminal treatment facilities, so that it better matches waste sorting categories and coordinates with the recycling of resources. For example, in February 2017, Beijing held an urban management working conference, which stated that Beijing will gradually promote the "big and small garbage can" model for waste sorting and implement the separation of dry and wet waste. Shanghai has fully implemented the compulsory sorting system for household waste since 2017. Guangzhou will pilot a compulsory sorting system for household waste in some areas.

Overall, China's waste sorting policy and system are being improved. As the state attaches importance to this issue, all local governments will speed up the formulation of local policies in light of local conditions. In China, a sound top-down policy framework will be established for waste sorting, and it is expected to be put into practice.

#### *4.1.1.4 Policies to encourage green travel*

Encouraging the purchase of small-displacement vehicles and new energy vehicles is an important area for the government to promote green travel.

The *Circular on Encouraging the Development of Energy-saving and Eco-friendly Small-Displacement Vehicles* was issued on December 25, 2005. In 2009 and 2010, the Ministry of Finance issued the *Circular on Reducing Vehicle Purchase Tax on Passenger Vehicles with Displacement of 1.6 Liters or Below*, which played a great role in stimulating consumer demand for small-displacement vehicles.

To promote new energy vehicles and change the energy structure in the consumption sector, competent ministries and commissions have issued a slew of guiding policies since 2009, including pilot demonstration and promotion programs, as well as pilot subsidy for encouraging individual purchases. From August 27, 2014 to December 19, 2014, three catalogs of new energy vehicle models exempted from purchase tax were released. Purchase of new energy vehicles on the catalog will be exempted from purchase tax. The *Circular on the Policy of Fiscal Support for the Promotion and Application of New Energy Vehicles from 2016 to 2020* issued in April 2015 gives strong financial support to new energy vehicles. Policy on related models of vehicles was released from 2016 to 2017. All of these indicate that vigorously promoting new energy vehicles has become an irresistible trend. There are comprehensive policies and regulations governing green transport, and specific implementation rules have been issued. While policies have continuously promoted the development of new energy vehicles, the demand for new energy vehicles remains to be enhanced.

On the whole, China got off to a late start in green consumption compared with developed countries, and its policy and system are still being improved. There is a lack of system of policies for waste sorting, and the policies to promote water and electricity saving and green purchasing remained to be improved. The policy on green travel is relatively perfect, but it has not achieved the expected effect.

### *4.1.2 Economic means to stimulate green consumption*

One of the essential principles of green consumption is the principle of equity, including intragenerational equity and intergenerational equity. It means that consumption should take into account the interests of others and future generations.

However, according to economic principles, consumers are rational man who will maximize their own interests. In other words, under the pure market conditions free from external intervention, green consumption has obvious positive externality, which will cause a severe shortage of supply. This is a typical manifestation of market failure. According to Keynesian theory, the government needs to actively intervene when a market failure occurs. Therefore, we shall not wholly rely on the market to realize green consumption. Appropriate government intervention is necessary. In addition to administrative intervention, adopting necessary economic means is useful international experience for promoting sustainable consumption.

#### *4.1.2.1 Fiscal subsidies*

Subsidizing producers with positive externalities are typical positive incentives, and the objective is to stimulate more similar practices. Due to factors such as technology and cost, the price of green products is usually slightly higher than that of similar ordinary products, hence little purchase. In order to raise consumer demand for green products, the government can reduce the price of eco-friendly products by directly subsidizing buyers, thereby attracting more consumers.

##### 4.1.2.1.1 PROJECT TO PROMOTE ENERGY-EFFICIENT PRODUCTS FOR THE BENEFIT OF THE PEOPLE

In order to expand consumer demand, enhance energy efficiency, and facilitate industrial upgrading, the National Development and Reform Commission and the Ministry of Finance have implemented the "project to promote energy-efficient products for the benefit of the people" since June 2009, which subsidizes the manufacturers of highly efficient energy-saving products through the central government funding. Then, production enterprises sell them at subsidy-adjusted prices. The standard for fiscal subsidy is primarily determined by the cost difference between energy-efficient products and the similar ordinary products. At the same time, local governments in areas where conditions permit are encouraged to provide certain funds in support of the promotion of highly energy-efficient products. The "project to promote energy-efficient products for the benefit of the people" is designed to subsize purchasers of energy-efficient products. The subsidy standards are primarily based on the price difference between highly energy-efficient products and ordinary products, with consideration to factors such as technological progress and scale effect. In order to save promotion cost, improve promotion efficiency, bring convenience to consumers, and facilitate supervision, this project indirectly subsidizes the producers of energy-efficient products. In other words, production enterprises sell energy-efficient products to consumers at promised promotion price minus the fiscal subsidies, and the ultimate beneficiaries are the consumer.

During the Twelfth Five-Year Plan period, the state continued to implement the "project to promote energy-efficient products for the benefit of the people." On May 18, 2009, the Ministry of Finance and the National Development and Reform Commission jointly issued the *Circular on Launching the Project to Promote*

*Energy-efficient Products for the Benefit of the People*, allocating 265 million yuan in special funds to support the promotion and application of energy-efficient products. Compared with the project to promote energy-efficient products for the benefit of the people for the 11th Five-Year Plan period, the project in the 12th Five-Year Plan period covered more products, including five categories of household appliances: energy-efficient flat-panel TVs, air conditioners, refrigerators, washing machines, and water heaters (including gas water heaters, heat pump water heaters, and solar water heaters). The existing subsidy policy for high-efficiency motors, energy-saving vehicles, and new energy vehicles is still in place. On September 9, 2012, another six categories of energy-saving products were included in the scope of fiscal subsidies – energy-efficient desktop computers and energy-efficient unit-type air conditioners in the field of consumer goods, and fans, water pumps, compressors, and transformers in the field of industrial products. At the same time, the state has issued the *Implementation Rules for the Promotion of Energy-efficient Room Air Conditioners in the Project to Promote Energy-efficient Products for the Benefit of the People*, *Implementation Rules for the Promotion of Energy-efficient Flat-panel TVs in the Project to Promote Energy-efficient Products for the Benefit of the People*, *Implementation Rules for the Promotion of Energy-efficient Household Gas Water Heaters in the Project to Promote Energy-efficient Products for the Benefit of the People*, *Implementation Rules for the Promotion of Energy-efficient Electric Washing Machines in the Project to Promote Energy-efficient Products for the Benefit of the People*, *Implementation Rules for the Promotion of Energy-efficient Household Refrigerators in the Project to Promote Energy-efficient Products for the Benefit of the People*, and *Implementation Rules for the Promotion of Energy-efficient Electric Motors in the Project to Promote Energy-efficient Products for the Benefit of the People*. In principle, energy-saving products with an energy efficiency grade 1 or 2 are subsidized, but the subsidy is inclined towards energy-efficient products with energy efficiency grade above grade 1. A subsidy of 300 to 650 yuan per unit (set) is given for room air conditioners with energy efficiency grade 2, and a subsidy of 500 to 850 yuan per unit (set) is given for room air conditioners with energy efficiency grade 1. On the basis of the previous experience in implementing the project to promote energy-efficient products for the benefit of the people, the state organized and implemented the verification of promotion information for the project, with a focus on supervising and verifying the promotion information on energy-saving products in the following three areas: The first is the production link. It mainly verifies the initial inventory, current production, and shipment of products promoted by manufacturers. The second is the distribution link. It mainly verifies the initial inventory, current shipments, and sales of products promoted by sales enterprises. The third is the consumer link. It primarily verifies the authenticity of information on consumers of energy-saving products. The subsidy supervision and verification work is gradually carried out on a routine and all-round basis. It was announced that the "project to promote energy-efficient products for the benefit of the people" would end on May 31, 2013. As from June 1, 2013, consumers will no longer receive state subsidies for the purchase of energy-saving household appliances. Regarding energy-saving vehicles, the Ministry of

Finance issued the *Circular on the Promotion of Energy-saving and Eco-friendly Vehicles with a Displacement of 1.6 Liters and Below*. It decided to implement the policy of promoting energy-saving and eco-friendly vehicles with a displacement of 1.6 liters or below from October 1, 2013 to December 31, 2015, and promotion subsidy standards remain unchanged. Green consumption, energy conservation, and emission reduction are promoted by means of subsidy policies.

#### 4.1.2.1.2 SUBSIDIES FOR NEW ENERGY VEHICLES

In 2009, the Ministry of Finance and the Ministry of Science and Technology issued the *Circular on Launching Pilot Work on Demonstration and Promotion of Energy-saving and New Energy Vehicles*. In September 2013, the Ministry of Finance and the Ministry of Science and Technology issued the *Circular on Continuing the Promotion and Application of New Energy Vehicles*, which stipulates that the maximum subsidy for new energy vehicles bought by individuals is kept at 60,000 yuan. Local pilot cities can increase subsidies in addition to the state subsidies or carry out other favorable measures, such as free licenses for individual purchase of electric vehicles in Shanghai. In April 2015, the Ministry of Finance, the Ministry of Science and Technology, the Ministry of Industry and Information Technology, and the National Development and Reform Commission jointly issued the *Policy on Fiscal Support for Promotion and Application of New Energy Vehicles in 2016-2020*, which stipulates the subsidized models of new energy vehicles and the extent of subsidies. The policy stipulates that the Ministry of Finance, the Ministry of Science and Technology, the Ministry of Industry and Information Technology, and the National Development and Reform Commission will launch the promotion and application of new energy vehicles nationwide, and central government funding will subsidize the purchase of new energy vehicles and the generalized system of preference will be implemented. Subsidies are targeted at consumers. When selling new energy vehicles, new energy vehicle manufacturers settle accounts with consumers at the price minus subsidies. Then, central government funding provides subsidy funds advanced by enterprises to the production enterprises according to procedures. The products subsidized by the central government funding are pure electric vehicles, plug-in hybrid electric vehicles, and fuel cell vehicles included in the "Catalogue of Recommended Models for the Promotion and Application of New Energy Vehicles." The subsidy standard is primarily based on the effect of energy saving and emission reduction, with consideration to factors such as production costs, scale effect, and technological advance. At the same time, a full variety of subsidy standards for new energy vehicles were promulgated in 2016. From 2017 to 2020, except for fuel cell vehicles, the subsidy standards for other automobile models were appropriately reduced. The subsidy standard in 2017 and 2018 fell by 20 percent from that of 2016, and the subsidy standard in 2019 and 2020 fell by 40 percent from that of 2016. Subsidy is intended to reduce prices for consumers, but in practice, some carmakers deliberately raise the prices of new energy vehicles to illegally obtain state subsidies. This will not motivate consumers and will also waste state funds.

In order to obtain good results in the field of green consumption, there must be some preconditions for the subsidy means:

1 Pay attention to the products for subsidy, generally high-value durable consumer goods. As the prices of low-value consumer goods are low, subsidies are usually small, making it difficult to effectively motivate consumers. Moreover, as the number of low-value commodities is numerous, it is objectively not easy to operate.
2 The setting of the subsidy amount. The subsidy will not play a motivating role if it is too low, and impose a heavy burden on the state finance if it is too high. The subsidy amount should be determined in the preliminary pilot period before large-scale promotion.
3 In the process of implementation, supervision should be in place to prevent enterprises from improperly obtaining subsidies and prevent fraudulent claims or repeated collection. The quality of subsidized products shall be strictly reviewed to ensure that products are eco-friendly products that meet the standards.

#### *4.1.2.2 Collection of taxes and fees*

Taxation is closely associated with people's lives. It imperceptibly influences people's consumption idea and ways of life through its regulation, guiding people to have a healthy life and live in harmony with nature. Since putting forward the concept of green consumption, China has formulated tax systems to promote green consumption, primarily including consumption tax, resource tax, and other taxes.

##### 4.1.2.2.1 CONSUMPTION TAX

Among the 15 taxable items (excluding automobile tires) of China's consumption tax related to green consumption are tobacco, cosmetics, gasoline, diesel, motorcycles, automobiles, firecrackers, fireworks, yachts, wooden disposable chopsticks, solid wood flooring, lead-acid batteries, and paints. Of these, the taxable items that can guide green consumption roughly fall into the following three categories: First, internalize the negative externalities of environment pollution, such as tobacco, cosmetics, firecrackers, fireworks, lead-acid batteries, and paints. Second, internalize the negative externalities of overconsumption of resources, such as wine, wooden disposable chopsticks, and solid wood flooring. Third, have both at the same time, such as gasoline, diesel, motorcycles, automobiles, and yachts. Levying taxes on products that are closely related to consumer demand and that will cause negative externalities in the process of production, processing, and consumption will increase the relative prices of such products, so as to inhibit taxpayers' production and consumption of such products to a certain extent, and encourage the selection of products that are pollution-free or cause little pollution. For example, regarding automobile consumption, the State Taxation Administration halves the vehicle purchase tax imposed on passenger cars with a displacement of 1.6 liters and below, or what are usually called small-displacement vehicles, and exempts new energy vehicles from vehicle purchase tax, thereby encouraging consumers to buy energy-saving and eco-friendly small-displacement cars. Since Guangxi Zhuang Autonomous Region Tax Service implemented the policy of halving the vehicle purchase tax imposed on small-displacement vehicles on October 1, 2015, the sales of small-displacement vehicles in the region increased by 28.5 percent year-on-year by the end of February 2016. The concept of green consumption has gained popular support. Another example is the tobacco consumption. Since May 2015, the state has significantly increased the consumption tax for cigarettes, increasing the price tax rate of the wholesale of cigarette from 5 percent to 11 percent, and increasing the volume tax from the original 0.003 yuan to 0.005 yuan per cigarette, which is aimed at tobacco control. Statistics from the State Taxation Administration show that cigarette sales steadily fall after the cigarette consumption tax was adjusted. It has basically achieved the purpose of tobacco control.

##### 4.1.2.2.2 RESOURCE TAX

As one of the most environmentally significant taxes in China, resource tax not only restricts the unregulated exploitation of resources by operators, reduce the loss and waste of resources, and conserve natural resources but also encourage resource-based enterprises to improve the development and utilization of resources out of their own interests, and address the imbalance between supply and demand of resources. In China, existing taxable resources fall into seven categories: crude oil, natural gas, coal, raw ore of other non-metallic ore, raw ore of ferrous metal ore, raw ore of non-ferrous metal ore as well as salt. The resource tax can restrain the conduct of enterprises at the beginning of green consumption, that is, the resource exploitation stage, and is significant for promoting green consumption. For the import and export of resource products, the state has reduced or revoked the export tax rebate rates for some energy-intensive products, highly polluting products, and resource-depleting products, restricted the export of products, and encouraged the use of foreign resources. Obviously, the "green tax policy" helps strengthen the regulatory role of taxation on environmental protection.

##### 4.1.2.2.3 OTHER TAXES

In addition to consumption tax and resource tax, which are directly related to resource and environmental protection as well as green consumption, other existing tax categories in China can also somewhat promote green consumption. Whether it be a positive or negative incentive, the value-added tax, corporate income tax, arable land occupation tax, real estate tax, urban land use tax, vehicle and vessel tax, and vehicle purchase tax are related to promoting green consumption.

As with subsidies, there are also preconditions for levying taxes to promote green consumption: (1) The determination of the object of taxation, or imposing taxes and fees such as resource tax on producers and consumers. However, the current scope of resource tax is limited, and most natural resources are not covered. Moreover, resource tax is usually levied on miners in poor and backward areas, rather than on the users of these resources. Therefore, it does not reflect the "compensation principle" in economics. It is recommended that the retail link is considered for the collection of various environmental taxes and fees, and a certain amount of tax is transferred to consumers. (2) Reasonably determine the amount of tax or fees. Excessively high tax rates will cause unnecessary losses that outweigh the social benefits of improved environment, reducing social welfare. Too low a tax rate cannot reflect the marginal social cost and cannot play a role in regulating consumers' purchasing behavior. The determination of the tax rate shall fully consider environmental impact of products in the life cycle, as well as acceptance by consumers. In order to inhibit the production and purchase of large-displacement vehicles and encourage the production and consumption of small-displacement ones, the state introduced a consumption tax on automobile purchasing in 2008, levying a consumption tax at a rate of 1 percent on passenger cars with a displacement of 1.0 liters and below, and a consumption tax at a rate of up to 40 percent on passenger cars with a displacement of over 4.0 liters.[2] In November 2016, the Ministry of Finance and the State Taxation Administration issued the *Circular on Matters Concerning Levying Consumption Tax on Ultra-Luxury Automobiles*, which stipulates the addition of a sub-tax item of "ultra-luxury automobiles" under the tax item of "automobiles." The scope of tax collection is passenger cars and medium and light commercial buses with a retail price of 1.3 million yuan (excluding value-added tax) or more per vehicle, that is, ultra-luxury automobiles under the sub-tax item of passenger cars and medium and light commercial buses. For ultra-luxury automobiles, a consumption tax will be added in the retail sector at a tax rate of 10 percent on top of the consumption tax levied at the current rate in the production (import) link. (3) Pay attention to the regulating role of tax differential and tax preferences. It is necessary to implement a tax-neutral policy, consider the impact of taxation on various industries and economic chain, and be sure to minimize the negative impact of taxation on the economy. For example, it is to reduce energy tax rates on public transport means, do not impose or impose little taxes on naturally degradable plastic bags, and so on.

Moreover, the acceptability of tax needs to be considered. Generally speaking, consumers are averse to rising prices, and may not understand the tax or even resist it. Conducting publicity among consumers is essential before the tax is collected.

Economic incentives can effectively regulate the cost of green consumption and change the contrast between costs and utility, thereby guiding consumers to make consumption conducive to environmental protection and resource conservation and reducing unsustainable consumption. Subsidies and taxes are economic incentives that can directly regulate consumer behavior. The principle of action is to adjust the price of a certain product to make it fully reflect the marginal social costs, including environmental costs, so as to maximize the total social benefits. Before employing these economic incentives, it is necessary to fully consider all factors. The beneficiaries and the level of the amount need to be carefully set. Supporting policies and measures as well as supervision and management are also indispensable. Since each means has its own characteristics, it needs to be used and innovated in light of actual conditions.

### *4.1.3 Encourage the popularization of information means for green consumption*

Given China's large population, raising awareness of green consumption is an important way to guide green consumption. Information means play a crucial role in this regard. At present, China's channels for publicizing green consumption include network information platforms, the environmental labeling system, the energy efficiency "leader" system, and publicity and education activities.

#### *4.1.3.1 Establishment of network information platforms*

At present, the online platforms for publicizing environmental protection and green consumption primarily include China Environmental Resources Network, cepn.cn, cgpn.org.cn, CES.CN, waterconserving.cn, and ditan360.com. China Environmental Resources Network is an environmental protection professional portal authorized by the executive committee of the "China Trans-century Environmental Protection Inspection Campaign" to link companies. It is also China's influential environmental protection professional portal with a high click rate (daily visits of over one million). In conjunction with the media supervision and legal supervision and publicity for "China Trans-century Environmental Protection Inspection Campaign," it organizes more than 300 television stations (channels), over 300 radio stations, and over 100 newspapers and periodicals nationwide every year to produce and publish public welfare TV, radio, and newspaper advertisements on environmental and resource conservation. CEPN.CN focuses on the issues in the field of environmental protection in China from multiple perspectives and releases laws and regulations as well as practical activities in a timely manner. Through programs such as special reports and expert views, it disseminates the ecological environmental issues of public concern as well as green consumption-related information such as protecting the Earth, co-building green homeland, Darth Day, Forest Day, Ocean Day, smart city, etc., in an easy-to-understand way. Public welfare programs publicize and report public welfare activities related to green consumption in a timely manner, expand public engagement, and give correct guidance to consumers. At the same time, special activities such as academic seminar, forums, and salons will be held. cgpn.org.cn focuses on the latest developments in the field of green procurement, as well as Chinese and foreign policies, regulations, and practices related to green procurement. The unique feature is its green product database in the "Green Product" column, which releases information related to green procurement of interest to consumers, including green office supplies, motor vehicles, furnishings, and building materials in a timely manner. CES.CN and waterconserving.cn focus on China's policies on energy and water saving, the practice of energy conservation and emission reduction in various fields, and information on new energy- and water-saving products. These fully promote energy conservation and emission reduction as well as sustainable production and sustainable consumption in China. ditan360.com is the world's earliest and most influential official portal on low-carbon economy, which aims to promote the development of low-carbon industry, low-carbon life and low-carbon technology, low-carbon projects, and low-carbon investment and financing.

#### *4.1.3.2 Environmental labeling system*

##### 4.1.3.2.1 ENVIRONMENTAL LABELING PLAN

Environmental label, also known as green mark (ten-ring label) and ecolabel, is a label affixed to a product or its packaging. It is a "certification mark" of a product, which indicates that such product is not only of satisfactory quality but also meets specific environmental requirements in the process of production, use, and disposal. It has environmental advantages such as low toxicity, little hazards, and resource conservation compared with like products. The pattern of China Environmental Label consists of green mountains, clear water, and the sun in the center and the peripheral ten rings, as shown in Figure 4.1. The pattern in the center represents the environment on which human beings rely for survival, and the surrounding ten interconnected rings indicate public engagement and protection of the environment. At the same time, the Chinese character "环" has both the meaning of ring and the environment, symbolizing "all people working together to protect the environment on which human beings rely for survival."

In 1993, China launched the environmental labeling program, and officially announced China Environmental Labeling – Ten-ring Label. On May 17, 1994, China Certification Committee for Environmental Labelling Products (CCCEL) was formally established, and the certification of China environmental labeling officially began. The program is somewhat of an official nature, because its management agencies are the state environmental protection agency and the environmental protection departments of provinces, autonomous regions, and municipalities. The Standards Division of the former State Bureau of Environmental Protection is responsible for formulating certification standards. The Industry Division is responsible for examining and approving projects, determining product types, and examining and approving the certification conclusions made by the

*Figure 4.1* China environmental labeling.

certification committee. Local environmental protection bureaus are responsible for preliminary examination and day-to-day supervision and administration. The CCCEL is the certification body for the program, with the responsibility for the re-examination of products under application, designating inspection agencies to perform product inspection, and organizing on-site inspection. The members of the CCCEL consist of experts from the departments of environmental protection, economy, scientific research, quality supervision, etc., and its supreme authority is the plenary committee meeting. Its personnel are from the State Bureau of Environmental Protection, the State Administration for Entry-Exit Inspection and Quarantine, Chinese Research Academy of Environmental Sciences, Ministry of Foreign Economic Relations and Trade, Chinese Society for Environmental Sciences, State Bureau of Quality and Technical Supervision, etc. Its leadership positions are held by the officials from the State Bureau of Environmental Protection.

Similar to management system certifications such as ISO9001, the procedures of environmental labeling certification (ten-ring certification and 10-ring label certification) are also divided into initial certification, annual supervision and inspection, re-evaluation certification, etc. Specifically,

4 The enterprise fills out the "Application Form of Environmental Labeling Product Certification" and submits it to China Environmental United Certification Center (CEC) together with the materials required for certification. If the requirements are met, the certification center will issue an "acceptance notice." The applicant will sign a contract with the certification center according to the "acceptance notice."
5 The certification center organizes on-site inspection in accordance with the *Guide to Safeguard Measures for Environmental Labeling Products* and the corresponding technical requirements for environmental labeling product certification.
6 The inspection team prepares a comprehensive evaluation report of environmental labeling products according to the application materials, the result of on-site inspection, and the environmental behavior inspection report of products, and submits it to the technical committee for review.
7 Upon receiving the review opinions of the technical committee, the certification center summarizes the review opinions and submits them for approval.
8 The certification center issues environmental labeling certificate, which are valid for three years, to qualified enterprises.
9 According to the issuance time of the certification certificate, the certification center prepares an annual inspection plan, issues an annual inspection notice to enterprises in advance, and conducts annual supervision and inspection.
10 Enterprises whose certificate expire in three years should again fill out the "Application Form" and submit it to the certification center together with relevant materials. The rest of the procedures is the same as that of initial certification.

4.1.3.2.2 GREEN FOOD PLAN

Green food refers to pollution-free, safe, high-quality edible agricultural products and processed products produced in an excellent environment according to the prescribed technical specifications, for which whole-process quality control is implemented and special marks are used. China Green Food Label is a quality certification mark officially registered by Green Food Development Center with the Trademark Office of the former State Administration for Industry and Commerce, as shown in Figure 4.2. It consists of three parts: the sun in the upper part, leaves in the lower part, and the bud in the center, symbolizing natural ecology. It is green in color, symbolizing life, agriculture, and environmental protection. It is perfectly round in shape, symbolizing protection. The whole graphic shows a scene of harmonious vitality under the brilliant sun. It shows that green food is safe, pollution-free food grown from a pure, good ecological environment, and can bring thriving vitality.

Established in 1992, China Green Food Development Center launched the certification of "Green Food" labeling. It is a specialized institution established under the Ministry of Agriculture (now the Ministry of Agriculture and Rural Affairs), responsible for setting certification standards, organizing reviews, signing use agreements with certified parties, and designating environmental protection and food monitoring departments for supervision. Green food is non-polluting safe, high-grade, and nutritious food that is produced in accordance with specific production methods under the principle of sustainable development, and that is authorized by a special agency to use the green food label trademark. It can be said that the certification of green food and the nature of the label are consistent with the environmental label. In May 1990, the Ministry of Agriculture officially prescribed the label and standards of green food. According to the standards: (1) The origin of the product or its raw materials must comply with the ecological environmental standards of green food; (2) Crop planting, livestock and poultry breeding, aquaculture, and food processing must comply with the production and operation procedures for green food; (3) Products must satisfy the quality and hygiene standards for green food; (4) The label of products must comply with the provisions in the *Manual of Standards for Green Food Label Design* prepared by the Ministry of Agriculture of China.

*Figure 4.2* China Green Food Label.

For the management of green food mark, the specific legal attributes of the trademark are proved according to the green food label. The use of the label shows that the production process and the quality of products meet the specific standards on green food, and enterprises that meet the standards are supervised regarding the implementation of the green food production and operation procedures, as well as the correct use of the green food label. The management of green food label has two characteristics: the basis of standard identification, and the basis of legal management. According to the standard identification, strict quantitative standards are set for the whole production process (from the soil to the table) that may affect the quality of the final product, and internationally accepted quality certification procedures are used to check whether they meet the standards, so as to ensure that the certification is scientific, authoritative, and impartial. In accordance with legal management, or in accordance with the *Trademark Law*, *Anti-Unfair Competition Law*, *Advertising Law*, and *Product Quality Law*, efforts are made to regulate the behavior of producers and business operators, crack down on counterfeit and shoddy products on the market, and safeguard the legitimate rights and interests of producers, business operators, and consumers. China Green Food Development Center will number products with green food label in a unified manner and issue the certificate of green food label.

The procedures for implementing the green food labeling: (1) The application is filed by the organization or individuals who are eligible to produce green food; (2) The preliminary examination shall be processed by the green food administrative department of the province (autonomous region, municipality, or city with independent planning status) where the applicant is located, and environmental evaluation is performed; (3) When the preliminary examination is successful, it is reported to China Green Food Development Center, which will review the materials in conjunction with authoritative environmental protection agencies; (4) For the successful applicants, the agency designated by China Green Food Development Center will carry out sampling and inspection, and the center shall be responsible for comprehensive review; (5) Certified applicants must sign a "Agreement on the Use of Green Food Label" with China Green Food Development Center.

Products certified as green food can use the green food label with a uniform pattern for a period of three years, starting from the date when the certificate is obtained. Upon expiration, the production enterprise must re-apply for certification, and it can continue to use the label only after the application is approved. At the same time, the number on the label will be changed. It takes half a year to go from re-application to the acquisition of certificate. Manufacturers are allowed to continue to use the green food label in the meantime. If the re-application is refused, the applicant must immediately stop using the label. Moreover, China Green Food Development Center will inspect products in accordance with the environmental, production, and quality standards for green food every year within the three-year validity period. If they do not comply with the regulations, the center will disqualify the use of product label.

#### *4.1.3.3 Energy efficiency "leader" system*

Energy efficiency "leader" refers to a product, enterprise or organization that achieves the highest energy efficiency among comparable competitors in the same range. The implementation of the energy efficiency leader system is important for motivating society in energy conservation and emission reduction, promoting the development of energy-saving and environmental protection industries, saving energy resources, and protecting the environment. By setting the benchmark, issuing incentive policies, and raising standards, it forms a long-term mechanism for improving energy efficiency for terminal energy-using products, energy-intensive industries, and public institutions, thereby promoting energy conservation and emission reduction. It sets energy efficiency benchmarks by publishing on a regular basis a catalog of terminal energy-using products with the highest energy efficiency, a list of manufacturers of energy-intensive products with the lowest energy consumption per unit of product, a list of public institutions with the highest energy efficiency, as well as energy efficiency indicators. It gives policy support to energy efficiency "leaders," guides enterprises and public institutions to become energy efficiency "leaders," incorporates energy efficiency "leader" indicators into mandatory national standards for energy efficiency and energy consumption limits in a timely manner, improves the dynamic update mechanism for standards, and continuously raises the access threshold for energy efficiency. Following the relevant requirements of the *Action Plan for Energy Conservation, Emission Reduction and Low-carbon Development from 2014 to 2015* (GBF [2014] No. 23), the *Opinions on Accelerating the Development of Energy Conservation and Environmental Protection Industries* (GF [2013] No. 30) and the *Air Pollution Prevention and Control Action Plan* (GF [2013] No. 37), the National Development and Reform Commission, the Ministry of Finance, the Ministry of Industry and Information Technology, the National Government Offices Administration, the National Energy Administration, the State Administration of Quality Supervision, Inspection and Quarantine and China Standardization Administration jointly issued the *Implementation Plan for the Energy Efficiency "Leader" System* on December 31, 2014, marking the official beginning of the implementation of the energy efficiency leader system in China.

The scope of implementation of the energy efficiency "leader" system covers terminal energy-using products (hereinafter "energy-using products"), energy-intensive industries, and public institutions. The energy efficiency "leaders" of energy-using products should meet the following requirements: (1) Products whose energy efficiency level reaches energy efficiency level 1 or above under national energy efficiency standards, and that have leading energy efficiency among comparable products of the same type; energy efficiency leader indicator should be improved year by year; (2) Products that use advanced and efficient energy-saving technology and spare parts, with low energy consumption in the life cycle; (3) Products that have nationally recognized energy-saving product certificate, with a third-party energy efficiency test report issued by a nationally recognized laboratory; (4) Products with excellent quality and performance; in the national supervision and random inspection of product quality conducted in the recent year, there are no unqualified products of this brand; (5) The product is an approved product for mass production; (6) The production enterprise is a lawful independent legal entity domiciled in mainland China, with a sound quality management system, a sound supply system and good after-sales service capabilities, which promises the normal supply of "leader" products via mainstream sales channels.

Energy-using products as energy efficiency "leaders" are selected by means of voluntary application by enterprises, expert review, public announcement, etc. Products listed in the catalog are authorized to place the energy efficiency "leader" label in a conspicuous position or on the packaging of the product. The label pattern is shown in Figure 4.3. The National Development and Reform Commission, in conjunction with relevant government departments, has issued incentive policies to encourage technological R&D, publicity, and promotion of energy efficiency "leader" products, and established a mechanism for aligning energy efficiency "leader" indicators with mandatory national standards for energy efficiency. Energy efficiency "leader" indicators are incorporated into the energy efficiency standard indicator system in a timely manner according to the developments of energy-saving technologies and market changes in energy efficiency levels, in conjunction with the specific situation of energy-using products. Greater efforts are made to inspect and supervise the energy efficiency, quality, and other performance indicators of energy-using products as energy efficiency "leaders." Energy efficiency "leaders" are regarded as the focus of the national quality supervision and random inspection of products, and harsher punishment is administered for violations. Energy efficiency label filing and management agencies, nationally recognized energy-saving product certification bodies, and relevant testing institutions shall carry out label filing, product certification, and performance testing in an objective and fair manner according to relevant regulations, and conduct effective follow-up investigation on the energy efficiency labels and quality certification of energy efficiency leaders. For products that provide false energy efficiency information, do not pass certification, or fail to meet quality standards, their shortlisted qualifications, the filing of energy efficiency labels, and energy-saving certificate shall be abolished and the practice shall be exposed. Manufacturers that provide false materials or give false publicity will be put on the negative list and will not be allowed to apply for energy efficiency "leader" label for energy-using products within three years.

On May 27, 2016, the National Development and Reform Commission, the Ministry of Industry and Information Technology, and the General Administration of Quality Supervision, Inspection and Quarantine (AQSIQ) jointly released the first catalog of energy efficiency "leader" products. The website and WeChat public account for energy efficiency "leader" program were also launched. The

*Figure 4.3* Energy efficiency "leader" label.

first batch of energy efficiency "leader" products include household refrigerators, flat-panel TVs, and variable-speed room air conditioners. Through enterprise application, local recommendation, initial selection, on-site energy efficiency testing, secondary evaluation, and public announcement, energy efficiency "leader" products of the year were selected from 477 participating models in 2016. China's National Energy Administration officially announced the site arrangement for 2017 (third batch) leader program, scale of site as well as timetable for the subsequent implementation plan. It is expected that 5GW application leader program will be launched by the end of 2018, and 1.5GW technology leader program will be launched on June 30, 2019.

#### *4.1.3.4 Publicity and education activities*

Publicity activities such as the national campaign on energy conservation and emission reduction, National Energy Conservation Publicity Week, National Water Conservation Publicity Week in Cities, as well as World Environment Day, Earth Day, and World Meteorological Day are organized and held, and China's resources and environment are publicized in order to raise public awareness of energy saving and environmental protection, thereby creating a social culture conducive to promoting green consumption. The publicity activities related to green consumption in China are shown in Table 4.2:

The case of NGO participation in environmental protection publicity: Global Village of Beijing Environmental Education Center.[3]

Founded in 1996, Global Village of Beijing Environmental Education Center (Global Village of Beijing for short) is a non-profit non-governmental environmental protection organization dedicated to public education on environmental protection.

Global Village of Beijing is the liaison station of the United Nations Environment Programme in China. The purpose of Global Village of Beijing is to promote sustainable development in China by creating a mass environmental culture. Global Village of Beijing mainly works to independently produce film and television programs on environmental protection, write and promote books and publicity materials on environmental protection, hold environmental protection forums, establish environmental education and training bases, and spread the theory and practice of green communities. At the same time, it has launched environmental protection projects such as green trains, green energy, circular economy, Green Angel Art Troupe, international exchanges, and recycling of consumables.

Environmental education provided by Global Village of Beijing has always been based on the community. In 1996, Global Village of Beijing helped Dachengxiang Family Committee in Xicheng District, Beijing establish a pilot waste sorting program and send waste sorting proposals to governments at all levels. In early 1999, it cooperated with Xuanwu District Government and the property company in establishing a green community model in Jiangong Nanli community, which involves community-level environmental protection facilities and public engagement mechanism. In 2001, the Beijing Olympic Games Bid Committee adopted the green

*Table 4.2* Overview of publicity and education activities on green consumption in China

| *Name* | *Description* |
|---|---|
| National campaign on energy conservation and emission reduction | Beginning in September 2007, the "National campaign on energy conservation and emission reduction" includes nine special initiatives: community and family initiative, youth initiative, enterprise initiative, school initiative, military quarters initiative, government organization initiative, science and technology initiative, science popularization initiative, and media initiative |
| National Energy Conservation Publicity Week | National Energy Conservation Publicity Week activity was initiated at the Sixth Energy Conservation Work Conference of the State Council in 1990. National Energy Conservation Publicity Week has been held every year since 1991 |
| National Water Conservation Publicity Week in Cities | It is held in the week to which May 15 belongs annually. Cities launch a series of activities to raise the public awareness of the important practical significance and long-term strategic significance of water conservation. Greater investment is made to develop and promote new water-saving processes, new technologies and new appliances. The comprehensive utilization of water use is improved in cities |
| World Environment Day | In 1972, the United Nations convened the United Nations Conference on the Human Environment in Stockholm, Sweden, in which representatives from 113 countries participated. The meeting discussed an action plan to protect the global environment and adopted the *Declaration on the Human Environment*. The meeting recommended that the UN General Assembly designate June 5, the day when the meeting opened, as World Environment Day |
| Earth Day | Earth Day, which falls on April 2, is a global environmental protection activity. The purpose is to arouse the human awareness of caring for the Earth and protecting the homeland, promote the coordination of resource exploitation and environmental protection, and improve the overall environment of the Earth |
| World Meteorological Day | World Meteorological Day, which falls on March 23, is established by the World Meteorological Organization in June 1960 to commemorate the establishment of the World Meteorological Organization and the entry into force of the *Convention of the World Meteorological Organization* (March 23, 1950) |

community promotion plan proposed by Global Village of Beijing, which became part of the Action Plan for Green Olympics. The concept and experience of Global Village of Beijing regarding green community have gained widespread government and social recognition. Global Village of Beijing has been invited to give lectures and training on green communities in over ten provinces and municipalities.

In order to bring the ideas of eco-friendly life and communities to rural areas, Global Village of Beijing rented 186 hectares of mountain forest as an environmental education base in the then Duijiushi Village, Jingzhuang Town, Yanqing County, Beijing in 1999. Farmers here sort garbage, use solar lamps, and plant pollution-free food. While getting close to nature, urban dwellers receive environmental education in various forms. This program also generates income for the poor villagers. This small village, which has mountains, forest land, wetlands, wilderness, and mountain streams and is inhabited by over 40 farmer households, has evolved into an ecological area integrating environmental protection, green tourism, and environmental education and training.

Global Village of Beijing also promotes environmental protection in life through large-scale citizen activities. In the "China Action on Earth Day in 2000" jointly initiated and organized by Global Village of Beijing and many non-governmental organizations across the country, nearly 10 million citizens made commitments in the event with the theme of "advocating sustainable consumption and living eco-friendly life." In the same year, 830,000 primary school students and their parents in Beijing completed the environmental protection commitment card issued by Global Village of Beijing and China Young Pioneers National Working Commission, spreading the concept of green Olympics and eco-friendly life among the people. The first national environmental protection song collection event, jointly held by Global Village of Beijing and *Music Weekly*, initiated a green movement in the music industry. In 2001, the "10 Million Green Volunteers in Action" survey and commitment event jointly planned by Global Village of Beijing and China Consumers Association had an impact on consumers nationwide. China Sustainable Consumption Forum sparked academic and policy research into sustainable consumption.

## 4.2 Evolution and practice of China's policies on green consumption

Since the beginning of reform and opening up, China has always upheld the basic principle of centering on economic development, made steady strides in building a moderately prosperous society in all respects, and improved the people's living standards. However, conflicts between economic development and resources and the environment have erupted, aggravating the fragile environment. Therefore, China begins to explore green consumption in the context of the international green trend. Of course, advocating green consumption is also closely associated with the grim challenges facing China after its accession to the World Trade Organization. As international economic integration becomes increasingly obvious, international trade, which is one of the main driving forces of economic development, has developed as never before. Trade between various countries has become more frequent and the relations have been closer. There is extremely fierce trade competition among countries. After China joined the World Trade Organization, the trend of green consumption has exerted a major impact on China. Foreign green consumer goods can easily enter China, intensifying the market competition. At the same time, developed countries are erecting increasingly higher green barriers, making it more difficult for Chinese products to enter the foreign markets. Green barriers are a means for Europe, the United States, and other countries to protect their domestic industries and markets by restricting import of goods through laws and regulations on the grounds of environmental protection. It mainly takes the form of regional environmental protection conventions, ISO14000 system certification, etc. The standards adopted by the EU and the North American Free Trade Area are basically the same, and even if there is a gap, it is small. Developed countries usually adopt regional free trade measures to keep out foreign products, including a wealth of Chinese products, on the grounds that such products do not meet their standards.

### *4.2.1 Proposal of green consumption in China*

Green consumption is put forward in the context of sharp conflict between China's population, resources, and the environment, intensifying international competition and mounting green barriers erected by developed countries.

In 1994, China formulated *China's Agenda 21 – White Paper on China's Population, Environment, and Development in the 21st Century*, which comprises 20 chapters. It expounds on the importance and significance of sustainable development. The white paper is roughly divided into four parts: sustainable development strategy, sustainable social development, sustainable economic development, and rational utilization of resources and environmental protection. Green consumption is closely related to population, household consumption and social services, the production and consumption of sustainable energy sources, the protection and sustainable use of natural resources, the harmless treatment of solid waste, etc.

The *China Trans-Century Green Project Plan* issued in 1996 is an important decision to incorporate environmental protection into the national economic plan. The plan calls on the governments to organize relevant government departments and enterprises to pool financial, material, and human resources in accordance with the requirements of international conventions to implement projects and measures in response to key areas and major ecological environmental problems, so as to address ecological environmental issues. According to the plan, ecological damage and environmental pollution shall be basically curbed by the end of the 20th century, so that the ecological environment in some cities and regions in China could be remediated to a certain extent, and the overall objective of ecological environmental protection could be achieved by 2010. The plan includes three phases over a period of 15 years. The principle of the plan is: highlight key environmental issues; be technically and economically feasible; take into account environmental, social, and economic benefits; "hold the polluter accountable," with capital investment mainly made by enterprises and local governments. The implementation of the project is managed according to the current investment management system.

In October 2005, the Fifth Plenary Session of the 16th CPC Central Committee put forward the building of a resource-conserving and environment-friendly society for the first time as one of the tasks of strategic significance. This was a major decision made by the CPC Central Committee with Hu Jintao as the General Secretary at that time in light of China's reality by drawing on advanced international experience. Thereafter, China has been committed to building a resource-conserving and environment-friendly society and worked to strike a balance between economic development, resources, and the environment. The Chinese government has always regarded "development as the fundamental principle," put forward the building of a resource-conserving and environment-friendly society, applied the Scientific Outlook on Development, coordinated the harmonious development of man and nature, advocated upgrading the consumption structure, and continuously promoted green consumption.

In 2007, the 17th CPC National Congress put forward "promoting an ecological conservation culture" for the first time, which marked a quantum leap in the CPC's concept of scientific development and harmonious development. The Scientific Outlook on Development is not just a simple change in the pattern of economic development. An essential meaning of applying the scientific outlook on development is to foster an ecological conservation culture. In terms of economic relations, green production and consumption for environmental protection is an important starting area for pursuing new-type industrialization as advocated by the scientific outlook on development. Promoting ecological conservation is a wide-ranging program, covering all factors of man, nature, and society. It is necessary to gradually change behavior and concepts of human beings, make rational and appropriate use of nature, take proven protective measures, and innovate the accounting system and relevant rules. Of course, addressing environmental inequity requires new environmental economic policies, including ecological compensation policies featuring financial transfer, and collection of environmental and resource taxes in due time. In the report of the 17th CPC National Congress, the task of promoting ecological conservation has the goals as the promotion of green consumption.

In June 2010, former president Hu Jintao said at the meeting of the Chinese Academy of Sciences and the Chinese Academy of Engineering that pursuing green development is to develop eco-friendly industries, reduce energy and material consumption, protect and remediate the ecological environment, develop circular economy and low-carbon technologies, and achieve the coordinated development of economy, society and nature. The Fifth Plenary Session of the 17th CPC Central Committee held in October 2010 stated the need to uphold the concept of green and low-carbon development, publicize green buildings and construction, develop green economy and green mining, promote green consumption model, implement green government procurement, and pursue green development.

In response to the call of the United Nations to advocate a green economy, China's former Ministry of Environmental Protection set the theme of the 2012 Environment Day as "Green Economy: Does it include you," in order to emphasize the philosophy of green consumption, call on the public to adopt new concept and behavior of consumption, buy eco-friendly commodities, save energy and resources, pay attention to environmental protection, and build a green homeland.

The necessity of green consumption has been recognized by the theoretical circles and was included in the *Outline of the 12th Five-Year Plan for National Economic and Social Development of the People's Republic of China*. The Outline requires building a resource-conserving and environment-friendly society, paying attention to ecological environmental protection, and continuously promoting green consumption. The Outline pointed out the need to promote the circular development in the production, consumption, and distribution fields, promote the all-round development of production and consumption, and put the focus of circular economy development on life and consumption, so as to achieve the goal of building a moderately prosperous society in all respects. Therefore, it is advocated that consumers opt for eco-friendly commodities, and the government implements green procurement, pays attention to resource and environmental conservation, and promotes green consumption.

In April and September 2015, the CPC Central Committee and the State Council successively issued the Opinions of the CPC Central Committee and the State Council on Accelerating the Promotion of Ecological Conservation and the Overall Plan for the Reform of the Ecological Civilization System. All regions and government departments are required to earnestly implement these in light of reality. These put forward the need to vigorously promote green development, circular development, and low-carbon development, uphold an ecological culture, advocate eco-friendly life, and accelerate the building of a beautiful China with blue skies, green mountains, and lucid waters and ensure sustainable development for the Chinese nation; vigorously develop energy-saving and environmental protection industries, guide consumers to choose energy-saving and new energy vehicles, energy-efficient household appliances, water-saving appliances and other energy-saving and eco-friendly low-carbon products, cut down the use of disposable supplies, and limit excessive packaging; vigorously promote green and low-carbon travel, advocate eco-friendly lifestyle and leisure model, strictly restrict the development of energy-intensive and water-intensive service industries, and launch-round anti-food waste campaign in catering enterprises, canteens, and households. Party and government institutions and state-owned enterprises should take the lead in practicing frugal consumption.

In November 2015, the State Council issued the Guiding Opinions of the State Council on Leveraging the Leading Role of New Consumption and Accelerating the Cultivation of New Supply and New Sources of Growth, stating that new-type consumption should play a leading role in driving the adjustment and upgrading of the industrial structure. Green consumption expands from ecological organic food to goods and services that help save resources and improve the environment such as air purifiers, water purifiers, energy-saving and water-saving appliances, eco-friendly household appliances, and green building materials. It has effectively promoted the development of circular economy, ecological economy, and low-carbon economy and provided a wealth of investment and entrepreneurship opportunities for technology R&D, enhancement of production and service capacity, and infrastructure construction in the fields of ecological agriculture, new energy, energy and water saving, comprehensive utilization of resources, environmental protection and pollution control, ecological protection and remediation, etc.

In 2016, ten government departments including the National Development and Reform Commission jointly issued the *Guiding Opinions on Promoting Green Consumption* to encourage the consumption of green products. According to the *Guiding Opinions*, by 2020, the market share of energy-saving household appliances such as air conditioners, refrigerators, and water heaters with energy efficiency level 2 or above will exceed 50 percent; greater efforts will be made to promote new energy vehicles and remanufactured products, implement the action plan for the production and application of eco-friendly building materials, and promote the use of eco-friendly building materials and decoration materials such as energy-saving doors and windows, and products made from construction waste.

### *4.2.2 The practice of China's policy on green consumption*

Driven and guided by China's green consumption policy, the practice of green consumption started with the "three-green program" jointly launched in 1999 by 12 central government departments including the Ministry of Commerce and the Publicity Department of the Communist Party of China. Following the implementation of activities such as the "Green Consumption Theme Year" held by China Consumers Association in 2001, the proposal of "promoting ecological conservation" at the 17th CPC National Congress and the proposal of the "green development" concept at the 18th CPC National Congress, green consumption practice is in full swing in China.

#### *4.2.1.1 Three-green program*

In 1999, six government departments including the State Environmental Protection Administration jointly launched the "Three-green program" – open up green channels, cultivate green markets, and advocate green consumption. It was vigorously promoted by local governments, and positive results have been achieved. In 2001, the six government departments further promoted the "three-green program" in order to implement the guiding principles of the national conference on rectifying and regulating the order of the market economy, realize the quality control of food "from the farm to the dining table," improve food hygiene and quality, and safeguard the health of consumers. The early "three-green program" was a systematic program that has the purpose of establishing a sound food safety guarantee system in the distribution field and the livestock and poultry slaughtering and processing industry, that focuses on establishing a strict market access system, and that features "opening up green channels, cultivating green markets, and advocating green consumption." Advocating green consumption is to increase publicity and reporting, organize activities of a public welfare nature, and establish a concept of pollution-free food consumption through harmonized policies and guiding measures. It is to raise the awareness of protecting rights and interests as well as the environment, promote the production and consumption of green food, and establish a scientific, eco-friendly food consumption model for the benefit of health. To cultivate a green market, it is necessary to strengthen the establishment of supporting market facilities in accordance with harmonized quality standards and ensure that green food produced still meets the "green" standards after processing, transport, wholesaling, retail, etc., in order to prevent contamination and spoilage. At the same time, it is necessary to perform strict inspection and testing, eliminate any fake and shoddy green food, and build a high-quality, pollution-free distribution network. Opening up green channels means building a "vegetable basket" commodity transport network that integrates multiple means of transport such as highways, railways, aviation, and water transport through coordination and organization of transport capacity, removing unnecessary checkpoints and unreasonable charges, and realizing efficient, pollution-free, and low-cost distribution.

The basic idea of the "three-green program" is to depart from the convention. The first is to start from consumption. It guides consumers to raise awareness of food safety, make new shopping choices, give equal priority to price and quality, and provide simple yet effective food testing means in the market, so that sub-standard food cannot be sold. This achieves the purpose of guiding the production of enterprises. The second is to implement whole-process hygiene quality control. Legal, economic, and administrative means will be employed, and a food safety guarantee system covering all links will be established. The third is that the government, enterprises, and consumers work together on the basis of labor division to form a synergy, with clearly defined responsibilities. The fourth is to consider food safety, human health, social credit, corporate culture, environmental protection, resource conservation, scientific consumption, etc., and make progress in a coordinated manner. The fifth is to give prominence to key points, take measures in light of local conditions, and implement them step by step. It is necessary to first focus on the hygiene quality of meat, vegetables, and wine commodities, and then expand to all types of food. We shall first ensure that the people have access to safe and secure food, and at the same time advocate the consumption of food that has national quality and safety certification such as organic food. Practice has proved that this is an innovative management method to address food safety issues in light of China's national conditions.

In order to further implement the "three-green program" and develop a green and low-carbon economy, the Ministry of Commerce issued the *Guiding Opinions on the Pilot Work of the Three-green Program* in October 2012. The guiding opinions put forward the following goals: to promote green and low-carbon procurement, create a number of green supply chains, expand the sales volume and market share of green low-carbon products, and ensure that the purchasing variety and quantity of green and low-carbon products for pilot enterprises should account for over 20 percent of the total number of similar commodities; to cultivate a number of green and low-carbon markets (restaurants) and ensure that pilot enterprises meet the national standards for green markets (restaurants) in terms of commodity access, business environment, facilities, and equipment, as well as operation and management; and guide green and low-carbon consumption, and promote consumers to embrace an idea and behavior of green and low-carbon consumption. At the same time, the Ministry of Commerce and the Ministry of Finance have launched the "three-green program" demonstration project in some areas featuring "promoting green and low-carbon procurement, cultivating green and low-carbon markets (restaurants), and guiding green and low-carbon consumption."

The main tasks during the 12th Five-Year Plan period are: (1) Promote green and low-carbon procurement. It supports pilot enterprises in cooperating with green and low-carbon commodity production enterprises (bases) and creates a green and low-carbon supply chain. It supports wholesale and retail enterprises in expanding the purchase of commodities with low-carbon labels, green labels, organic labels, environmental labels, geographical indications label, energy-saving label level II or above and well-known trademarks, and increasing the sales volume and market share of green and low-carbon products. It supports pilot enterprises in establishing standards and norms for green and low-carbon procurement, establishes strict market access mechanism, guides green, standardized, and branded production, and develops green and low-carbon distribution. (2) Cultivate green and low-carbon markets (restaurants). It supports pilot enterprises in upgrading the site environment, facilities, and equipment in accordance with the national requirements and standards for green markets (restaurants), and motivates pilot enterprises to participate in green and low-carbon market certification. It supports pilot enterprises in launching green and low-carbon marketing, setting up sales zones and counters for green and low-carbon products, and expanding exhibitions, promotion, and sales of green, low-carbon products. It supports pilot enterprises in establishing scientific, standardized, and efficient processes and mechanisms for green and low-carbon operation and management, establishing a sound traceability and labeling system for green and low-carbon products, completing the inspection, testing, and handling of unqualified products, and improving the management level. (3) Guide green and low-carbon consumption. It supports the publicity of green and low-carbon consumption, promotes green and low-carbon brands, provides information services to consumers to purchase green and low-carbon products and services, and guides the general public to develop green and low-carbon consumption habits and value orientation. It encourages consumers to buy green and low-carbon products and promotes energy-efficient household appliances, office supplies, and high-efficiency lighting products. It reduces standby energy consumption, reduces the use of disposable supplies, implements regulations restricting the excessive packaging of commodities as well as the production and sales of ultra-thin plastic shopping bags, and advocates green and low-carbon lifestyles and consumption model.

#### *4.2.1.2 Promotion and use of new energy vehicles*

New energy vehicles refer to vehicles with advanced technology principles, new technologies, and new structure that use unconventional vehicle fuel as the power source (or use conventional vehicle fuel and new-type on-board power devices) and that integrate advanced vehicle power control and drive, including hybrid electric vehicles (HEVs), battery electric vehicles (BEVs), fuel cell electric vehicles (FCEVs), hydrogen engine vehicles, as well as gas vehicles and alcohol ether vehicles. At an executive meeting of the State Council held on September 29, 2015, Premier Li Keqiang stressed that no local government should impose restrictions on the operation and purchase of new energy vehicles, and existing restrictions should be abolished. On October 25, 2015, Beijing Municipal Office of Regulation and Management of Indicators for Passenger Vehicles issued an announcement, which states that in order to implement the guiding principles of the executive meeting of the State Council and promote the development of new energy vehicles, the indicators for new energy passenger cars for demonstration application are directly allocated to all applicants who have passed the qualification examination. On February 16, 2016, the Ministry of Industry and Information Technology released data on the factory certificate of motor vehicles, which show that China's production output of new energy vehicles in January 2016 was 1.61 million, a year-on-year increase of 144 percent.

New energy vehicles mainly have two stages of development: In the first stage, hybrid vehicles are the main direction of development, supplemented by new energy vehicles such as fuel cell vehicles, and the new energy vehicle market is developed. In the second stage, on the basis of the mature technology of BEVs, BEVs gradually replace hybrid vehicles and fuel cell vehicles and even completely occupy the new energy vehicle market, and zero emissions are achieved.

China has stepped up its support for new energy vehicles since 2010. On June 1, 2010, five cities of Shanghai, Changchun, Shenzhen, Hangzhou, and Hefei piloted subsidies for purchase of new energy vehicles by individuals. In July 2010, the number of pilot cities for the demonstration and promotion of energy-saving and new energy vehicles in China was increased from 20 to 25. Given environmental protection, energy security, and other reasons, it is a strategic move for China to vigorously develop emerging industry of new energy vehicles. Since 2013, the National Development and Reform Commission, the Ministry of Finance, the Ministry of Industry and Information Technology, the Ministry of Science and Technology, etc., have issued many policies to encourage and promote the development of new energy vehicles, including high subsidies for the purchase of new energy vehicles, and no restrictions on odd-and-even license plate rule and traffic control. During the 12th Five-Year Plan period, the state has greatly increased the cumulative production and sales volume of BEVs and plug-in hybrid vehicles, and basically developed a charging facility system and a commercial operation mode for new energy vehicles in line with the market scale. According to the Ministry of Finance's *Circular on the Policy of Fiscal Support for the Promotion and Application of New Energy Vehicles from 2016 to 2020*, in order to increase industrial demand and expand industrial space economically, the state spares no effort to support the development of BEVs, plug-in hybrid (including extended-range hybrid) vehicles, and fuel vehicles and has set a road map for the gradual withdrawal of subsidies in the next five years.

In 2015, China saw explosive growth in new energy vehicles, with an output of 379,000 vehicles, a year-on-year increase of 3.5 times, making China the world's largest incremental market for new energy vehicles. By 2020, the cumulative output and sales of BEVs and plug-in hybrid vehicles reached a new height compared to that of 2015, and large-scale commercial operations were realized.

**Case study: natural gas light Trucks in Chengdu reach a large-scale, "three-green program" acts as a booster**[4]

Favorable policies for new energy vehicles were introduced in 2015, and as a result enterprises attached increasing importance to the R&D and production of new energy vehicle models. The supermarket delivery trucks at Chengdu branch of 360che.com enterprise include Longju single-row box-type light trucks produced by Dongfeng Nanchong, which have CNG sign on the vehicle bumper and cylindrical gas storage tanks underneath.

The cargo compartment of Longju truck bears the words "Shiyitong," which refers to an e-commerce platform specializing in transporting commodities for supermarkets, including beverages, beer, snacks, convenience foods, grain and oils, household chemicals, etc. It should be routine transport with standard load. Natural gas light trucks in Chengdu have achieved large-scale development. "Shiyitong" has made bulk purchase of CNG models for the "last-mile" logistics distribution. As the terrain in urban areas is generally flat, natural gas light trucks should perform well under standard loading. Compared with diesel fuel-powered light trucks, the price of natural gas light trucks may be prohibitive to individual buyers. Therefore, this model is still mainly purchased by enterprises for short-and middle-distance distribution services or as municipal sanitation vehicles. The CNG mark on the bumper of Longju vehicles indicates that it is a model fueled by compressed natural gas and meets the National Stage V emission standards. The implementation of the Beijing Stage V emission standard has sent out a message that China will have more stringent requirements for emission standards. The next stage emission standards will be implemented nationwide to strictly control vehicle exhaust pollution. CNG-powered light trucks undoubtedly lead the implementation of the policy. Even if China Stage V standards are implemented in Chengdu, there is no need to upgrade vehicles, because clean energy has already minimized environmental pollution in the city.

Moreover, this model has the freight vehicle driving certificate in urban roads in Chengdu City, as a result of the "three-green program." Vehicles with the "three-green program" license are allowed to drive on some roads in the city, regardless of the restrictions on morning and evening rush hour traffic control. Licensed vehicles transporting goods can temporarily park to load or unload goods on small and medium-sized streets and branch roads within designated periods, as well as on main trunk roads and busy streets. Special privileges for temporary parking are of help for last-mile delivery services.

#### *4.2.1.3 Waste sorting*

Municipal household waste sorting has been promoted in China for many years. The *Regulations on the Administration of City Appearance and Environmental Sanitation* were promulgated in August 1992, which detail the specific practices of collecting, transporting, and disposing of urban household waste under the principles of environmental protection and harmless treatment. In 1993, the Ministry of Construction formulated and promulgated the *Measures for the Management of Urban Household Waste* (revised in 2007) (hereinafter the Measures) in accordance with the *Regulations*, which is the first special normative document on the administration of municipal household waste in China. The *Measures* clearly define the responsibilities of management by construction departments and supervision by environmental sanitation departments and stipulate that urban residents are required to put household waste into garbage containers or designated household waste places at the prescribed location and time as required. In 2000, the Ministry of Construction issued the *Circular on Pilot Cities for the Sorting and Collection of Household Waste* (JCH [2000] No. 12), which chose the eight cities of Beijing, Shanghai, Guangzhou, Shenzhen, Hangzhou, Nanjing, Xiamen, and Guilin as pilot cities for the sorting and collection of household waste. It officially marked a prelude to the pilot program of waste sorting and collection in China. At the same time, a charging system for household waste disposal is implemented. This fee is charged as a business service fee instead of administrative fee, and a bidding mechanism is introduced for the disposal of municipal household waste.

Thereafter, the relevant ministries and commissions have successively formulated and issued many departmental-level regulations. In 2006, the Ministry of Commerce formulated and promulgated the *Measures for the Management of Renewable Resources Recycling*. The National Development and Reform Commission, the Ministry of Finance, the Ministry of Construction, and the State Environmental Protection Administration jointly formulated and issued the *Circular on Operating the Charging System for the Municipal Household Waste Disposal and Promoting the Development of Waste Disposal as an Industry*. The National Development and Reform Commission issued the *Circular on Establishing a Statistical Reporting System for Information Relating to Municipal Household Waste Disposal and Charging*. The Ministry of Environmental Protection spearheaded the drafting of the *Regulations on the Management of the Recycling and Disposal of Waste Electrical and Electronic Products*, which was issued in 2009 with the approval of the State Council. It is also the second administrative regulation issued by the State Council in the field of solid waste following the *Regulations on the Administration of City Appearance and Environmental Sanitation*. As the problem of urban household waste became more prominent and the management of urban solid waste deepened, the State Council approved and forwarded in 2011 the *Opinions on Strengthening the Disposal of Municipal Household Waste* jointly issued by 16 ministries and commissions, including the Ministry of Housing and Urban-Rural Development and the Ministry of Environmental Protection. In April 2015, five ministries and commissions including the Ministry of Housing and Urban-Rural Development issued a document, identifying 26 cities (districts) including Dongcheng District of Beijing, Jing'an District of Shanghai, Guangzhou City of Guangdong Province, and Hangzhou City of Zhejiang Province as the first group of demonstration cities (districts) for household waste sorting. In September 2015, the CPC Central Committee and the State Council issued the *Overall Plan for the Reform of the Ecological Civilization System*, which explicitly stated the need to "accelerate the establishment of a compulsory waste sorting system." On June 15, 2016, according to the plan made by the central government, the National Development and Reform Commission and the Ministry of Housing and Urban-Rural Development jointly issued the *Scheme for a Compulsory Waste Sorting System (Draft for Comments)*, requiring the establishment of a compulsory sorting system for municipal household garbage. After extensive solicitation of opinions, the General Office of the State Council forwarded on March 30, 2017 the *Implementation*

*Plan for the Household Waste Sorting System* (hereinafter referred to as the "Plan") promulgated by the National Development and Reform Commission and the Ministry of Housing and Urban-Rural Development. The *Plan* requires the implementation of compulsory sorting of household waste in municipalities directly under the Central Government, provincial capitals, cities with independent planning status as well as the first batch of demonstration cities for household waste sorting designated by the Ministry of Housing and Urban-Rural Development and other government departments. It is stated that by the end of 2020, in the key cities that implement mandatory sorting of household garbage, the coverage of household waste sorting and collection shall exceed 90 percent, and the recycling and utilization rate of household waste shall exceed 35 percent.

Regrettably, despite the many years' practice of waste sorting in China, the overall effect still needs to be improved for a host of reasons. Although we now enter an era of mandatory waste sorting, the Plan stipulates that compulsory waste sorting is mainly targeted at Party and government institutions, schools, scientific research, cultural and other public institutions, as well as some units or enterprises managing public places in the pilot cities. For residents, it adopts the methods of guidance and encouragement. In other words, residents who generate the most household waste and find it most difficult to sort waste will continue to be an obstacle to implementing the waste sorting system in the future.

**Case introduction: Chengdu green earth creates "Internet +" waste sorting**[5]

Wang Jianchao, who served as a research and development engineer in Microsoft China for five years, never thought that his career would involve waste disposal. Wang Jianchao is engaged in promoting household waste sorting in an institution called "Green Earth" in Chengdu. Through real-name registration and the practice of waste sorting in exchange for points, this institution has promoted 200,000 households in 584 communities in Chengdu to engage in waste sorting. A total of 10,520 metric tons of garbage had been collected from 2012 to 2016.

> We position the new company as a waste sorting technology company. We work to establish a new-generation municipal waste sorting and resource-oriented recycling system by means of a market-oriented approach with the aid of mobile Internet technologies such as WeChat and Apps, so as to help the government effectively reduce waste, and enhance the sustainable management of municipal waste and public engagement,
>
> said Wang Jianchao

Sorting waste is easier said than done. Despite the rich practical experience, Wang Jianchao and his colleagues still confront a host of problems and conflicts. Waste sorting is inevitably accompanied by the issue of recycling renewable resources. "We used to have the waste recycling service at the on trance of the community, but it becomes increasingly difficult to find them!" A resident living in Xicheng District, Beijing complained to the reporter: To dispose of an old sofa, I have to dial the government service hotline 12345. When it is not allowed in the community, and there is no recycling service nearby, what do you say is the way?

The practical dilemma leads to the possibility of using "Internet +" for intelligent waste sorting. According to the introduction, the current "Internet + waste sorting" roughly falls into two categories of applications: First, after community residents sort dry and wet garbage at home, the exclusive QR code containing family registration information is affixed to the garbage, which is then put in the garbage bin. Residents receive the corresponding points in the app. These points can be used for purchase at supermarkets or in exchange for daily necessities. Second, residents make an appointment for door-to-door recycling services via the relevant websites or mobile apps, and give the sorted recyclable garbage to the recycling staff in exchange for corresponding points or other rewards. The services provided by the website operators or mobile clients vary, depending on the situation of the operators or clients. The applications are based on real-name registration. If the waste is not properly sorted, the staff can find the "owner" of the waste according to the QR code or registered information, and give guidance or supervision.

According to Wang Jianchao, feedback opinions can be bound to the points system through the residents' accounts so that detailed guidance on sorting can be provided. Residents get one point for every 100 grams of renewable garbage. The points can be exchanged for daily necessities such as soap, laundry detergent, and even mobile phones. Residents have a game-like experience in waste sorting and recycling. Similar models operate other provinces and cities such as Beijing, Jiangsu, Sichuan, and Zhejiang. In 2014, Beijing launched the "Intelligent Waste Sorting" program, whereby residents can scan the QR code on the smart kitchen waste garbage bin or recycling cabinet to receive the intelligent waste sorting bag and then pack the waste, affix the QR code to the bag, and put it into the recycling cabinet.

## Notes

1 Jiang Hongbing, He Lu. How to universally implement waste sorting system. http://sh.people.com.cn/n2/2017/0311/c134768-29837629.html.
2 Circular of the Ministry of Finance and the State Taxation Administration on Adjusting the Policy on Consumption Tax for Passenger Cars (CS [2008] No. 105), effective September 1, 2008.
3 Wu Jing. Research on China's policy on the development of green consumption, A Chinese Master Degree Thesis. 2013.
4 Based on news reports.
5 Based on news reports and Wang Jianchao's speech.

# 5 Practices of green consumption in China's communities

## 5.1 Green community as well as practice in Shenzhen

The concept of green community was first introduced to China by Global Village, a non-governmental environmental organization. Since Dachengxiang community in Beijing adopted the practice of establishing a waste sorting and recycling station in 1999, green community has gradually been recognized and supported by the Chinese government. By 2001, the establishment of green communities became a national program covering 47 key cities nationwide. The 21st century will be a green century. The concept of green is felt all over the world, covering production, manufacturing, sales, and other links, as well as the concept of living and residence. As a result, we have undergone fundamental changes in living, from which mankind has benefitted tremendously. The demand for a better living environment is increasing, and the concept of a green community just satisfies such a demand. In an ideal green community, there is fresh air, green grass, vibrant birdsong, and blooming flowers; contaminants are properly disposed of; surrounding natural landscape, cultural sites, as well as natural lakes, rivers, and wetlands are well conserved; society and economy develop steadily at the community level; and there is sustainable environmental, social, and economic development.[1]

### *5.1.1 Concept of green community*

Green community[2] refers to a community that independently establishes and maintains a community environmental management system and public engagement mechanism in the long term. Guided by the idea of sustainable development, it advocates that residents choose a green and fashionable way of life, becoming one of the basic functional units of green city building. The basic criteria for becoming a green community are: (1) It must be an established, relatively independent community with a certain scale and well-functioning management institutions (residents' committee, community management committee, property company, etc.); (2) There must be a good environmental management and supervision system in the community that can protect the environmental rights and interests of residents; (3) It has well-functioning environmental protection facilities, without environmental pollution or environmental disturbance to the residents. Its

DOI: 10.4324/9781003433040-5

environmental noise values meet the standards for functional area, and domestic sewage enters the pipeline collection system or disposal facilities; (4) Measures are put in place to save energy and reuse resources, and it actively promotes and uses clean energy; science education and publicity activities on the environment are carried out; (5) There is a clean and beautiful living environment; trees, grass, and flowers are planted; there are public green spaces and places for public entertainment, recreation, and communication; residents have high environmental awareness. Green community is the community-level place, base point, and foundation for public engagement mechanism for environmental protection. It also provides strong support for advocating green consumption. It plays a pivotal role in establishing a sound public engagement mechanism and achieving sustainable social development.

A green community serves four functions: (1) supervise environmental law enforcement. A community-based public engagement mechanism is established to leverage the role of community residents in supervising law enforcement, and protect the environmental rights and interests of citizens. (2) Offer policy recommendations. The government communicates with the public through the joint meeting system, hearing the opinions of the masses, etc., allowing residents to make suggestions, understand government decisions, and put them into action. (3) Provide environmental education. Through the community environmental protection education and self-management mechanism, residents receive continuous environmental education in daily life and raise environmental awareness. (4) Advocate a green life. A green community can effectively promote environmental protection campaign at the community level, practice the concept of environmental protection into daily life and community culture, and involve residents on a large scale. Such green civilization not only reduces the consumption of resources and environmental pollution, builds a natural and harmonious living environment, but also helps to create a "green market," promote green consumption, and build a green industrial chain.

### *5.1.2 Requirements for the building of green communities*

There are explicit requirements for building green communities, which are summarized into the following six areas:

1 A joint committee involving the government and all walks of life. The joint committee is the core of the green community environmental management system, responsible for the environmental management and implementation at the community. According to the characteristics of its management entities, it roughly includes three modes:

   First, a community environmental management model that involves relevant government departments, non-governmental organizations, and property management companies. The joint committee is composed of relevant government departments (including the cultural-ethical office, environmental protection bureau, sanitation bureau, and sub-district office), non-governmental environmental protection organizations, residents' committees, and relevant enterprises (property management companies). The members of the joint committee fulfill their respective responsibilities: The cultural-ethical office is in charge of the overall environmental civilization progress at the community. The environmental protection bureau is responsible for community environmental protection and pollution control affairs. The sanitation bureau is responsible for the facilities and cleaning of sorted waste and publicizing waste sorting and recycling. Non-governmental environmental protection organizations are responsible for raising residents' environmental awareness and guiding the public to participate in environmental protection. Sub-district offices and residents' committees are responsible for administrative matters related to the community environment and organizing environmental protection activities. The property management company is responsible for property management. The feature of this model is that the participation of relevant government departments strengthens the environmental management of the community, thereby coordinating with the surrounding organizations when it comes to environmental problems. Jiangong Nanli in Xuanwu District, Beijing, is a pilot area using this model.

The second is a community environmental management model based on residents' committees. Residents' committees often launch environmental publicity and education activities, organize activities related to environmental protection, and implement waste sorting. Social organizations play a role in planning, promoting, assisting, and communicating. Under this model, residents' committees exercise environmental management and organize residents to participate in environmental protection activities and advocate that residents choose a green lifestyle to achieve the goals of self-education, self-management, and public participation for green community. Dachengxiang in Xicheng District, Beijing, is a pilot place using this model.

The third is the community environmental management model based on the property management company and the owners' committee. Under this model, property management companies must have high environmental awareness and environmental management capabilities and proactively communicate with environmental protection departments and environmental protection organizations, carry out environmental protection activities, and embrace a green lifestyle. Under this model, a real estate company integrates the concept of eco-friendly buildings into the design, construction, and management process from the beginning of house development, so that the community has high-standard environmental protection facilities from the outset. After the owners move in, the property management company and environmental protection organizations work together to establish a software system for the green community. Jiamingyuan in Beijing is a pilot place using this model.

As green communities are being promoted, all sectors of society are more involved in this regard, and more organizations and institutions participate in the building of green communities. Therefore, the joint committee can take various forms. The key is to establish an environmental management system and a public engagement mechanism at the community level.

2 A waste sorting and transport system. As a component of a green community, waste sorting is an important part of infrastructure construction and requires the installation of sorted garbage cans, biological waste disposal machines, etc. It is also a software project in environmental education, involving all residents. As a special system project, it requires the cooperation of governments, residents, and enterprises.

First, the government should put in place a diversified investment and market operation mechanism. Diversified investment models should be introduced for the construction of household waste disposal facilities. A new mechanism featuring the government guidance and the enterprise participation is adopted. It allows enterprises to better participate in investment and operation under the overall guidance of government planning. Specific measures include: (1) Increase input, including the introduction of foreign capital and high technologies, to improve the infrastructure and capacity of waste disposal. The use of biowaste reduction facilities is promoted in communities where conditions permit. (2) Coordinate and adjust the functions of relevant government departments, draw up qualification standards and management methods for waste sorting and treatment enterprises, put the cleaning of residential communities under the scope of enterprise management, and establish an industrial operation mechanism that is coordinated by the government, with the participation of enterprises. (3) Add systematic facilities, such as purchasing specialized waste sorting and transport vehicles (dedicated vehicle signs for enterprise use, and the pass for transport vehicles issued on demand), and building a special site for waste sorting (or solved by industrialization methods). (4) Formulate policies to support and reduce taxes and fees for enterprises. For example, in the areas of service, the waste and cleaning fee and transport fee paid by each household every year are assigned to enterprises for use, and no management fee shall be levied on enterprises, so as to make this field more attractive to enterprises. As a result, the growing number of enterprises will rapidly increase the waste sorting and transport services. (5) Purchase biowaste treatment facilities in communities where conditions permit, and treat biowaste at source, so that garbage quantity is actually reduced. Residents can truly feel the benefits of waste sorting, and as a result will be motivated to participate in waste sorting. (6) Publicity and education, such as increasing media publicity of waste sorting and recycling, and setting up waste sorting and recycling publicity teams responsible for publicizing and guiding waste sorting and recycling. Waste sorting manuals, publicity materials, and posters are printed and distributed to enterprises, schools, and communities to facilitate waste sorting. In addition, attention should be paid to the education of minors on environmental protection, so that they influence their parents, families, and communities. (7) Give rewards and penalties strictly. Communities, schools, government departments, and individuals who do a good job in waste sorting receive material rewards and moral encouragement, as well as publicized through the mass media. Communities, households, and individuals who do not sort garbage should receive patient education and guidance. Those who refuse to sort garbage despite education should be given appropriate financial fines.

Second, enterprises should bear corresponding responsibilities and obligations, and fulfill social responsibilities while seeking interests. The specific measures include: (1) Undertake some functions of waste sorting previously operated by the government. (2) Work with the government to explore feasible tax and favorable policies for the recycling industry. (3) Responsible for the collection, acquisition, transport, and treatment of sorted waste, and be responsible for the cleaning of residential communities, and the transport and disposal of non-recyclables. (4) Actively develop and adopt high and new technologies, and promote the technologies of reuse and harmless treatment of waste. (5) Sum up experience, transition from a stage of government support to a market-oriented mechanism, and finally expand the service area to the whole city.

3 A plot of green space with a certain area and extensive greening. Greening is a key indicator of the quality of living environment, as it plays the role of purifying the air and beautifying the landscape. According to the regulations, the green area of the community should account for 30 percent of the total area of the community. Various greening methods can be used (such as vertical planting greening and roof greening). Green space should have abundant sunshine duration and meet the requirements for resident activities; should be close to residential buildings for the sake of viewing; should have a certain number of venues for activity (such as playground), and have seats, paved stones, etc., for the sake of recreation, walking, sports, and fitness; should match the natural, cultural landscape and ecological environment in and around the community. Green space in green communities should be planned under the principles of convenience, safety, cleanliness, and environmental friendliness. It is mainly equipped with plant communities, supported by lawns; it should be both practical and artistically pleasing.

4 A team of volunteers. The team of volunteers is the mainstay for environmental protection in the green community, who participates in environmental protection activities, and is responsible for taking the lead in becoming green household and acting as role model for other households. The leader of the volunteer team, as a member of the Green Community Joint Committee, should proactively participate in the environmental management in the community, and work to enhance the residents' sense of identity with the green community, and build close and harmonious neighborhood relations. Children in the community are a positive force. We can educate them and arrange them to participate in a great variety of environmental activities. The practice of building a green community has educational significance for children, who influence the family and then the community. This is a proven way of environmental education. The team of children volunteers can be combined with school environmental protection efforts. Middle and elementary schools can work with a nearby community, so that the environmental education and practice at schools can apply to the community. Schools can also be invited to participate in environmental protection activities at the community.

5 A place for disseminating environmental protection knowledge. Publicity venue can be used for the following activities: green community training, such as

training for relevant personnel from sub-district offices, cadres of residents' committee, and community volunteers. It can be used to organize environmental protection activities, such as garbage exhibition, promoting energy-saving lamps and phosphorus-free washing powder, discussing policy recommendations, and holding citizen hearings. It can also be used to hold household environmental protection competitions, select green households, and hold green community networking events.

6 A certain number of environmental conscious households. The *Green Community Guidebook* compiled by Global Village prescribes ten pieces of requirements for a green household: save water; protect water sources and reduce pollution; save energy; take public transport or travel by bicycle; use recycled paper; buy green products and green food; cut down the use of disposable items; waste sorting and recycling; care for animals and protect nature; participate in environmental protection activities such as afforestation.

The main purpose of building a green community is to enable citizens to learn about and exercise their rights and responsibilities regarding environmental protection. Environmental management is incorporated into community management through cooperation between the government, social organizations, and the public, and a public engagement mechanism at the community level is established to raise residents' environmental awareness and civility level, and promote public participation in environmental protection. In the process of creating a green community, a full range of activities are held to enhance the cohesive force of the community, and create a community atmosphere of friendly environment, intimate neighbors, and harmonious coexistence.

### *5.1.3 The practice of green community in Shenzhen*

The practice of green communities is vigorously promoted in Shenzhen. By means of the extensive use of green low-carbon technologies such as planting rooftop flowers and grass, using solar lighting, and recycling domestic sewage in communities, Shenzhen created 305 green communities in 2012 such as Heyi Community, Donghai Community, South China Electric Vehicle City, Yitian Village, and OCT Community, accounting for 48.9 percent of the total number of communities in Shenzhen, putting Shenzhen top in China. The practice of green community has also become a key cell project for Shenzhen to build a harmonious society, a resource-conserving and environment-friendly society, and an eco-city. Back in 2007, Shenzhen was the first city in China to set the assessment and acceptance criteria for green communities. The competent authorities commission professional institutions to conduct a pre-assessment of the applicant communities and then form an assessment team composed of ecological experts, deputies to the municipal people's congress, CPPCC members, etc., to conduct on-site assessment and scoring. The OCT community, as one of the first "National Advanced Communities for Building Green Community," has consistently invested in environmental improvement, environmental publicity, and education, with an urban greening coverage of 52 percent and the per capita public green space area of 48 square meters, equal to the world-leading urban greening rate.

#### *5.1.3.1 Shenzhen assessment standards for green community3*

In Shenzhen, a green community refers to an incorporated community that has certain infrastructure facilities that meet environmental protection criteria (including green buildings, community greening, waste sorting, sewage treatment, water and energy conservation, and new energy facilities), and that has established a sound environmental management system and public engagement mechanism.

Based on international experience and local characteristics, Shenzhen has formulated sound assessment standards for green community by taking into account infrastructure facilities and environmental cultural.

The basic conditions for meeting Shenzhen standards for green community are as follows:

1 A perfect environmental management and supervision system.

   1 Establish a leadership body. The leadership body is led by the sub-district office where the incorporated community is located and is composed of functional departments such as the cultural-ethical office, the urban construction section, the publicity department, and the women's federation under the sub-district office, as well as relevant organizations such as environmental protection agency, schools, and community-based units.
   2 Create a working body. The working body, which is based on the community, is composed of the residents' committee or property management company, representative residents, and relevant personnel of the school and community-based units.
   3 Draw up a work plan. A work plan for creating a "green community" has been formulated, or the community work plan covers environmental protection and contains specific measures for creating a "green community," and the task is implemented by the relevant departments and responsibility is assigned to the designated person according to the plan.
   4 Create a work portfolio. The basic materials on the community are complete. The work plan for building a green community, meeting minutes, activity introduction, work summary, background information, etc., are complete, accompanied by photos, audio-visual, and other materials. The archives are properly managed by designated personnel.
   5 Establish a team of "green volunteers." It has established one or more teams of "green volunteers," mainly community residents, and actively carries out activities.
   6 Organize the study and training for personnel on a regular basis. It organizes the personnel of the leading body and executive agencies to undergo learning and training through classroom training, field visits, participation in exchange activities, etc.

7 Establish a coordination mechanism for environmental management. It has established a system of regular joint meetings with government departments, residents, and resident units in the community in order to discuss community-related environmental affairs and solicit opinions from or inform residents of the creation and implementation plans in the form of residents' meetings, announcements, etc.
8 Establish a self-improvement system for sustainable improvement. The community conducts self-assessment and summary by stages, puts right any problem that arises, makes self-improvement, and establishes a healthy and continuous improvement mechanism.

All pollution sources are discharged according to standards.

2 It abides by the laws and regulations governing environmental protection. There are no violations of laws and regulations governing environmental protection. Environmental disputes have been properly resolved.

1 Domestic sewage. All sewage in the community is discharged into the municipal sewage collection pipeline or the community's self-built sewage treatment facilities, and there is no sewage overflow in the community.
2 Air pollution. The cooking fumes emitted by the commercial catering, entertainment service, or canteen businesses in the community should be specially treated and discharged according to standards. Dust prevention measures are put in place for construction, demolition, and other projects.
3 Noise pollution. All commercial noise sources (central air conditioning, cooling towers, and fans) in the community meet the standards. Construction and decoration activities in the community are carried out according to national laws and regulations as well as requirements for working hours, and no noise pollution is caused.
4 Solid waste. Household waste is put in bags. There are sorting and recycling devices and obvious signs. Waste put in designated places is cleaned on the same day it is generated. Residents sort garbage and put it in designated places as required. Construction waste is sorted, collected, and transported in a timely manner, and no garbage is exposed in the community.

3 The community environment is clean and beautiful.

1 The community environment is tidy and clean. All public facilities are in good condition. There are no haphazardly parked vehicles, no open-air markets or illegal construction, and no mobile stalls or unregulated postings. There is no burning of garbage or leaves, open-air barbecues, etc.
2 The community is greened and beautified in a pleasing manner. The greening rate (including vertical greening) in the community reaches 35 percent. There is no damage to greening. Ancient and famous trees are well-preserved. There are public places for recreation, entertainment and other activities in the community.

4 Actively carry out environmental publicity and education.

   1 Environmental promotion measures are in place. The community is equipped with fixed environmental publicity and education facilities such as environmental protection windows, and bulletin boards. Environmental information is released in a timely manner. It organizes environmental protection activities with more than 100 participants at least twice a year.
   2 Routine environmental education. The community carries out activities on green households and green consumption. There are over 20 kinds of books, audio-visual, and graphic materials on environmental protection in the community. It conducts regular environmental education activities for residents in the form of environmental protection classes, participatory activities, field trips, etc., at least once a quarter, in light of the reality of the community.

5 Residents have high environmental awareness.

   1 Community residents have high environmental awareness and protect the environment on their own initiative. All organizations and residents in the community abide by laws and regulations governing environmental protection. Residents care for environmental protection facilities and other public facilities in the community. There is no practice of selling or consuming wild animals and plants placed under state protection. Residents adopt eco-friendly behavior, such as saving water and electricity, and recycling resources.
   2 Use eco-friendly products. Organizations and residents in the community say no to disposable foam tableware. It advocates the use of eco-friendly phosphorus-free washing powder with ecolabels or energy-saving labels, as well as eco-friendly electrical appliances such as refrigerators and air conditioners.

6 Plus points.

   1 It is rated as a national and/or provincial "culturally advanced community," "demonstration area community construction," "ecological community," "quiet community," etc.
   2 It has passed ISO14000 environmental management system certification.
   3 The community carries out special activities in light of its cultural, region, and other characteristics and achieves good results. The planning and design of community meets the requirements of environmental protection, and eco-friendly building materials and energy-saving equipment are used.

#### *5.1.3.2 Introduction to green community case in Shenzhen*

As an epitome of Shenzhen's green communities, Longjing Community in Xin'an Sub-district Office, Bao'an District, Shenzhen exercises jurisdiction over seven communities 23,000 permanent residents, covering an area of 0.9 square kilometers.

In the process of creating green community, it combines people-centered approach and ecology, proceeds from the goal of sustainable community development, upholds green management, guides residents to make green consumption, operates in an eco-friendly way, and creates a green culture in the community.

First of all, the residents of Longjing community are engaged in building a green community on their own initiative. "In order to build a green community, whoever sees the litter must pick it up, whether it be a piece of waste paper or a cigarette end." In the surprise inspections of community sanitation conducted by residents' committees, there is no littering or piling of household waste, etc. Community residents have a strong environmental awareness. Residents participate in various environmental protection public welfare activities at the community, and everyone is involved in building a green community.

Second, the Longjing community has three active environmental protection volunteer teams: elderly people, young people, and adolescents. The elderly volunteer team composed of 32 retired people is responsible for morning and evening sanitation inspection and door-to-door environmental protection publicity. The youth volunteer team composed of 21 young people from residents' committees and property management office is responsible for making sanitation signs, planning greening activities, giving consulting on environmental protection knowledge, etc. The adolescent volunteer team is composed of 30 elementary school students in the community, who carry out environmental protection publicity at schools.

Finally, community garbage is sorted and collected, and green civilization is advocated. Community residents promote the planting of flowers and grasses on the balcony, make large-scale greening, and publicize environmental protection. 30 colored waste sorting and recycling bins are placed in the community. Based on the green concept and in conjunction with the community's natural and cultural conditions, Longjing Community vigorously builds a green community. It stimulates their enthusiasm for participating in environmental protection and has realized the sustainable development of the community.

Shenzhen Municipal Commission for Human Settlements has made steady progress in promoting ecological conservation. In 2010, it organized and launched the activities of building "National Ecological District," "Shenzhen Ecological Sub-district Office," "Shenzhen Green Community" and "Shenzhen Ecological Industrial Park." It explored the content, methods and priorities of the national pilot region for promoting ecological conservation. It has compiled the *Shenzhen Indicator System for Promoting Ecological Conservation*, revised the *Shenzhen Evaluation Standards for Ecological Sub-district Offices*, *Shenzhen Evaluation Standards for Green Communities* and other ecological improvement standard system with local characteristics, and established supporting assessment and acceptance procedures. In 2012, Shenzhen had 305 green communities, 49 ecological sub-district offices, 15 national-level green schools, and 95 provincial-level green schools, putting Shenzhen top in the country.[4] 208 projects with a total building area of over 21 million square meters have been awarded the green building evaluation label. It ranks first among major cities in China in terms of the number and scale of projects that have been awarded the green building evaluation label. On

July 16, 2015, Guangdong Province issued and implemented the *Evaluation standard for the construction of a livable community* (DB44T1577-2015). Shenzhen launched the "micro-renewal" to transform villages in the city to explore a new path for building green and livable communities.

## 5.2 Practice and promotion of green consumption in Beijing

In recent years, Beijing has promulgated a slew of policies related to green consumption. In 2012, Beijing released the *Beijing Municipal Action Plan for Energy Conservation and Emission Reduction during the 12th Five-Year Plan Period*, which promotes energy-saving and low-carbon lifestyles. In 2013, the Beijing Municipal People's Government promulgated the *Beijing Municipal Clean Air Action Plan in 2013-2017*, which requires compiling the *Green Consumption Guide* to encourage citizens to embrace green food, green home (choosing eco-friendly products and energy-saving household appliances, etc.), and a green life (encouraging water and electricity saving, such as reducing standby time and cutting down the use of air conditioning). The first part of the *Several Policies and Measures to Promote Consumption Growth in 2015* issued by Beijing Commission of Commerce focuses on guiding energy conservation and emission reduction and promoting consumption. Specifically, the measures include: (1) Promoting energy-saving household appliances, launching "energy-saving products entering supermarkets" activity, awarding special marks to energy-saving supermarkets, and giving certain financial support. (2) Promoting new energy vehicles. Specifically, the measures include purchase subsidies, no restrictions based on odd-and-even license plate rule, discounts for charging facilities, 30 percent subsidies for property management companies that install public charging piles, query of charging facilities via the app, charging network with an average service radius of 5 kilometers within the scope of the sixth ring road, etc.; (3) Subsidies for the elimination of old cars; (4) Promote eco-friendly oil fume purifiers.

In addition to introducing the green consumption policy, Beijing has actively carried out practical green consumption activities. The action plan for "Green Beijing" is one of top priorities. *"Green Beijing" Action Plan (2010-2012)* requires the establishment of a citywide green consumption system, covering green government service, green business, and green living. Green life is achieved through two ways: (1) Advocate a green lifestyle. Specific actions include helping citizens consciously engage in energy and water conservation, and resource recycling, guiding citizens to travel by public transport, bicycle, or walking, encouraging citizens to develop habits such as turning off lights, sorting waste, and saving water, and strengthening waste sorting at source and reduction. (2) Guide green consumption. Specific measures include guiding the public to buy and use energy-saving eco-friendly household products; encouraging the public to buy energy-saving appliances with energy efficiency level 2 or above; encouraging the public to buy small-displacement, low-emission vehicles; encouraging the public to use cloth bags and baskets, avoid over-packaged products as far as possible, and reduce the use of disposable tableware and daily necessities, etc. According to the *Beijing*

*Municipal Plan for Building and Developing Green Beijing during the 12th Five-Year Plan Period*, as citizens raise their environmental awareness and have a higher demand for environmental quality, the demands for the ecological environment extend from basic areas such as landscaping and pollution treatment to higher-level new areas such as forest carbon sequestration, green food, biomass energy, and recreation and leisure. To this end, Beijing shall make initial progress in building an eco-friendly green consumption system during the 12th Five-Year Plan period. The scale of green buildings further expands, the source of indoor air pollution is effectively controlled, the energy and resource consumption per unit of building area is further reduced, and citizens enjoy a more comfortable and eco-friendly living environment. The modern integrated transport system is basically established, the proportion of travel by public transport keeps rising, urban transport becomes significantly more efficient, and citizens have access to more efficient and convenient travel. There is effective supply of green and eco-friendly food, a sound food safety management system is established, the ability to prevent and control food safety risks is enhanced, and citizens have a safer and healthier diet. The green market service system is being improved, more prominence is given to the leading role of green models, and the proportion of green products consumed by citizens keeps increasing.

This section summarizes the practice and promotion of green consumption in Beijing based on the definition and research scope of green consumption in the first chapter.

### *5.2.1 Resource conservation and green purchase*

In Beijing, citizens are encouraged to save resources and make green purchases mainly through water-saving management, tiered electricity pricing, subsidies for energy-saving household appliances, and other measures. Beijing faces an acute shortage of water resources, with per capita water volume only 1/80 of the world's per capita water volume. Over the years, Beijing has taken water-saving measures and continuously improved the water-saving policy system, as shown in Table 5.1. Beijing builds a water-saving city mainly through four measures: (1) Raise the public awareness of water conservation. Beijing has launched publicity and education work on a large scale, such as compiling readers on water saving, publicizing water saving at primary and secondary school classrooms, selecting 100 water-saving households, organizing and observing water-saving projects, building water-saving education bases, holding water-saving short message competitions, and selecting "water-saving stars." (2) Subsidize residents in using water-saving appliances. Since 2014, six districts of Beijing have piloted the promotion of water-efficient household water appliances with water efficiency level 2 or above. Residents can obtain government subsidies of 1–200 yuan for the purchase of water-efficient shower heads or nozzle restrictors. During the 13th Five-Year Plan period, Beijing also plans to use 100,000 sets of replacement water-saving household water appliances every year.[5] (3) Tiered water pricing policy. After the tiered water pricing was implemented in May 2014, the water consumption of urban households from

June to October 2014 declined by 1.3 percent compared with the same period of the previous year. After the water price for special industries increased sharply, the water consumption for car washing decreased by 20 percent compared with 2014, the water consumption for golf courses decreased by 39 percent compared to the same period last year, and the water consumption for bathing decreased by 31 percent. (4) Establish water-saving organizations (enterprises). In Beijing, nearly 12,000 organizations (enterprises) and communities are engaged in water-saving program. Of this, water-saving organizations (enterprises) account for 25 percent and water-saving communities nearly 34 percent.[6]

A tiered pricing for household electricity consumption similar to the tiered water pricing has also been implemented in Beijing. The results of research show that

*Table 5.1* Policy framework for water conservation in Beijing

| *Policy type* | | *Specific measures* |
|---|---|---|
| Concept | Publicity and education | Knowledge popularization, non-profit advertising, information disclosure, publicity of models |
| | Create water-saving organizations | Create water-saving enterprises, communities, parks, households, and industries |
| Mechanisms | Optimize the industrial structure | *Catalogue of Newly Added Industries for Prohibition and Restricted Development in Beijing*<br>*Catalogue of Industrial Pollution Industries, Production Process Adjustment and Withdrawal as well as Equipment Elimination in Beijing* |
| | Strengthen the assessment mechanism | *Opinions on Comprehensively Promoting the Building of a Water-Saving Society.* Formulate eight water-saving incentive measures such as assessment standards and self-built rainwater utilization facilities by organizations |
| | Water utilization quota management | Nearly 30,000 social organizations in the city are included in the management of water use plan. Accountability assessment and performance management are implemented. Monthly monitoring and bi-monthly assessment are carried out |
| | Water impact assessment review | Demonstration (evaluation) report approval for water resources for construction projects, approval of soil and water conservation plans for production and construction projects, and approval of flood impact assessment report for non-flood control construction projects |
| | New water pricing policy | Tiered water pricing, higher charging standards, and higher water prices for special industries |
| Science and technology | Promote water-saving appliances | Subsidize high-efficiency shower devices, toilets, etc. |

the current tiered electricity pricing has basically reasonable grading standards, which helps curb the household electricity demand outside a reasonable range, plays a good role in electricity saving, and also meets the electricity purchase costs of electric power enterprises.[7]

The *Beijing Work Plan for Piloting the Promotion of Energy-Efficient Household Appliances* (issued in 2011) expired in 2013. In order to promote green consumption in Beijing, and spur energy conservation, emission reduction, and the development of the circular economy, the subsidy policy for energy-saving products was re-launched on November 27, 2015 after a two-year hiatus. The new Beijing municipal subsidy policy for energy-saving household appliances subsidizes nine types of products that meet national quality standards such as TV sets, air purifiers, and refrigerators at 8 to 12 percent. The *Administrative Measures for the Allocation of Central Government Subsidy Funds for the Promotion of Energy-efficient Industrial Products in Beijing Project to Promote Energy-efficient Products for the Benefit of the People* reflect Beijing's determination to promote energy-saving products and also provide financial support for the promotion of energy-saving products.

In terms of the promotion of organic/green food, the *Beijing Municipal Plan for Building and Developing Green Beijing during the 12th Five-Year Plan Period* states the need to ensure an effective supply of green and eco-friendly food, establish a sound food safety management system, further enhance the ability to prevent and control food safety risks, and allow citizens to have access to safer and healthier diet. In addition, the *2014 Action Plan for the Implementation of the Quality Development Outline of Beijing* also mentions the need to establish a sound supervision mechanism for the geographical indications certification for organic food. However, only Haidian District mentioned the promotion of green and organic food in the "vegetable basket" system program, but it still lacks specific promotion measures.

In addition to the aforesaid policies, Beijing has also launched some campaigns to advocate resource conservation and green procurement. In 2011, the Beijing Government officially issued the *Beijing Municipal Action Plan for Energy Conservation and Emission Reduction during the 12th Five-Year Plan Period*, which stresses that all people shall engage in energy conservation and emission reduction; the focus is on implementing ten initiatives for energy conservation and emission reduction involving households, communities, and enterprises; culturally advanced, economical, green and low-carbon production models, consumption models and living habits should be promoted; and all people are mobilized to participate in energy conservation and emission reduction. To this end, Beijing launches a pilot program for energy-saving supermarkets, publicity activities for energy saving, environmental protection and low-carbon life in Beijing, etc. Energy-saving supermarkets open up the sales channels of green products by linking the three major stakeholders of energy-saving product manufacturers, distributors, and consumers. Innovative energy-saving supermarket activities are continuously launched: First, the number of energy-saving supermarkets rose from two in 2010 to 11 in 2012. Second, more business forms are available. Specialty stores of building materials and e-commerce websites have been added. Third, the mode of activity is being innovated, and the campaign to become "demonstration store for energy-saving product promotion" in Beijing has been further carried out. Fourth, the comprehensive benefits are obvious. The annual sales of energy-saving products in energy-saving supermarkets increased by 148 percent year-on-year, and the proportion of customers who prefer energy-saving products increased from 60 percent to 99 percent. Pilot enterprises such as Suning Appliance have taken the lead in banning the sales of non-energy-saving products, which is a good exemplary role. In 2015, Beijing had 26 energy-saving supermarkets in 16 districts. By the end of 2014, nearly 140,000 electricity-saving products in ten categories were sold in major energy-saving supermarkets in Beijing, and the market share of energy-saving household appliances at energy efficiency level II (new national standard) or above reached 53.44 percent.[8] In 2014, the fourth publicity event for energy conservation and environmental protection in Beijing featured four brand activities: "caravan," "green classroom," "entrepreneurship season," and "model conduct." By increasing public participation, popularizing knowledge on environmental protection, and promoting the innovative application of technology products, it further guides the public to participate in energy conservation, environmental protection, and low-carbon life.

#### *5.2.1.1 Waste sorting*

Beijing has been improving the waste sorting management system. The *Beijing Municipal Regulations on Household Waste Management* was promulgated in November 2011 and entered into force on March 1, 2012. Thereafter, Beijing has successively issued policies such as the *Circular of the Beijing Municipal People's Government on Issuing the Key Work Division Plan for the 2016 Report on the Work of the Municipal Government*, and the *Proposal of the Beijing Municipal Party Committee on Formulating Beijing 13th Five-Year Plan for the National Economic and Social Development*, which set the goal of 56 percent for the household waste recycling rate.

The work of waste sorting has been underway since 2000. As shown in Table 5.2, Beijing promulgated the work plan as well as assessment and evaluation plan for the sorting and collection of household waste from 2000 to 2002. Waste sorting was limited to rough categorization and the on-site treatment of kitchen waste. It was not until 2010 that the measure of establishing teams of waste sorting guides was put forward. In recent years, certain subsidies have been given for the waste sorting, collection, and transport system. In 2012, the implementation of the *Beijing Municipal Regulations for Household Waste Management* led to the law-based management of household waste in Beijing. For the first time, the regulations define the waste sorting system, as well as the principles of waste sorting, the standards for garbage. It is also stipulated:

> In accordance with the principles of more fees for more discharge, less fees for less discharge, more fees for mixed waste, and less fees for sorted waste,

> Beijing gradually establishes a system of household waste disposal charging that features metering-based charging, classified pricing, and easy collection; strengthens the management of fees, and promotes the reduction, sorting, and recycling of household garbage. Organizations and individuals that generate household waste shall pay waste disposal fees in accordance with regulations.

The *Circular on Matters Concerning the Adjustment of Non-Household Waste Disposal Charges in Beijing*, which entered into effect on January 1, 2014, also contains relevant provisions. The *Plan for Compulsory Waste Sorting System* may offer an opportunity for more people to pay attention to waste management issues and realize their responsibilities. After all, "whoever generates waste pays" is the basic principle of waste management in countries all over the world.

The work of waste sorting and management in Beijing mainly focuses on three areas: the construction of storage places for sorted waste, collection and transport vehicles for sorted waste, and the construction of sorted waste treatment facilities. In terms of putting garbage in the garbage can, Beijing adopts the waste sorting mode of "large-scale sorting and small-scale sorting." Kitchen waste, decoration

*Table 5.2* List of Beijing policies on waste sorting

| *Name* | *Promulgation date* | *Main points* |
|---|---|---|
| *Beijing Municipal Action Plan for Improving the Quality of Consumer-oriented Service Industries* | July 29, 2015 | Propose incorporating the renewable resource recycling system into the waste sorting management system |
| *Interim Regulations on the Management of Municipal Special Subsidy Fund for Waste Sorting, Collection and Transport System Construction Project in Residential Communities in Urban Areas of Beijing* | April 17, 2011 | Determine the source of subsidy funds, scope of subsidy, subsidy amount, etc., regarding the waste sorting, collection, and transport system |
| *Guiding Opinions on the Establishment of Teams of Waste Reduction and Sorting Instructors in 600 Pilot Communities in the City* | May 31, 2010 | Establish a team of waste reduction and sorting instructors in a pilot community that meets waste sorting standards |
| *Interim Measures for the Assessment and Evaluation of Household Waste Sorting, Collection and Disposal* | September 20, 2002 | Specific assessment and evaluation plans for waste sorting and collection work |
| *Circular on Household Waste Sorting, Collection and Treatment* | April 9, 2002 | Sorting and treatment principles of rough categorization and on-site disposal of kitchen waste |
| *Beijing Municipal Work Plan for Municipal Waste Sorting, Collection, Recycling and Comprehensive Utilization* | January 22, 2000 | The focus of waste sorting is waste paper, waste plastics and waste batteries |

waste, bulk waste, dead branches and leaves, etc., are treated as large-scale waste, while the waste produced by residents, enterprises, and public institutions is regarded as small-scale waste. For small-scale waste in communities, trash cans for sorted waste are provided, together with special recycling stations such as low-value goods collection points. In terms of waste sorting, collection, and transport, Beijing allocates special vehicles for sorted kitchen waste, recyclables, and hazardous waste on top of the waste collection and transport system. In terms of sorting and treatment, the terminal treatment of household waste in Beijing mainly takes the form of landfill and incineration. For the separated kitchen waste, it adopts the methods of small biochemical treatment stations mainly based on composting as well as kitchen waste treatment plants, and some waste is biochemically processed on site.

Waste sorting is mainly processed in three steps: rough sorting by sanitation workers, the recycling of useful waste by waste scavengers, and waste sorting done by residents at home as advocated by the state. Due to a lack of concrete implementation plans and guiding measures for waste sorting, Beijing is still at the second level for waste sorting, namely relying on waste scavengers for waste sorting. In this way, only items that can be sold are collected, while the rest is not differentiated. Moreover, sorted garbage cans and garbage stations do not play a role in the process. According to a survey conducted by Friends of Nature, an environmental protection organization, the number of pilot communities for waste sorting in Beijing has been increasing since a new round of waste sorting was promoted in 2010: it was 600 in the first year, but exceeded 3,000 in 2016, accounting for more than half of the total residential communities in the city. Despite an increase in the number of pilot communities, the effect of waste sorting did not reach expectations. Although there are nominally three types of waste – kitchen waste, recyclables, and other waste – for waste sorting in pilot communities in Beijing, the municipal sanitation department is responsible for sorting and transporting only two categories: kitchen waste and other waste. As a result, the main sorting model promoted in pilot communities in Beijing includes only "dry and wet waste." In other words, kitchen waste is separated from other mixed waste and transported by the municipal sanitation department to suburban composting yards for treatment.

Despite the fact that the municipal sanitation department ensures that most of the pilot communities are equipped with special kitchen waste transport vehicles and communities are staffed with "secondary sorters" for secondary sorting of kitchen waste, residents are generally ignorant about this work. Conversely, residents usually see trash bins for mixed garbage and garbage trucks for mixed transport. As a result, most residents mistakenly think that waste sorting is useless when sorted waste is transported in a mixed way. Therefore, few people take the initiative to sort waste. It can be seen that the community lacks sustained and targeted efforts for publicity and mobilization, and it is difficult to raise residents' awareness and mobilize them. Over-reliance on secondary sorters in the long term has serious weaknesses, such as increasing the financial burden on the government, making it difficult to develop a sense of responsibility among residents, and discouraging residents from making waste sorting. The original intention of "guidance role in waste sorting" is practically nonexistent. It is suggested that it is necessary to define the responsibilities and roles of "green armbands" and secondary sorters, effectively evaluate the significance and effect of "green armbands" in sorting guidance, and adjust relevant policies in a timely manner.

In addition to the aforesaid policies, Beijing piloted the "intelligent waste sorting model" in 350 communities in 2016. Under this model, community residents only need to scan the QR code via WeChat and put the sorted household waste into the renewables recycling cabinet for points, which can be used in exchange for shopping cards, daily necessities, telephone cards, etc.

Furthermore, Beijing has established a green recycling system for waste household appliances in energy-saving supermarkets, promoted cooperation between waste household appliance recycling institutions and energy-saving supermarkets, and regulated the recycling, dismantling, and utilization of waste household appliances. The number of energy-saving supermarkets in Beijing increased from 16 in 2013 to 20 in 2014, covering 11 districts in the city.

### *5.2.2 Green travel*

In recent years, Beijing has shifted the focus of green transport from increasing the supply of transport facilities to developing public transport and advocating green travel. According to Beijing municipal transport development plan, in 2015, it works to ensure that the "green travel" consisting of rail transit, ground buses and bicycles will account for 65 percent. In particular, the proportion of travel by "bicycle + public transport" will be increased. Since 2014, promoting new energy vehicles has become one of the priorities for Beijing. Beijing has issued a slew of policies to subsidize the purchase of new energy vehicles, regulate the management of new energy vehicle manufacturers and products, and invest in and manage supporting charging facilities, as shown in Figure 5.1.

Economic incentive policies are the main measure for Beijing to promote new energy vehicles. After the subsidy standards for new energy vehicles are stipulated in the *Circular on Doing a Good Job in the Promotion and Application of New Energy Vehicles* issued by the Ministry of Finance, the Ministry of Science and Technology, the Ministry of Industry and Information Technology, and the National Development and Reform Commission, Beijing issued many specific subsidy policies and plans for the promotion of electric vehicles, and put into practice the "state + local" dual subsidy policy citywide. The ratio of Beijing municipal to state fiscal subsidies is 1:1. Although the purchase subsidy is the main way to promote new energy vehicles, the subsidy withdrawal mechanism has also been launched since the subsidy policy was implemented in 2013, and the decline increases year by year. In addition to subsidies, measures such as exemption from purchase tax, no traffic restrictions, and direct allocation without the need for license plate lottery have greatly stimulated the sales of new energy vehicles. As shown in Figure 5.2, the number of license plates used for pure electric passenger cars began to rise after the separate allocation of indicators was implemented in early 2014. After the purchase tax exemption policy was implemented in August 2014, the number of license plates for pure electric passenger cars in Beijing saw a second round of significant increases.

Before the subsidy policy was phased out at the end of 2014, the number of license plates for pure electric passenger cars shot up from 578 to 2,507. After subsidies were lowered in 2015, the number of license plates used plummeted to 477. When the policy of no traffic restriction was announced five months later, the number of license plates for pure electric passenger cars increased again, reaching 1,955.

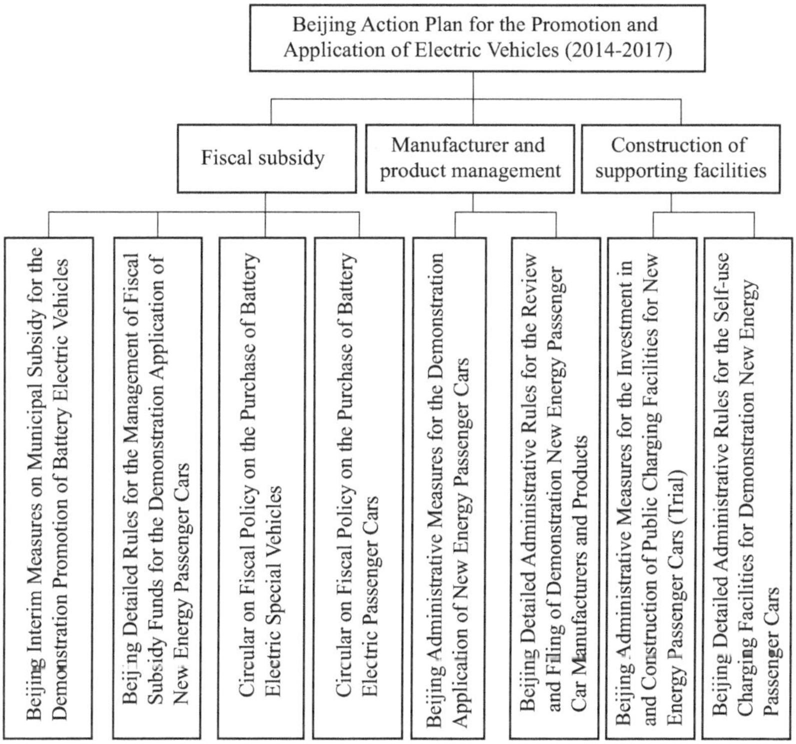


*Figure 5.1* Framework of Beijing policies on new energy vehicles.

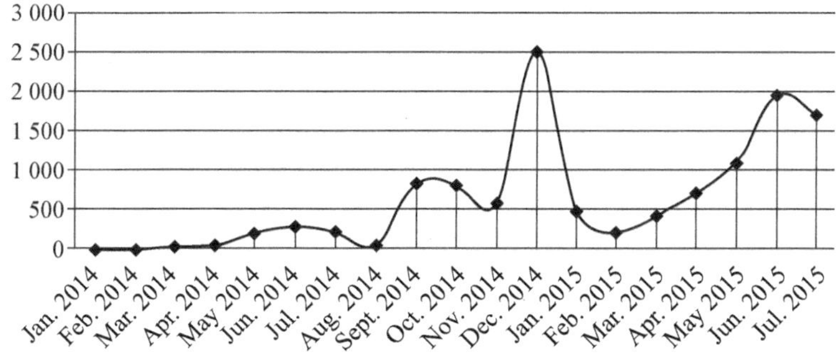


*Figure 5.2* Monthly number of license plates for pure electric passenger cars in Beijing.

Source: Beijing New Energy Vehicle Development Promotion Center.

In order to deal with the decline in sales caused by dwindling subsidies, Beijing formulated detailed management rules for the construction of charging facilities for passenger cars. By the end of 2015, Beijing had built 17,795 charging piles of various types, of which 10,272 were privately owned, with a supporting ratio of 63.9 percent. At the 2nd Electric Vehicle & Charging Infrastructure China Summit Forum held in 2017, Niu Jinming, director of the Beijing New Energy Vehicle Development and Promotion Center, said that Beijing had planned to build over 90,000 charging piles. Beijing is committed to exploring new models for promoting new energy vehicles, such as short-time rental of pure electric vehicles, whereby a pure electric vehicle can be leased to different users at different times. It encourages short-term and connection-type use of vehicles, maximizing the efficiency of pure electric vehicles in cities.

In terms of action, Beijing has built a service platform for self-use charging facilities, so that residents can keep abreast of charging piles under construction. It supports State Grid in releasing the "e-charging network" and "Beijing charging facility distribution map." Charging experience events held in cooperation with automakers are also underway.

## 5.3 Survey on green consumption awareness among community residents in Beijing

### *5.3.1 Overview of the survey*

Public engagement in environmental protection is a proven practice by all countries in the world. Raising the awareness and concept of green consumption at the community level allows citizens to learn about and exercise their environmental rights and responsibilities. The practice of fostering cooperation between the government, non-governmental organizations, and the public, incorporating green consumption into government decisions and community management, and building a public engagement mechanism at the community level will help residents embrace green consumption, raise residents' awareness of green consumption, and improve residents' civility and quality. The survey is an important way to gauge the green consumption awareness of community residents, their recognition of green consumption behavior, and the factors that influence the green consumption behavior of community residents.

Based on the idea of sustainable consumption, consumer psychology, and behavioral theory, in conjunction with China's policy on sustainable consumption and the practice of "green community," as well as the practice and promotion of sustainable consumption in China and Beijing, the survey focuses on the policy needs of the Chinese government (particularly the Beijing government) to promote green consumption and the priorities of recent work (resource conservation and green purchase, waste sorting, and green travel). Questionnaires and research analysis are conducted to analyze community residents' knowledge of the aforesaid sustainable consumption areas, sustainable behavior in residents' consumption, and residents' willingness to make sustainable consumption and their influencing factors. The survey mainly includes the following areas:

residents' awareness of green consumption and recognition of different areas of green consumption; residents' awareness and consumption behavior in the three key areas of green consumption: resource conservation and green purchase, waste sorting, and green travel; their willingness to make sustainable consumption and their influencing factors (including publicity and education, laws and regulations, policies, and economic means); residents' acceptance of state and Beijing local policies and measures to promote green consumption as well as the effect of implementation. The specific technology roadmap is shown in Figure 5.3.

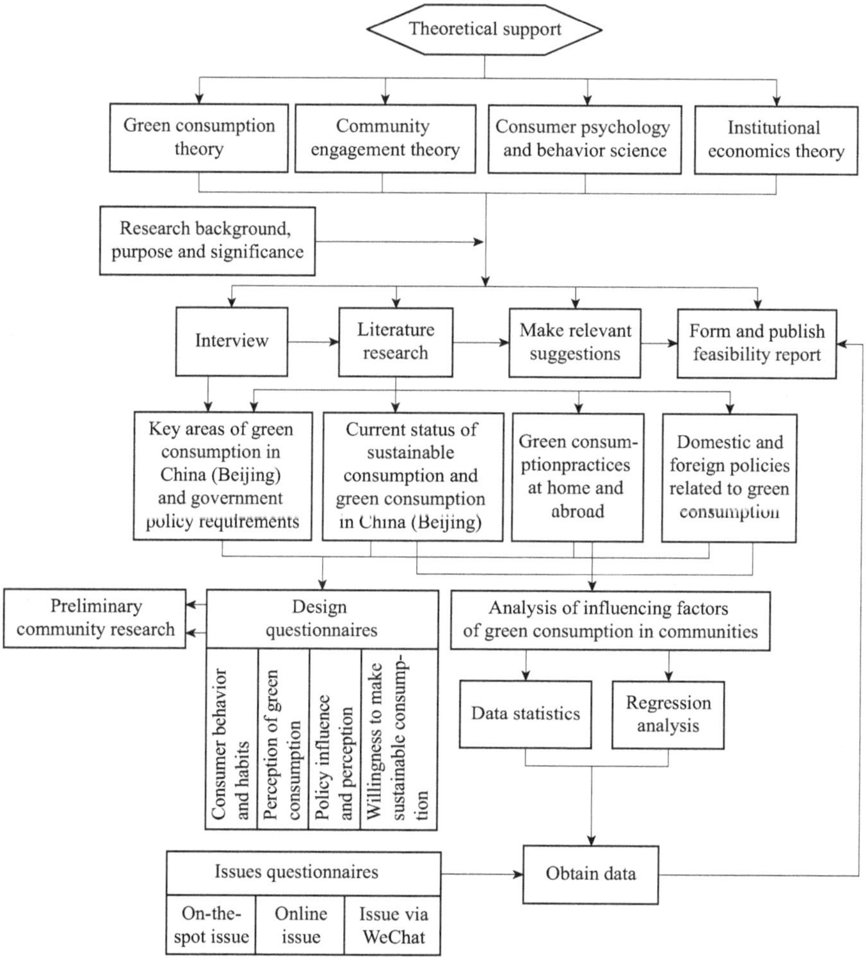


*Figure 5.3* Technical roadmap for research into the current situation of green consumption in Beijing communities.

*Sources:* All-China Environment Federation, School of Environment and Natural Resources of Renmin University of China, Survey on Beijing Community Household Awareness of Sustainability Consumption and Policy Advocacy Project Research Report, 2015

*5.3.1.1 Community selection*

In the survey, communities are selected mainly based on the following two principles: (1) Fully reflect the level of economic and social development and current situation in various urban areas of Beijing, and fully reflect the differences between the central urban area and the suburbs of Beijing; (2) Fully consider the difference in the development levels of the north and south of Beijing caused by geographical location, and select two different communities in the central urban area in the north and the suburbs in the south.

Based on the above two principles, the survey selected Bajiaobeili Community in Shijingshan District, Beijing and Wangjing Community composed of five small communities in Wangjing, Chaoyang District, Beijing.

Bajiaobeili Community is an old community independently organized by residents, and the residents' committee has limited funds, whereas the new Wangjing Community in Chaoyang District adopts the management model led by the residents' committee, which has sufficient funds. The overview of the two communities are as follows:

Bajiaobeili Community is located to the west of Shijingshan Amusement Park, covering an area of 200,000 square meters. Shijingshan District Experimental Elementary School is located in the community. Built as a closed community in 1984, it has a total of 47 buildings, and 3,557 households with 11,000 people. It is inhabited by 15 ethnic minority people, including Manchu, Mongolian, Hui, Tibetan, Miao, and Zhuang. The residents' committee has 13 members. The community's Party committee has 479 Party members and eight Party branches. Bajiaobeili Community has been awarded titles such as "National Advanced Cultural Society," "Advanced Unit of the National Family Planning Association," "Culturally Advanced Residential Community in the Capital," "Culturally Advanced Citizen School in the Capital," "Advanced Unit for Ethnic Unity and Progress in the Capital," and "Model Community with Law Popularization Characteristics in Shijingshan District." In 2003, it was awarded the title of "Advanced Community-level Party Organization in Shijingshan District in Fighting 'SARS'." In 2005, it was awarded the title of "Beijing Model Collective."

Wangjing community in Chaoyang District consist of Nanhuxili Community, Nanhuxiyuan Zone 2 Community, Huajiadixili Zone 3 Community, Shengxing Community and Wangjing Xiyuan Zone 3 Community. Nanhuxili Community is located in the west of Wangjing Area, bordering Wangjing West Road in the east and Nanhu West Road in the south, and adjacent to Jijingxiangsong community across the road in the west and north, covering an area of over 100,000 square meters. The community has jurisdiction over buildings and bungalows in Nanhuxili Community courtyard, No. 6 Courtyard, and Nanhu Third Lane, as well as Zhongguang Yijingwan, with a total of 38 residential buildings. The community has 3,227 households, with a permanent population of 6,333 and a floating population of 1,650. Nanhuxiyuan Zone 2 Community includes two communities of Jijingqinyuan and Beijing Xiangsong, with a total of 3,013 households. Jijingqinyuan Community covers an area of 77,000 square meters, with a building area of 170,000 square meters and 1,895 households. Beijing Xiangsong Community covers an area of 88,000 square meters, with a building area of 310,000 square meters and 1,100 households. It was put into use at the end of 2007. The two communities boast beautiful environment, sound management, complete infrastructure facilities, and people-oriented services. Jijingqinyuan Community has outdoor basketball court, football pitch, and tennis courts, as well as a picnic field where owners can have barbecue at the weekends. There is an indoor recreation and fitness club, including a swimming pool, table tennis tables, etc. Huajiadixili Zone 3 Community is located in the southwest of Wangjing Area, bounded by Nanhu South Road in the east, Nanhu North Street in the south, Wangjing West Road in the west, and Nanhu Comprehensive Market in the north, covering an area of 0.18 square kilometers. The community has 26 buildings, one bungalow courtyard, and 2,849 households with 7,122 permanent residents. The community boasts a resident activity room, a library and a cultural room, and a venue for physical exercise for the benefit of community residents and students. There are seven cultural and sports teams and four volunteer service teams in the community. Shengxing Community is located at 9 Nanhu South Road, adjacent to Daxiyang Community in the east, Wangjing West Road in the west, Zone C of Zhiyu City in the south, and Huguang Middle Street in the north. It is a high-quality community overall, belonging to the friendly and neighborly service business district. The community has jurisdiction over three communities of Shengxindadi Home, Xinghai Mingzhu, and Zhiyu City, covering an area of 0.23 square kilometers. There are 18 residential buildings and 2,325 permanent households, with a permanent population of over 6,000. The community has jurisdiction over more than 80 social units, two schools, and five quarter-hour certified service providers. The services covered include hairdressing, drugstores, convenience supermarkets, accommodation, etc. Wangjingxiyuan Zone 3 Community covers an area of 17.4 hectares, with a total building area of 560,000 square meters and a greening area of 58,000 square meters. It has 22 residential buildings and 3,567 households, with a resident population of about 11,000. The community is characterized by a large foreign population, diverse volunteer activities, and many volunteer groups.[9]

### *5.3.1.2 Research methods*

Three methods are used for this survey: (1) Distribute questionnaires in the community, interact with community residents to learn about their awareness of and willingness to make green consumption; (2) Issue questionnaires online, involve more residents through community network, and ensure the representation of the community and the participation of residents; (3) Use research methods such as the Internet and WeChat to learn about the green consumption made by residents in Beijing communities other than the selected communities, so as to fully understand the status of green consumption made by residents in Beijing and supplement the survey on selected communities.

#### 5.3.1.3 Questionnaire design

In terms of questionnaire design, this survey tries to reflect the facts about community residents in terms of green consumption awareness, recognition, and willingness to consume, as well as the relationship with the level of urban development, residents' spending level and income level, education level, etc. The basic framework of the questionnaire is shown in Table 5.3:

*Table 5.3* Basic framework of the questionnaire

| | | |
|---|---|---|
| Basic household information | The size and composition of the household | Number of people<br>Educational level |
| | Employment and income | Occupation<br>Income level |
| | Housing | Total area of housing<br>Per capita housing area |
| | Medical coverage | Whether covered by medical insurance<br>Average annual medical spending |
| | Personal information | Age, gender, marital status |
| Recognition of green consumption | Whether aware of green consumption | |
| | Ways of learning about green consumption | TV<br>Newspapers<br>Internet<br>Communication with friends and neighbors<br>Community or street publicity<br>Others |
| | How to interpret green consumption | Give options (saving water and electricity, sorting garbage, buying eco-friendly products, moderate consumption, saving resources, green travel, etc.) |
| | Attitude towards current consumption pattern | Whether consumption pattern needs to be improved |
| Consumer behavior and habits | Annual or monthly expenditures | Select and rank options (basic food, apparel, shoes and hats, medical treatment, water and electricity, communications, transport, recreation and entertainment, tourism, education, housing/car repayment, etc.) |
| | Green consumption in daily consumption | Give options [low-carbon and frugal consumption, waste sorting (e-waste separately), waste re-use, purchase of eco-friendly products, green travel, etc.] |
| Willingness to make green consumption | Are you willing to make green consumption | Pay attention to information on green consumption (including information on whether products are eco-friendly, waste sorting, e-waste recycling and low-carbon transport, etc.) |
| | What factors affect green consumption | Easy operation<br>Government consumption policy (price/economic incentive)<br>Relevant public publicity<br>Whether others do so<br>Whether such act is socially accepted<br>Mandated by the government |

*Source: Survey on Sustainable Consumption Awareness of Community Households in Beijing and Policy Advocacy Project,* jointly conducted by All-China Environment Federation and the United Nations Environment Programme.

*5.3.1.4 Data processing methods*

The statistical analysis for this book was most performed using IBM SPSS Statistics 22, and some charts were plotted using Microsoft Office Excel 2013.

In terms of data processing, explanation is needed regarding the following points:

The first is the processing of missing values. Questionnaires that are not completed or that are not filled out according to the requirements are considered invalid. The question is a missing value and is not considered in the statistical analysis of such question. However, if the multiple-answer question requires at least N items to be selected, and the number of items selected by the respondent is less than N, it is still treated as a valid answer.

The second is the case of invalid questionnaires. For questionnaires in which all or most of the answers are the same and are filled on the same day and the survey is conducted in the same community, only one copy is retained, while the rest are regarded invalid. If the questionnaire is not analytically significant due to the absence of most information or a little of key information, it is regarded as invalid. Invalid questionnaires are not considered in the statistical analysis of each question.

Third, questionnaires contain obvious clerical errors. Clerical errors in questionnaires made by the respondents are corrected in the data processing. For example, if you select "Yes" but give the reason for "No," the answer is corrected as "No." If the age is over 65 years old, the occupation is corrected as a retiree, and so on.

The fourth is the issue of proportion. Regarding the question of travel proportion, if the sum of the various proportions is not 100, it is subject to scale processing. In the case of a vacant item, the value of the item shall be calculated and recorded according to the sum of 100. If there are two or more vacant items and the sum of the remaining items is not 100, the answer will be invalid and is not recorded.

When inferring the mean difference between comparison groups, the data are processed in the following ways to facilitate analysis:

The first is the sequencing problem with three options. For questions with the "Yes," "No," and "Unclear" answers, "Unclear" answers are treated as missing values. For questions with the "Clear," "Relatively clear," and "Unclear" answers, "Clear" and "Relatively clear" answers are treated as the same value.

The second is the grouping of the population characteristics. Gender and community are the norms and are not repeated here. According to age, it is divided into three groups: elderly (over 55 years old), middle-aged (35 to 55 years old), and young (18 to 35 years old). The population is differentiated based on expenditure. The upper tertile and lower tertile of the average monthly expenditure of the sample population are selected as the grouping basis. It is divided into three groups: low expenditure (monthly expenditure below 2,000 yuan), medium expenditure (2,001 to 3,000 yuan), and high expenditure (over 3,001 yuan).

In terms of the selection of classified variable for inferential statistics, exogenous variables on population and socioeconomic information are mainly used as categorical variables in this analysis in order to avoid the statistical errors caused by endogenous variable analysis. In addition, classification based on social and economic information variables can also provide different characteristics of different cohorts regarding green consumption patterns. Therefore, in addition to classification by community, the age, gender, and monthly living expenditure (and marital status) are used as categorical variables.

##### *5.3.1.5 Basic situation of the survey*

This survey focuses on three areas: the awareness of green consumption, green consumption behavior, and willingness to make green consumption by community residents in Beijing, as well as the impact of green consumption policies. At the level of consumer behavior and willingness as well as policy impact, it analyzes the three key areas of green consumption: resource conservation and green purchase, waste sorting, and green travel. In analyzing the survey results, the author first makes descriptive statistics of the overall data on the two communities and analyzes the green consumption cognition, behavior, and willingness of community residents in Beijing as well as the status of policy implementation. Then, inferential statistics are performed for different groups of people (mainly by age, gender, and monthly expenditure) and different communities, in order to learn about the differences in green consumption perception, behavior, and willingness of different cohorts as well as residents in different communities, and policy effects, thereby judging the target group of policies, and providing a factual basis for targeted policy recommendations in light of the communities.

A total of 1,200 questionnaires were distributed and 1,167 questionnaires were collected, with a recovery rate of 97.25 percent. Of these, 1,115 questionnaires were valid, with a rate of effective questionnaires of 95.54 percent. These include 496 valid questionnaires for Bajiaobeili Community in Shijingshan District, 504 valid questionnaires for Wangjing Community in Chaoyang District, and 115 valid questionnaires collected via WeChat, as shown in Table 5.4:

### *5.3.2 The results of the survey*

##### *5.3.2.1 Basic information of respondents*

The basic information of the sample respondents is shown in Table 5.5:

Information on the sample population and social and economic statistics are shown in Table 5.6:

*Table 5.4* Statistics on the number of questionnaires distributed and valid questionnaires

| | | | |
|---|---|---|---|
| Number of questionnaires issued and collected | 1,167 | Valid questionnaires | 1,115 |
| Bajiaobeili Community, Shijingshan District | 530 | Bajiaobeili Community, Shijingshan District | 496 |
| Wangjing Community | 521 | Wangjing Community | 504 |
| WeChat | 116 | WeChat | 115 |

*Table 5.5* Basic information about the sample respondents as a whole

| | *Frequency* | *Percentage (%)* |
|---|---|---|
| Age (years) | | |
| 18–24 | 97 | 8.8 |
| 25–34 | 219 | 19.9 |
| 35–44 | 202 | 18.4 |
| 45–54 | 129 | 11.7 |
| 55–64 | 189 | 17.2 |
| >65 | 264 | 24 |
| Gender | | |
| Female | 679 | 63.5 |
| Male | 391 | 36.5 |
| Marital status | | |
| Unmarried | 58 | 11.8 |
| Married | 382 | 78 |
| Divorced or widowed | 50 | 10.2 |
| Educational level | | |
| Junior high school and below | 116 | 24 |
| High school/vocational high school | 131 | 27.1 |
| Junior college | 108 | 22.3 |
| Undergraduates | 116 | 24 |
| Master's degree or above | 13 | 2.7 |
| Occupation | | |
| Company employee | 96 | 19.6 |
| Government staff | 31 | 6.3 |
| Self-employed | 13 | 2.6 |
| Professional and technical personnel | 14 | 2.9 |
| Student | 13 | 2.6 |
| Teacher | 7 | 1.4 |
| Freelancer | 12 | 2.4 |
| Migrant workers in the city | 4 | 0.8 |
| Serviceman | 1 | 0.2 |
| Retiree | 271 | 55.5 |
| Unemployed | 19 | 3.9 |
| Other | 10 | 2 |

*Table 5.6* Information on the overall sample population and social and economic statistics

| | *Valid answer* | *Minimum value* | *Maximum value* | *Mean* | *Standard deviation* |
|---|---|---|---|---|---|
| Population | 1,097 | 1 | 8 | 3.15 | 1.176 |
| Housing area | 1,071 | 2 | 2,000 | 80.62 | 68.79689 |
| Living expenses | 1,080 | 0 | 30,000 | 3,262.52 | 2,731.328 |
| Medical expenditures | 1,015 | 0 | 300,000 | 4,987.45 | 14,148.58 |

*5.3.2.2 Awareness of green consumption*

51 percent of respondents have heard of the conception of green consumption, and nearly half of residents are ignorant about this, indicating that the concept of green consumption remains to be further publicized. Figure 5.4 shows the ways community residents learn about green consumption as well as their corresponding proportions. 35.25 percent of the respondents learn about the concept of green consumption through TV and broadcasting, ranking top. The Internet and newspapers are the second and third most important ways for community residents to learn about green consumption. It shows that television broadcasting, the Internet, and newspapers have a good publicity effect, while community publicity, publicity at schools or educational institutions, and communication with friends and neighbors have a poor effect of popularization. This shows that it is necessary to strengthen the publicity through communities, schools, or educational institutions in the field of green consumption.

The results of community residents' perception of green consumption are shown in Figure 5.5. The proportion of residents who believe that water and electricity saving, and waste sorting belong to green consumption behavior is the highest, accounting for 69.80 percent and 59.20 percent, respectively. The recycling of waste household appliances and waste batteries, and the purchase of energy-saving and eco-friendly products are also regarded by nearly half of the residents as green consumption behavior. The proportions of people who use no or less disposable products, reuse idle goods, and reduce travel by private car are similar, accounting for about 37 percent. This shows that in order to promote green consumption in China, we can choose widely recognized areas, such as water and electricity saving, waste sorting, recycling of waste electrical and electronic products, green purchase, and green travel.

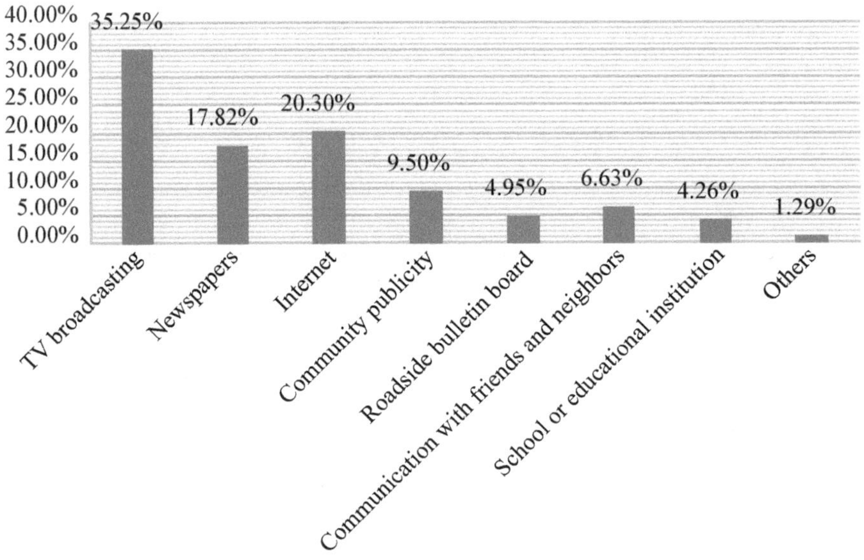


*Figure 5.4* Ways for community residents to learn about green consumption.

Moreover, 80 percent of community residents agreed to abandon the current consumption model; 16 percent said they were unclear; only four percent said that there is no need to change existing consumption patterns. At the same time, 96 percent of residents are in favor of embracing new consumption patterns, while only four percent disagree with this view. It can be seen that most residents are aware of the drawbacks of the current consumption pattern and are in favor of establishing a green consumption model.

#### *5.3.2.3 Green consumption behavior and willingness*

##### 5.3.2.3.1 RESOURCE CONSERVATION AND GREEN PURCHASE

A survey on the types of drinking water used by community residents (see Figure 5.6) found that 63 percent of residents use tap water, 17 percent have their own purifiers installed, and 19 percent choose barreled or bottled water, showing that nearly 40 percent of respondents lack basic trust in government-run water

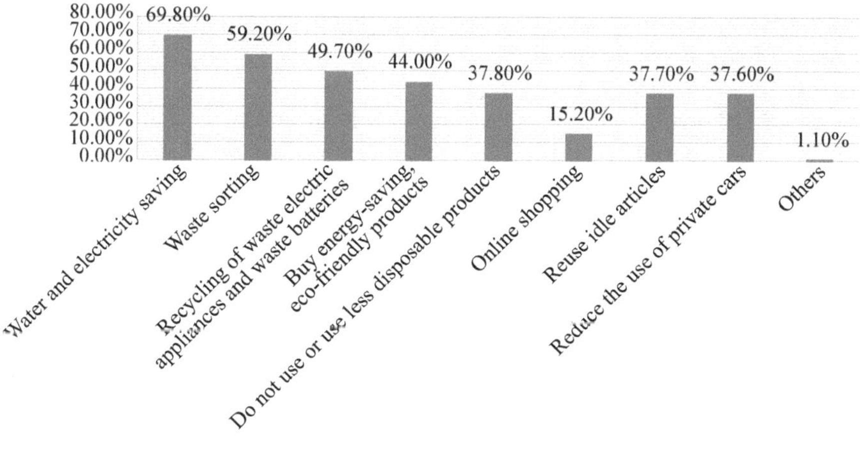


*Figure 5.5* Community residents' perception of green consumption behavior.

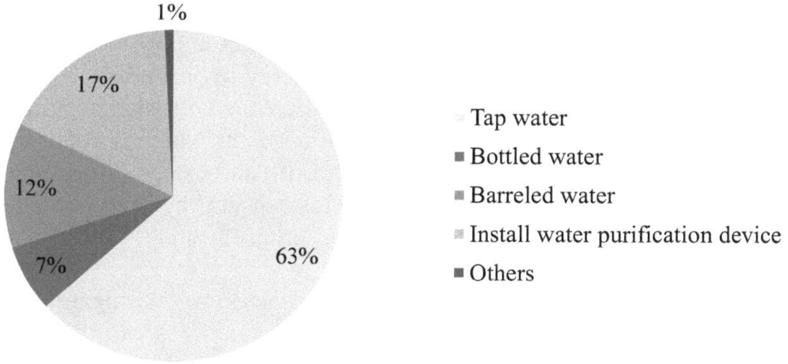


*Figure 5.6* Types of drinking water used by community residents.

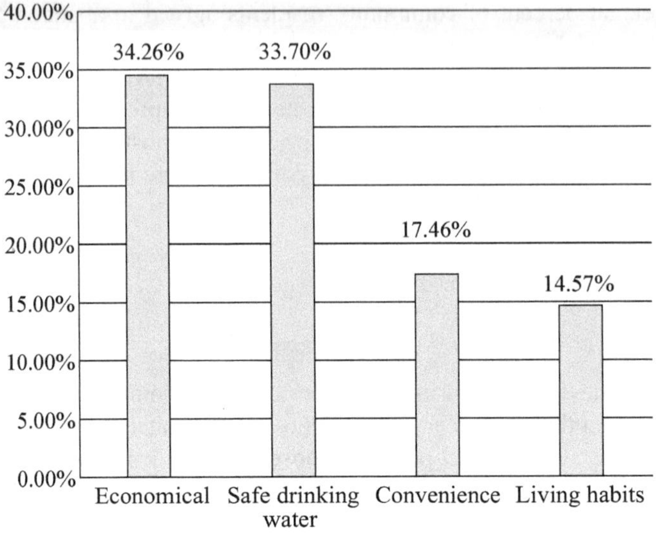


*Figure 5.7* Reasons why community residents choose drinking water.

systems. As shown in Figure 5.7, the options of affordability and safe drinking water ranked first and second (34.26 percent and 33.70 percent respectively), indicating that affordability and safety are top considerations for respondents when choosing drinking water.

A survey on factors that influence water and electricity conservation by residents (respondents choose at most three options) (see Figure 5.8) shows that an easy-to-operate method ranked first, followed by tiered pricing, living habits developed from an early age, and material incentives for water and electricity saving. The number of respondents who choose the "others do the same" option is the lowest. It can be seen that easy-to-operate methods, tiered pricing, and the living habits developed from an early age are the main factors promoting residents to save water and electricity.

A survey on the circumstances under which residents buy energy-saving products (see Figure 5.9) shows that over 40 percent of the respondents choose to buy energy-saving products when the government subsidizes energy-saving products. The proportion of respondents who purchase energy-saving products based on product safety consideration and small price difference with similar products is neither large nor small, while the proportion of residents who buy energy-saving products as a result of media publicity is small. It can be seen that government economic subsidy is an important way to guide residents to buy energy-saving/eco-friendly products, and the high safety level and price advantages are also selling points of energy-saving products.

The survey contains seven options (multiple choices) to investigate residents' perception of measures that promote green consumption. As can be seen from Figure 5.10, 74.90 percent of residents agree that trade-in of old goods for new products are green consumption measures, and 42.80 percent, 41.50 percent, and

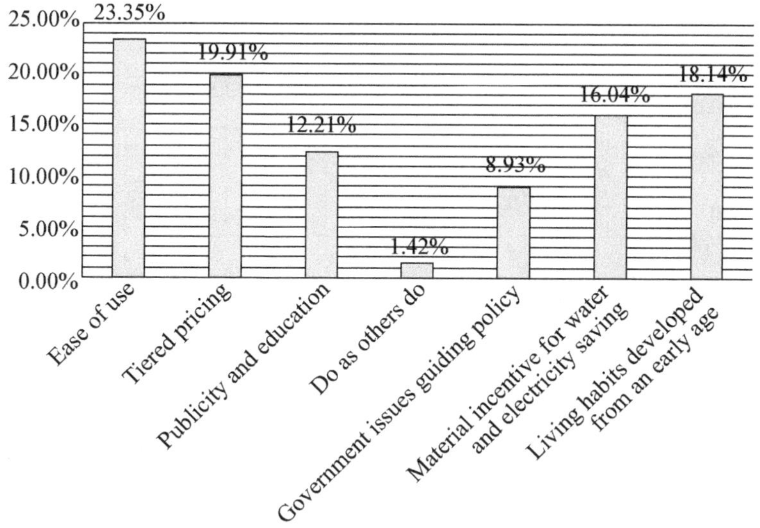


*Figure 5.8* Factors affecting water and electricity conservation by community residents.

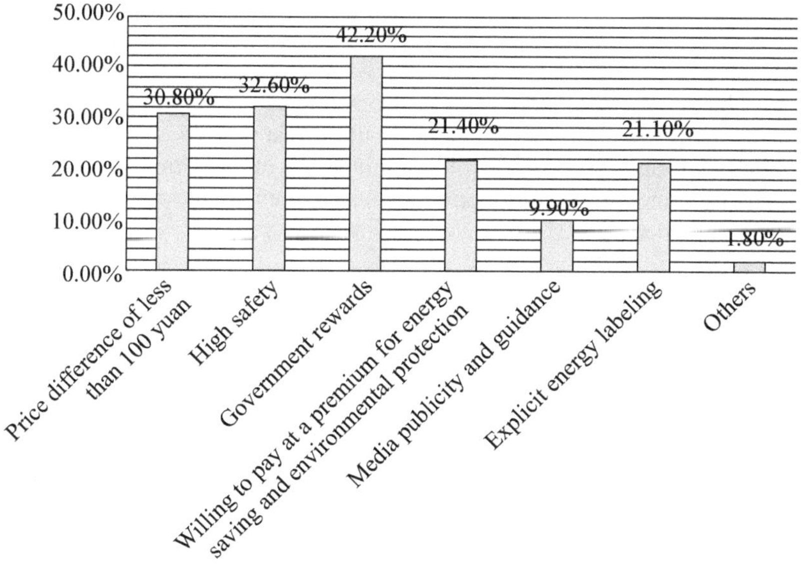


*Figure 5.9* Factors affecting community residents who purchase energy-saving/green products.

40.50 percent of residents choose forcibly eliminating disposable products, establishing community platform for second-hand products and government-funded housing renovation, respectively. Residents have a low level of approval for relevant energy conservation publicity and increase in disposable product prices. It is inferred from this that the trade-in energy-saving measures can greatly mobilize

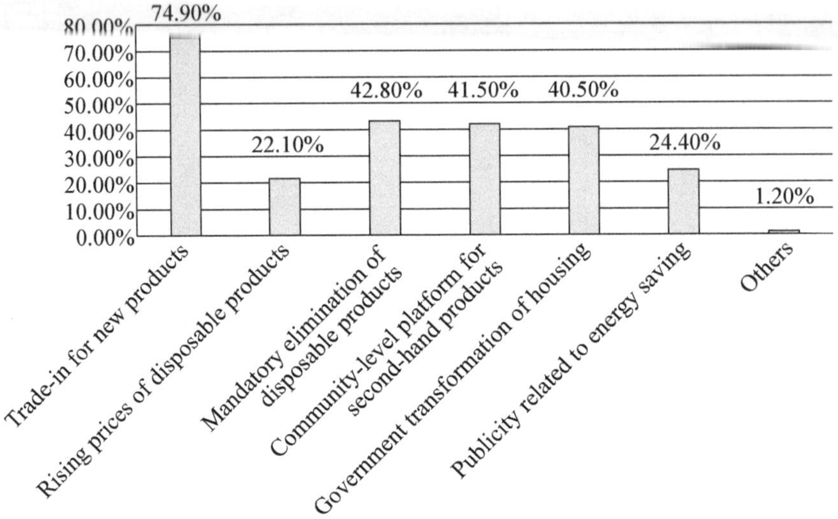


*Figure 5.10* Measures to save resources and energy according to the awareness of community residents.

residents and achieve good effect of energy saving. It is easier to cut down the use of disposable products by mandating the phase-out of disposable products than by increasing their prices. The government should invest funds and efforts in housing renovation and the establishment of community-level platforms for second-hand goods and promote green consumption by means of energy conservation and recycling of waste goods.

##### 5.3.2.3.2 WASTE SORTING

In Beijing, household waste is sorted and recycled under four categories: recyclables, kitchen waste, hazardous waste, and other waste. For the question of types of household waste sorted and recycled, only 4.04 percent of the community residents chose the right answers, while the other ones missed options or gave wrong answers. This shows that the residents are ignorant of the knowledge of regulations of municipal household waste sorting and recycling. As can be seen from Figure 5.11, 41.97 percent of the respondents missed one option, and 22.16 percent missed two options. Residents are unclear about the rules of correct sorting, indicating that it is urgent to publicize the knowledge of waste sorting. Figure 5.12 shows the level of knowledge of community residents about household waste recycling. It can be seen that the number of residents who missed A (recyclables) was the smallest, and the number of residents who missed F (hazardous waste) was the most (73.71 percent of the total). It shows that knowledge related to hazardous waste is the least publicized, followed by the knowledge of kitchen waste and other waste. This also confirms the lack of knowledge of community residents about correct waste sorting.

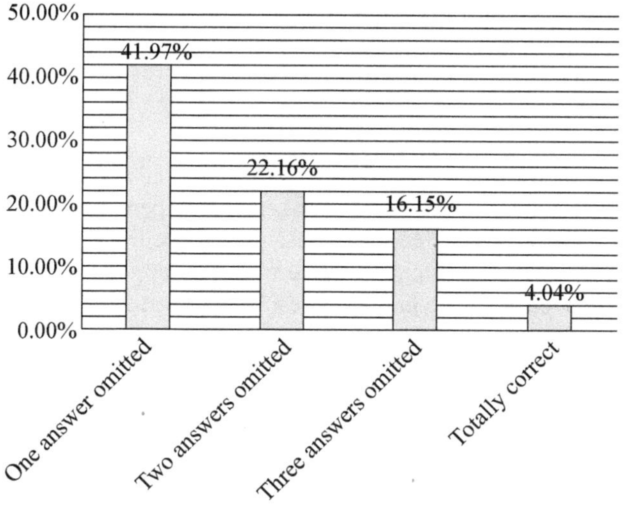


*Figure 5.11* Perception of household waste sorting.

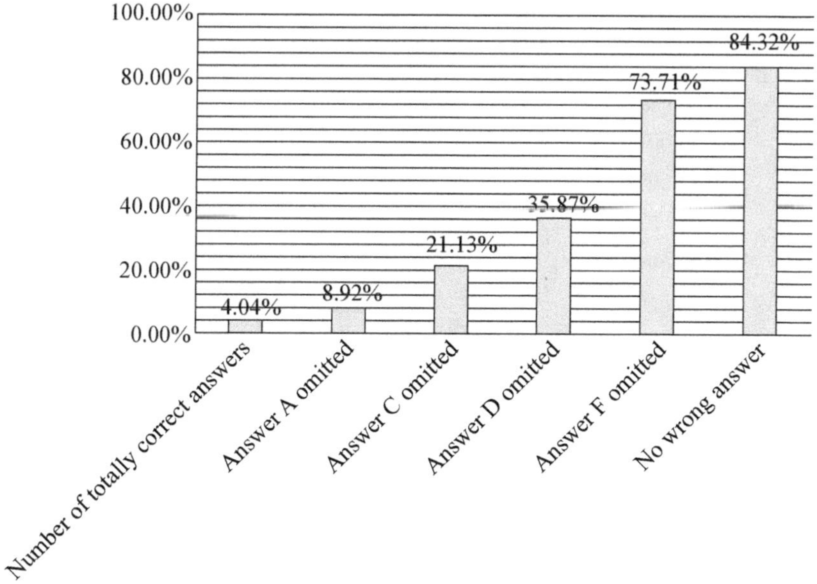


*Figure 5.12* Perception of household waste sorting through questionnaires.

In terms of disposing of household waste, 50 percent of the respondents put it in the garbage cans without sorting and another 50 percent sort and put it in designated garbage cans. This reflects that half of the residents have the awareness and behavior of waste sorting, while another half dispose of waste indiscriminately and urgent action is needed in this regard.

On the issue of how to dispose of large waste electrical appliances, 73 percent of respondents choose door-to-door recycling service, 36 percent give them to others, and only 23.5 percent send these to professional recycling points. It can be seen that the current recycling system of waste electrical appliances is immature and needs to be improved, so that community residents prioritize professional recycling stations.

The selection of measures that promote community residents to sort waste is shown in Figure 5.13. Ranked in descending order, the answers are as follows: special recycling service stations in the community (recycling of electronic waste, product leasing, replacement of old items, etc.); the government promulgates laws/regulations to mandate waste sorting, and gives detailed instructions on waste sorting; the media step up efforts to publicize and educate the general public about the significance and process of waste sorting; certain material reward for waste sorting; other people do so. 73.00 percent of respondents believe

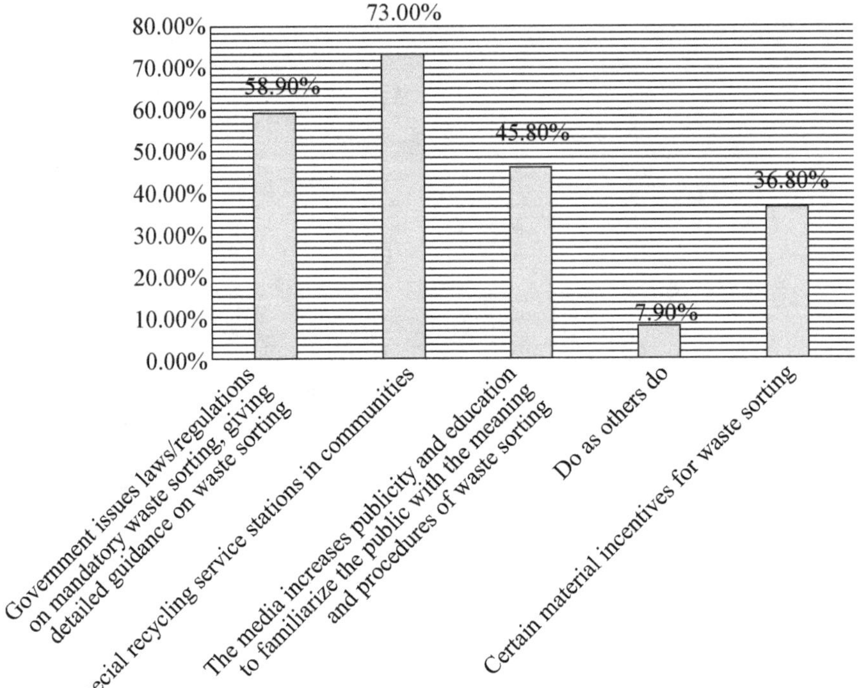


*Figure 5.13* Selection of measures that motivate community residents to sort garbage.

that the establishment of special recycling service stations in the community will promote waste sorting and disposal. 58.90 percent believe that the laws/regulations that mandate waste sorting as well as detailed guidance on waste sorting can also promote waste sorting.

On the issue of important measures to promote waste sorting, 33 percent of residents believe that the most important is to establish special recycling stations in the community, and 26 percent believe that the government-mandated waste sorting has the best effect, which confirm the importance of these two measures in the eyes of residents.

According to a survey on economic measures to promote waste sorting (see Figure 5.14), community residents believe that government material incentives for waste sorting and dedicated personnel responsible for waste sorting in the community (paid by residents) are the most effective, while the government's fines for failure to sort garbage in accordance with regulations are the least effective. In addition, 35.30 percent and 38.20 percent chose "more charge for more waste, and less charge for less waste" and "more charge for mixed waste, and less charge for sorted waste," respectively. Of course, this has a lot to do with respondents' preference for material rewards rather than financial fines and does not fully explain that payment measures are less effective than incentives.

###### 5.3.2.3.3 GREEN TRAVEL

Figure 5.15 shows the proportion of travel modes for community residents. The range of the proportion of four travel modes is 0–100 percent, indicating huge differences between individuals. The largest mean of the proportion of various travel

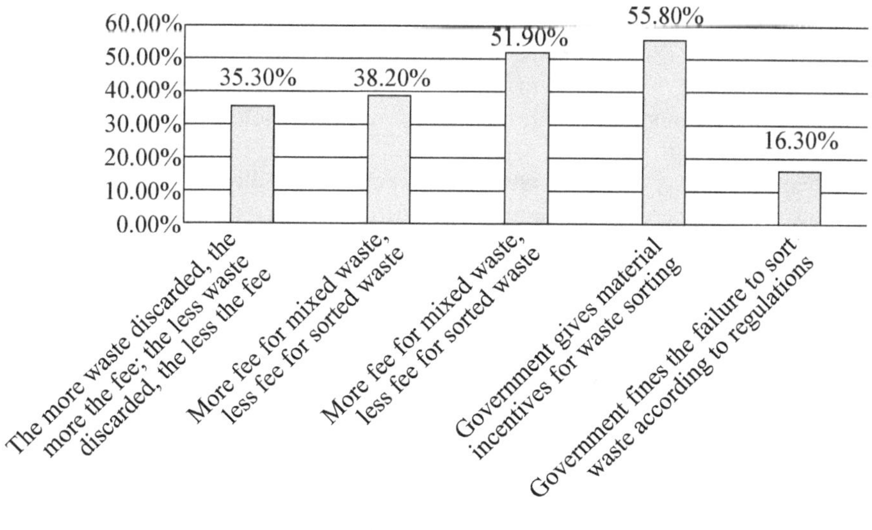


*Figure 5.14* Economic measures to promote waste sorting.

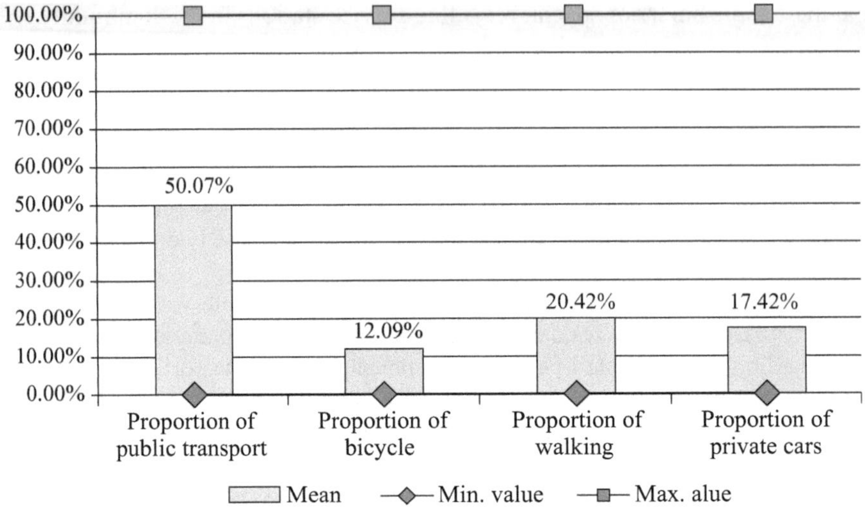


*Figure 5.15* Proportion of travel modes for community residents.

modes is the public transport (bus and subway), accounting for 50.07 percent, followed by walking and private cars, accounting for 20.42 percent and 17.42 percent. Bicycle has the smallest proportion, accounting for 12.09 percent. This is related to the high proportion of elderly people in the sample respondents, who generally prefer public transport or walking for getting around.

From the perspective of the types of community residents' private cars, the survey shows that ordinary fuel-powered vehicles are in the majority (accounting for 89 percent), while only a small number are gasoline-electric hybrid vehicles (accounting for 6 percent) and battery electric vehicles (accounting for 5 percent). Residents prefer ordinary fuel-powered vehicles, while electric vehicles are rarely used.

When community residents were asked if they are willing to buy a small-displacement car, 49 percent answered yes, 24 percent no, and the rest said it was hard to say. When asked about their willingness to buy new energy vehicles, 42 percent answered yes, 28 percent said no, and 30 percent said it was hard to say, reflecting that residents are somewhat willing to buy new energy vehicles, but only 11 percent of residents choose new energy vehicles when buying cars. It shows a huge difference between their willingness and what they do.

In descending order of importance, the factors driving residents to reduce private car use are: convenient public transport, reduced or subsidized public transport fare, community shuttle bus, free bicycles in communities and transport hubs, traffic restrictions on private cars, increased parking fees, increased gasoline prices, media education, and increased fuel consumption taxes (see Figure 5.16). It can be seen that public transport, community shuttle buses, and bicycles are considered as most important factors affecting residents' travel.

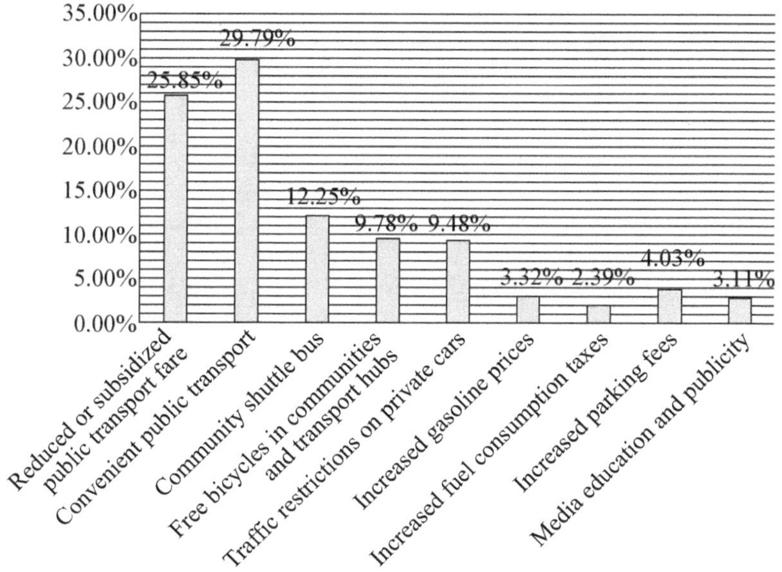


*Figure 5.16* Contributing factors that reduce the use of private car.

A survey on the contributors to reducing travel by private car found that the proportion of people who choose convenient public transport and reduced or subsidized public transport fare is the largest (69.73 percent for the two factors) (see Figure 5.17), which confirms the importance of public transport and community shuttle buses in reducing travel by private car.

### *5.3.2.4 The popularization of green consumption-related policies and implementation effect*

#### 5.3.2.4.1 RESOURCE CONSERVATION AND GREEN PURCHASE

Among the respondents, the proportion of residents who are generally aware of the tiered water and electricity pricing standards is the largest (43 percent aware of water pricing standards, and 42.60 percent aware of electricity pricing standards), and the proportion of residents who are ignorant of the standards was the smallest (21.30 percent ignorant of water pricing standards, and 17.40 percent ignorant of electricity pricing standards), as shown in Figure 5.18. Overall, most residents have a certain knowledge of the tiered water and electricity pricing policies, and the tiered electricity pricing standards are more known to residents than the tiered water pricing standard, but they have little knowledge of specific standards.

The implementation effect of the tiered water pricing and electricity pricing policy is shown in Figure 5.19. About 60 percent of respondents believe that tiered water pricing and electricity pricing can prompt them to save water and electricity, but nearly 20 percent still believe that these policies do not have a facilitating

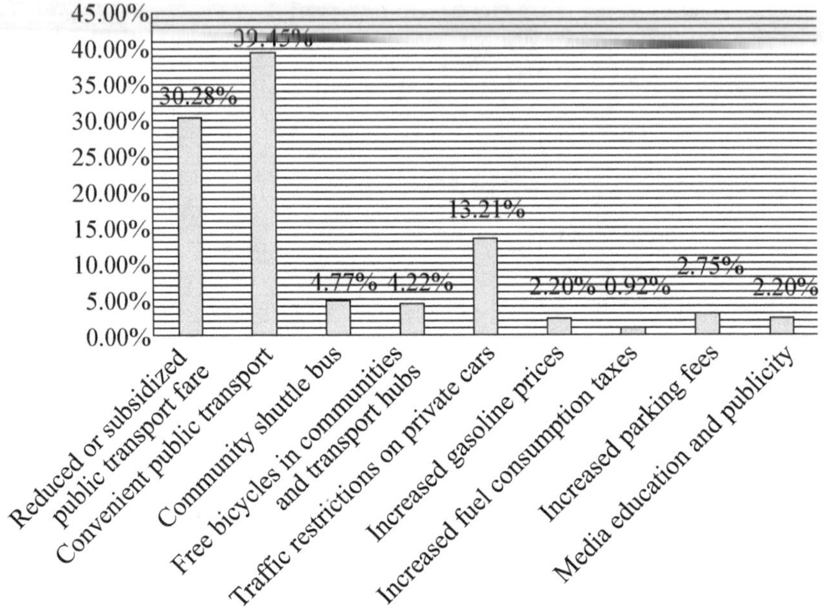


*Figure 5.17* The biggest contributing factors to reducing travel by private car.

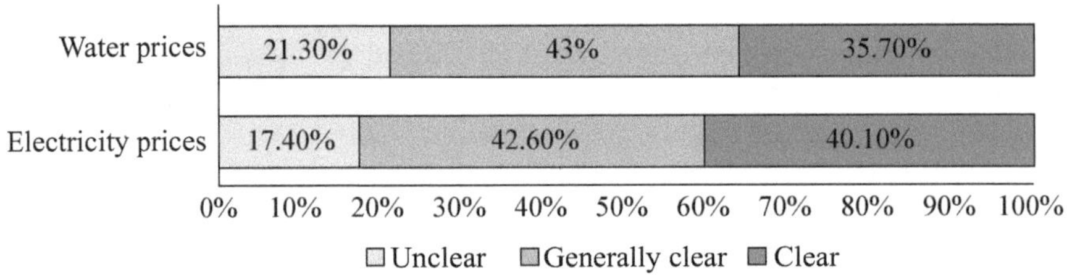


*Figure 5.18* Community residents' perception of tiered water pricing and electricity pricing standards.

effect. It can be seen that the tiered water pricing and pricing price standards have certain effects in promoting water and electricity saving, but other policies are needed to guide the residents to save resources.

The survey shows that 72 percent of residents purchased subsidized energy-saving household appliances when the state operated subsidies for such appliances, and 28 percent never purchased these. The public have a good response to this policy.

#### 5.3.2.4.2 WASTE SORTING

59 percent of the respondents are aware of the provisions on the urban waste sorting and recycling in the *Law of the People's Republic of China on the Prevention*

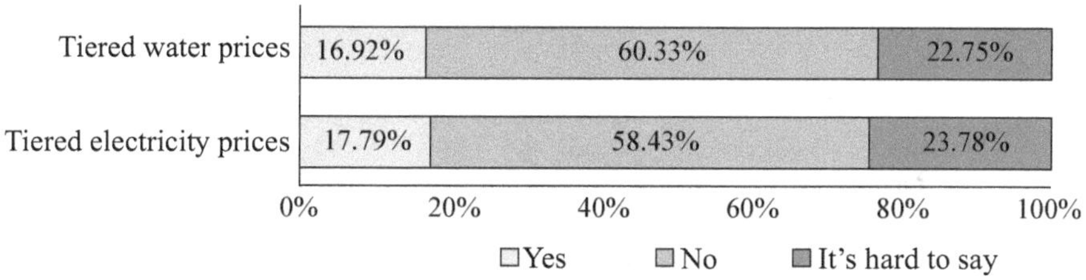


*Figure 5.19* Effect of tiered water pricing and electricity pricing policy.

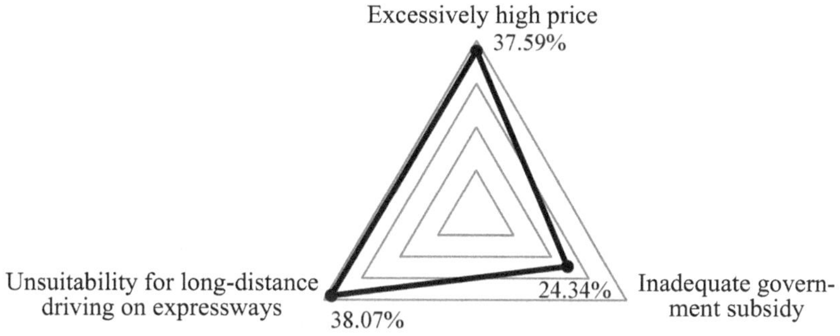


*Figure 5.20* Reasons for not buying small displacement cars by community residents.

*and Control of Environmental Pollution by Solid Waste* (hereinafter the *Solid Waste Law*), but about 40 percent still do not know about it or are completely ignorant of it. The survey results show that the *Solid Waste Law* is not yet widely known, giving rise to the need to educate the public in this regard.

In addition, more than 60 percent have heard of the *Beijing Administrative Regulations for Household Waste*, and 33 percent are not aware of this. It shows that it is necessary to further publicize and popularize such regulations, which are immediately related to the everyday life of residents.

##### 5.3.2.4.3 GREEN TRAVEL

45.2 percent of the respondents have heard of the subsidy policy on small-displacement cars; the number of people who are ignorant about it is neither large nor small. Only 23.34 percent of the respondents are aware of the policy details. A survey on whether the subsidy policy can prompt residents to buy small-displacement cars shows that only 40 percent support the subsidy policy for small-displacement vehicles, 36 percent take a wait-and-see attitude, and 24 percent think that the subsidy policy is ineffective. A further survey on respondents who do not buy small-displacement cars (see Figure 5.20) shows that the reasons are unsuitability for long-distance driving on expressways, high prices, and inadequate government subsidies. It can be seen that the functional weakness of small-displacement cars is the biggest hurdle to consumer purchase. Therefore, if the functional defect is

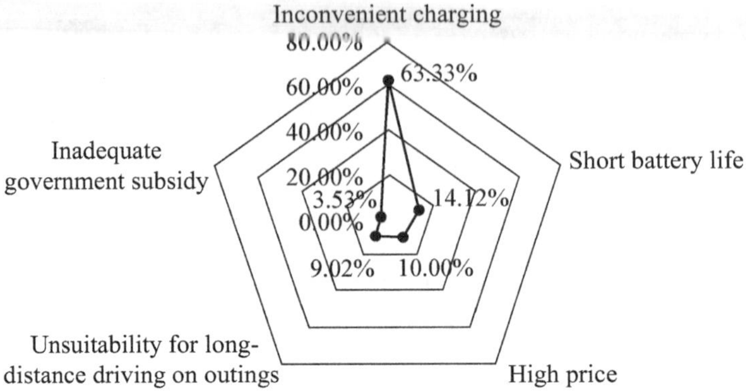


*Figure 5.21* Reasons for not buying new energy vehicles by community residents.

not solved, it is difficult for the diverse policies on small-displacement vehicles to achieve the expected results alone.

Community residents are generally aware of subsidy policy for new energy vehicles. 75 percent of residents have heard of or are aware of the policy details. However, similar to the subsidy policy for small-displacement vehicles, subsidy policy for new energy vehicles only prompts one-third of residents to buy new energy vehicles, while other residents choose to wait and see or do not buy new energy vehicles. A further survey on respondents who do not buy new energy vehicles (see Figure 5.21) reveals that the reasons are: convenient charging, short battery life, high price, unsuitability for long-distance driving on outings, and inadequate government subsidies. The reason of inconvenient charging ranks far ahead of other reasons, indicating that residents do not buy new energy vehicles because it is inconvenient and lacks rich functions. The second reason, a short battery life, also confirms this view.

### *5.3.3 Analysis of differences between different groups of people*

#### *5.3.3.1 Analysis of differences between different age groups*

In this survey, respondents fall into three groups according to age: young (18–34 years old), middle-aged (35–54 years old), and elderly (55 years old and above). Questions with significant differences are selected for comparison based on the mean difference between the comparison groups through inferential statistics. The results are as follows:

In the survey on the perception of green consumption, the elderly are not as much aware of green consumption as young and middle-aged people, while elderly people are slightly more in favor of the establishment of a green consumption model than young and middle-aged people.

In the survey on willingness and behavior regarding green consumption, the three groups showed differences in terms of green purchase, household waste sorting, and green travel. In terms of green purchase, elderly residents recognize the role of trade-in services, while young and middle-aged residents more agree with the role of increasing the prices of disposable products. In terms of household waste sorting, more young and middle-aged people engage in waste sorting than middle-aged and elderly people. In terms of green travel, the highest proportion of people taking public transportation is the elderly people, followed by young people. In terms of travel by private car, the proportion of middle-aged people is far higher than that of the elderly people.

In the survey on the perception of green consumption policy, the differences between different age groups are mainly reflected in the perception of policies such as tiered water pricing and tiered electricity pricing standards, waste sorting regulations and green travel, as well as their impact on green consumption. The middle-aged and elderly groups are more aware of the tiered water and electricity pricing standard than the young people, and the tiered electricity pricing better prompt the elderly people to save electricity. In the case of *Beijing Administrative Regulations on Household Waste*, the regulations are better known to middle-aged and elderly groups than to young people. In a survey on the subsidy policy on small-displacement vehicles and new energy vehicles, it was revealed that the middle-aged group has the highest level of awareness of this policy, followed by the young people and the elderly people. The new energy vehicle subsidy policy has a better promotion effect on the young and elderly people than on the middle-aged group.

#### *5.3.3.2 Analysis of difference between groups of different genders*

All respondents were compared by gender. Questions with significant differences are selected for comparison based on the mean difference between the comparison groups through inferential statistics. The results are as follows:

In the survey on perception of green consumption, the difference between the people of both sexes is mainly as follows: On the issue of perception of green consumption behavior, more women think that water and electricity saving is a kind of green consumption behavior. Similarly, more women are in favor of establishing a green consumption pattern compared to men.

In the survey on willingness and behavior regarding green consumption, the difference between the two sexes is mainly reflected in the identification of measures that promote green consumption as well as the identification of household waste sorting and recycling. A survey on the measures recognized by respondents for promoting green consumption revealed that more women think that rising prices of disposable items and building community-level second-hand markets and platforms contribute to green consumption compared to men.

In the survey on perception of green consumption policy, the differences between the two sexes are mainly as follows: In terms of water pricing standards, women are more sensitive to the tiered water pricing standards and have a better knowledge in this regard. In terms of low-carbon travel, men are more aware of the subsidy policy on small-displacement cars, but this policy prompts more women to buy small-displacement cars than men. Men are more aware of the subsidy policy for new energy vehicles than women, and the difference is significant.

#### *5.3.3.3 Analysis of differences between people with different monthly expenditure levels*

The upper tertile and lower tertile of the monthly expenditure of the respondents are selected as the grouping basis. They are divided into three groups: low expenditure (monthly expenditure of less than 2,000 yuan), medium-level expenditure (2,001–3,000 yuan), and high expenditure (more than 3,001 yuan). According to the results of inferential statistics, the differences between groups are mainly as follows:

In the survey on the perception of green consumption, people with high expenditure are more aware of the concept of green consumption than people with middle and low spending, and more of them believe that waste sorting and battery recycling belong to green consumption.

In the survey on willingness and behavior regarding green consumption, the differences between groups with different spending are mainly reflected in low-carbon travel. Significantly more people with middle and low spending choose walking and public transportation that groups with high spending, while significantly more groups with high spending travel by private car than groups with middle and low spending.

In the survey on the perception of green consumption policy, the people with middle and low spending are more sensitive to the tiered water and electricity pricing, thinking that the tiered pricing can effectively promote water and electricity conservation. People with low and middle spending are more inclined to buy energy-saving products. People with high spending are more informed of the subsidy policies for small-displacement vehicles and new energy vehicles.

### *5.3.4 Analysis of differences between communities*

#### *5.3.4.1 Comparison of basic information on respondents*

The demographic and financial differences between the two communities are mainly reflected in the following areas: respondents in Bajiaobeili Community in Shijingshan District are mainly middle-aged and elderly people over 55 years of age, while those in Wangjing Community in Chaoyang District are mainly people aged 25 to 44 years of age. Therefore, the education level for Wangjing community is significantly higher than that of Bajiaobeili community, and Wangjing community has more residents who hold junior college degree, bachelor's degree, master's degree, or above. In terms of occupation, Wangjing Community has more company employees than Bajiaobeili Community, but has less retirees than Bajiaobeili Community. In terms of per capita housing area, the average housing area of Wangjing Community is 10 square meters more than that of Bajiaobeili Community. Bajiaobeili community has more residents who receive public health services than Wangjing community, and this has something to do with the large number of retired cadres there. The monthly expenditure level of residents in the two communities approximates normal distribution, mainly in the 3,000–4,999 yuan group. The difference is that the income distribution is relatively concentrated in Bajiaobeili community, and the proportions of low-income and high-income people are less than those of Wangjing community.

### *5.3.4.2 Community comparison in terms of perception of green consumption*

A comparative analysis of the perception of green consumption among residents in the two communities reveals that the perception of green consumption among residents in the two communities is basically similar. The following two points are noteworthy:

7 In terms of ways to learn about green consumption, the residents of Bajiaobeili community rely more on television, while more residents of Wangjing community learn about green consumption through traditional media and communication such as community, street publicity, and friends compared with those in Bajiaobeili community, as shown in Figure 5.22.

8 The awareness of the concept and behavior of green consumption is slightly higher among residents of Wangjing Community than among those of Bajiaobeili Community. The eight options in Figure 5.23 all belong to green consumption behavior. In this book, one point is assigned to each option. The higher the score (more selected options), the higher the awareness of green consumption behavior. The average score for Bajiaobeili community is 3.29, and that of Wangjing community is 3.44, which is slightly higher than the former. Moreover, the proportion of residents who chose three options is the highest, while less

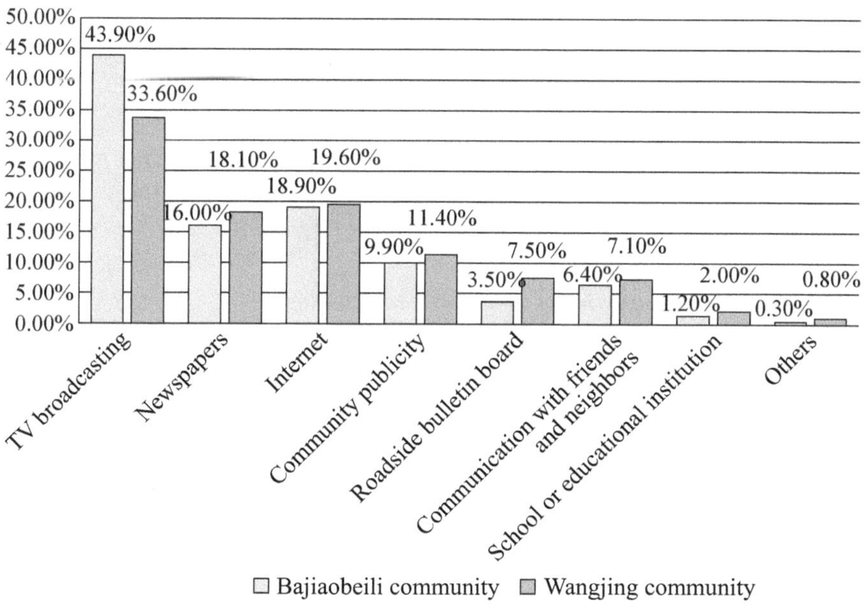


*Figure 5.22* Differences in ways community residents learn about green consumption.

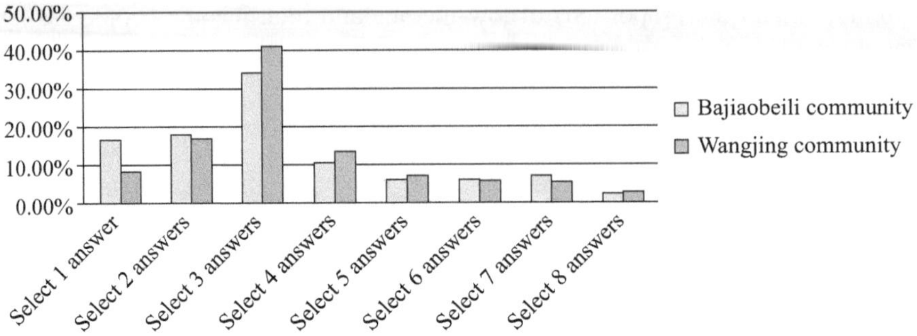


*Figure 5.23* Differences in community residents' perception of green consumption behavior.

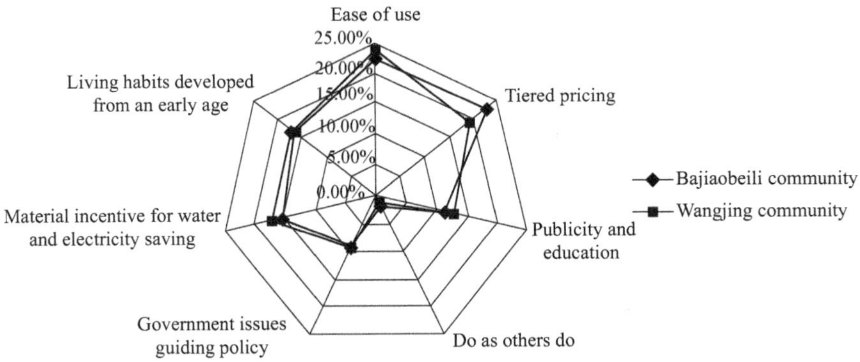


*Figure 5.24* Community comparison of residents' preferences for measures promoting water and electricity saving.

*Note:* A refers to recyclables, C kitchen waste, D other waste, and F hazardous waste.

than 3 percent chose all the options, indicating that residents are not fully aware of the green consumption behavior. It is urgent to disseminate the concept and connotation of green consumption and related knowledge.

### *5.3.4.3 Community comparison of willingness and behavior regarding green consumption*

In terms of resource saving and green purchase, the differences in the willingness and behavior of residents in the two communities regarding green consumption are mainly reflected in the following areas: (1) Residents in the two communities have the same preference for various measures to promote water and electricity conservation, and the promotion effects in descending order are: convenient operation, tiered pricing, reward for water, and electricity saving, living habits developed from an early age, publicity and education, government guidance policies, and similar practice by others. The residents of Bajiaobeili community more prefer tiered pricing (see Figure 5.24). (2) According to the comparative analysis of the selection of measures that best promote water and electricity saving, the number of residents in the two communities who chose "convenient operation" is the largest, perhaps because people are more inclined to easy operation in the fast-paced life. In addition, residents of Bajiaobeili community are more willing to spend more money on energy-saving/eco-friendly products. Residents of Wangjing community believe that the establishment of community second-hand platform is the second choice to promote resource conservation, while respondents of Bajiaobeili community are more inclined to regard the government-mandated elimination of disposable products and housing renovation as the second choice.

After analyzing the differences between the two communities in waste sorting, the following conclusions can be drawn: (1) 4.33 percent of the respondents in Wangjing community are aware of the methods of waste sorting in Beijing, as against 1.51 percent for Bajiaobeili community. In terms of the disposal of household waste, 54.09 percent of the residents of Wangjing Community do not perform waste sorting, while 39.43 percent of residents of Bajiaobeili community perform waste sorting. It can be seen that the residents of Bajiaobeili community have higher awareness of waste sorting than those of Wangjing community. Through interviews with residents' committees of the communities, the research team found that high-end communities in Wangjing engage workers to perform household waste sorting. (2) The preferences of residents of the two communities for financial incentives that promote waste sorting are generally the same.

In terms of green travel, the differences between the two communities are mainly shown below: (1) Residents of Bajiaobeili Community prefer low-carbon public transport more than residents of Wangjing Community. This is associated with the higher proportion of middle-aged elderly residents and retirees in Bajiaobeili community, and more accessible and convenient public transportation compared to Wangjing Community. In order to promote low-carbon public transport, Wangjing community needs to improve public transport services (such as the "last mile connection" from the community to bus stops). (2) Residents of Bajiaobeili Community are more inclined to buy small-displacement vehicles and new energy vehicles than residents of Wangjing Community, and there are significant differences. (3) In a survey on the best measures to reduce the use of private cars, it was revealed that residents of Bajiaobeili community highly approve of the two measures of "community shuttle bus" and "free bicycles in the community and bus hubs," while the residents of Wangjing community prefer "convenient public transport" and "traffic restrictions on private cars." Therefore, different incentive mechanisms that encourage residents to choose low-carbon travel should be established for different communities, and stereotyped policy measures should be avoided.

#### *5.3.4.4 Community comparison of the effects of green consumption policies*

Of the policies, only the tiered water pricing and new energy vehicle subsidy have significantly different implementation effect in the two communities. More than half of the residents of both communities (67.1 percent for Bajiaobeili Community and 57.5 percent for Wangjing Community) believe that the tiered water pricing policy can prompt them to save water, indicating that the tiered water pricing has a certain effect and role in promoting water conservation. This effect is more significant in old communities such as Bajiaobeili community, where the proportion of elderly people and retirees is high.

In terms of the subsidy policy for new energy vehicles, the proportion of residents in Wangjing community who choose to buy new energy vehicles is the smallest, the number of residents who will not buy is neither large nor small, and the number of residents who choose "it's hard to say" is the largest. In Bajiaobeili community, the number of residents who choose to buy new energy vehicles is the largest, the number of residents who choose "it's hard to say" is neither large nor small, and the number of residents who choose not to buy is the smallest. The residents of Bajiaobeili Community readily accept the subsidy policy for new energy vehicles, and the policy effect is better here than in Wangjing community. This may be attributed to income disparity and different geographic distance from the central area, as well as different lifestyles.

### *5.3.5 Conclusions*

#### *5.3.5.1 Summary of the sample survey results*

The survey reveals that 51 percent of the respondents have heard of green consumption, while less than three percent give correct answers regarding green consumption behavior, and most respondents can only select three to four options related to green consumption. This indicates that Beijing residents are generally not aware of the concept of green consumption. Half of the residents have a smattering of green consumption, while the other half are totally ignorant of green consumption. There is great room for popularizing green consumption in the community. It is necessary to strengthen publicity at the community level. The survey also reveals that television and the Internet are the two most effective channels for promoting green consumption. Therefore, the two should be the key media for popularizing green consumption. Of course, extensive publicity at the community level is also necessary.

In terms of behavior, the behavior of respondents regarding green consumption is generally insufficient. In terms of resource conservation and green purchase, waste sorting, and green travel, respondents perform best in resource conservation and green purchase, while waste sorting and green travel are rarely carried out. In terms of resource conservation and green purchase, over 60 percent of residents use tap water and show certain trust in the quality of government-run water supply, but another 40 percent choose barreled water and bottled water or have water purification equipment installed to purify tap water, resulting in huge waste of funds and materials. This is unsustainable consumption behavior and underscores the need for the government to improve the quality of tap water for Beijing residents. In terms of waste sorting, only four percent of residents are aware of state and Beijing local regulations on waste sorting. It is urgent to carry out publicity in this regard. In terms of the ways to dispose of household waste, nearly half of the respondents, which is a high proportion, said that they would perform waste sorting. In terms of treatment of waste household appliances, 73 percent choose door-to-door recycling services. It is urgent to establish a sound recycling system of waste electrical appliances to improve the efficiency of resource use and prevent secondary pollution caused by waste electrical appliances. In terms of green travel, the proportion of travel by private cars accounts for 20.42 percent. Of the private cars, ordinary fuel-powered vehicles account for over 90 percent, while small-displacement vehicles and new energy vehicles are not popular. This works against the control of air pollution in Beijing. However, this is also a potential area for Beijing to promote green consumption. The municipal government needs to make coordinated plans to develop public transport and its supporting facilities to prompt the residents of communities in Beijing, especially newly built large communities such as Wangjing Community, which are far from the urban center, to choose public transport. Moreover, it is necessary to reasonably guide the development of small-displacement vehicles and new energy vehicles.

In terms of the willingness to make green consumption, the respondents show high willingness, but there is a large difference between their willingness and what they do. Overall, in terms of incentives for green consumption, respondents prefer economic policies, particularly subsidy policies, rather than government-mandated policies. Respondents generally believe that communities play a key role in promoting green consumption. Specifically, residents are highly willing to save resources, mainly because of the habits developed from an early age. Easy methods and the implementation of tiered pricing also play a certain promoting role. Regarding the choice of eco-friendly/energy-saving products, economic measures are most favored. Respondents prefer eco-friendly/energy-saving products with government subsidies or with little price differences from similar products. Regarding measures to promote resource and energy saving, respondents tend to agree with trade-in and the establishment of community-level platforms for second-hand products. In terms of waste sorting, economic incentives and subsidies are more popular with residents than mandatory fees. The establishment of community-level recycling stations and recycling by dedicated personnel have also been recognized by many people. In terms of green travel, nearly half of the respondents expressed their willingness to buy small-displacement vehicles and new energy vehicles, but only 11 percent actually bought new energy vehicles. This shows a big difference between what they do and willingness. Public transport plays the greatest role in reducing the use of private cars. Community residents also have a certain demand for community shuttle bus.

Different groups of people perceive green consumption differently. Young and middle-aged people have a slightly higher level of perception of green consumption than the elderly, but the consumption behavior of middle-aged and elderly people better meets the standards of green consumption, whether it be in resource conservation, waste sorting, or travel. There are no obvious differences between people of both sexes regarding the perception, behavior, and awareness of green consumption. The difference between the people with different monthly spending is mainly reflected in the perception of green consumption and green travel. People with high spending are significantly more aware of green consumption than people with low spending, but the travel mode of people with low spending is obviously more eco-friendly than that of people with high spending.

In terms of the implementation of green consumption policies, existing policies on green consumption are rarely popularized and their implementation produce little results. From the perspective of residents' knowledge, the tiered water and electricity pricing policy is the most popularized, followed by energy-saving subsidy policy, small-displacement vehicles and new energy vehicles, and waste sorting policy. From the perspective of results, the energy-saving subsidy policy is highly favored. The tiered water and electricity pricing policy also has a certain promoting effect. The waste sorting policy is not perfect and is not easily operable, and therefore it plays a small role. The effect of subsidy policy for small-displacement vehicles and new energy vehicles leaves a lot to be desired.

#### *5.3.5.2 Summary of results of community comparison*

The difference in the sample demographic and economic status between Bajiaobeili Community and Wangjing Community is mainly reflected in the average age of respondents. Respondents in Bajiaobeili Community are older in age and have slightly lower educational level than those of Wangjing Community. The difference in the average income of respondents in the two communities is small, but the income distribution of residents in Bajiaobeili community is more concentrated, while residents of Wangjing community have a greater income disparity, perhaps due to the fact that Wangjing community comprises five different small communities. From the perspective of geographical location and history, Bajiaobeili community is located in the west, and Wangjing community in the east. The residents of Bajiaobeili community are mostly elderly locals, while Wangjing community has a larger non-local population.

In terms of perception of green consumption, the level of perception of green consumption in the two communities varies slightly. Residents of Wangjing community have a slightly higher level of perception than those of Bajiaobeili community and are more willingness to see the establishment of a green consumption model. In terms of ways of learning about green consumption, television and the Internet are the main media for residents of the two communities to learn about green consumption, but the residents of Wangjing community favor community publicity.

In terms of green consumption behavior, residents of Wangjing community have a slightly higher awareness of waste sorting due to the young average age. However, when it comes to the action of disposing of household waste, garbage sorting is better performed in Bajiaobeili community than in Wangjing community, and residents of Bajiaobeili community also prefer eco-friendly public transport in terms of travel.

In terms of willingness to make green consumption, residents of the two communities exhibit strong willingness to make green consumption. They also prefer economic incentives, but the residents of Bajiaobeili community are more willing to buy small-displacement vehicles and new energy vehicles.

*5.3.5.3 Analysis of influencing factors of survey results*

The factors affecting the results of this survey are mainly:

1 Institutional system. At present, China's institutional system related to green consumption lack laws or policies that stipulate the legal liability of consumers. Therefore, consumers are not required to bear legal responsibility for their action, whether it be in terms of green purchase, waste sorting, or low-carbon travel, and they are rarely affected by the policy. Specifically, the weaknesses of the institutional system include a lack of mandatory policies and the lack of cohesion between policies. Waste sorting cannot be carried out mainly because it is not mandatory. The lack of matching between the subsidy policy for new energy vehicles and other relevant policies and measures also causes unsatisfactory results.
2 Economic policy. The economic policies related to green consumption significantly influence the green consumption behavior of residents. For example, the tiered water and electricity pricing policy has promoted residents to save water and electricity, and the subsidy policy for energy-saving household appliances has greatly boosted residents' willingness to buy energy-saving products. However, the subsidy policy for small-displacement vehicles and new energy vehicles fails to play an incentivizing role. This shows that economic policy can only play a certain role within a certain scope. For technically limited products such as small-displacement vehicles and new energy vehicles, the incentives of subsidy policies cannot compensate the weaknesses of vehicles such as being suitable for long-distance driving and inconvenient charging.
3 Technical support. Regarding the failure of subsidy policy for new energy vehicles, technical hurdle is the primary reason. Due to the insurmountable technical problems of new energy vehicles, it is different from ordinary automobiles in terms of functionality and convenience of use. Heavy government subsidy cannot make up for their own shortcomings. It shows that technical support is a key influencing factor for promoting green consumption (including the promotion of electric vehicles).
4 Operability. In a survey on the willingness to make green consumption, residents spoke of the important role of ease of operation. In terms of the choice of water types, the disposal of waste electronic products and the choice of means of transport, residents generally value the ease of operation and opt for easy-to-operate options. Therefore, making green consumption more operable is an important way to promote green consumption.

#### *5.3.5.4 Conclusions and recommendations*

Field research, questionnaires, and interviews conducted in the two communities reveal the following differences between the two communities:

9 Bajiaobeili Community is an old community independently organized by the residents. It has a full range of supporting facilities and easy access to transport, but its funds are limited, and community activities are mainly organized by residents on their own initiative. Wangjing community adopts the management mode led by the residents' committee, and underdeveloped supporting facilities and public transport support, but the residents' committee has sufficient funds.
10 The residents of Bajiaobeili community are older, mainly local middle-aged people and elderly retirees, with a low spending capacity. The residents of Wangjing community are relatively young, mainly middle-aged and young people and non-local people, with a high spending level.
11 The residents of Bajiaobeili community have a high awareness of conservation and environmental protection and are more engaged in green consumption such as water and electricity saving and green travel and are better aware of green consumption policies. Residents of Wangjing community need to be more aware of green consumption, and they make relatively fewer green consumption.

Therefore, in view of the problems facing Bajiaobeili community, the policies and suggestions for promoting green consumption are proposed below:

12 Establish a team of community volunteers for green consumption. The residents of Bajiaobeili community are mostly retirees, who have abundant time and a high awareness of green consumption. As there is a lack of funds for hiring professionals, a team of volunteers is the best means of publicity and guidance. The volunteer team can proactively participate in community environmental management, organize, and participate in community publicity and education activities, and guide neighbors to become aware of green consumption.
13 Help community residents perform waste sorting at home. In terms of waste sorting, it can adopt the methods of "not setting garbage cans, performing waste sorting at home, and door-to-door sorting and recycling by dedicated personnel" or "garbage cans for sorted waste under the supervision of dedicated personnel." The volunteer team spreads the knowledge of waste sorting and supervises and helps other residents to complete waste sorting at home in accordance with regulations. At the same time, it gradually achieves alignment with the municipal recycling system.
14 Regularly hold publicity lectures on green consumption. Publicity and education activities on green consumption are held regularly in the community, with different themes for each session, including knowledge of environmental protection and energy conservation, publicity of environmental protection policy, and energy conservation tips. It can also cooperate with schools nearby,

and residents serve as keynote speakers. At the same time, a WeChat public account of the community is opened to share green consumption-related knowledge every day, including policy on green consumption, tips on household energy conservation and environmental protection, and identification and promotion of eco-friendly products, etc.

15 Establish community market for second-hand products. A monthly or quarterly second-hand product fair is held in the community. Residents are invited to operate stalls in the place designated by the management committee for trading in second-hand products. The residents of Bajiaobeili community make frugal consumption, with a high demand for second-hand products. Residents can trade second-hand products under the condition that the management committee provides a venue.

In view of the problems facing Wangjing community, the following suggestions are made:

16 Open a WeChat public account of the community. Green consumption-related knowledge is pushed on the WeChat platform every day, including policy on green consumption, tips for household energy conservation and environmental protection, and identification and recommendation of eco-friendly products. The residents of Wangjing community are young, mostly office workers, and have less time to take part in large-scale activities organized by the community. Publicity and promotion through new media such as WeChat are the most effective for them. Of course, based on the current good community work, it is necessary to strengthen publicity and demonstration on green consumption.

17 Establish sorting and recycling stations for waste articles. Because Wangjing community adopts a management model led by the residents' committee, residents pay high property management fees. Therefore, the residents' committee has the financial resources to hire social personnel to perform waste sorting, and residents are not required to perform waste sorting independently. Given sufficient funds, Wangjing community should also establish sorting and recycling stations for waste articles, cooperate with municipal waste removal and transport as well as waste recycling enterprises, and participate in the establishment of a municipal waste and waste recycling system.

18 Provide community shuttle bus services to solve the "last mile" problem. Since Wangjing community is far from the city center, and supporting infrastructure and public transport are underdeveloped, it is necessary to operate community shuttle bus on a regular basis every day. The route of shuttle bus covers nearby metro stations, bus stops, large markets, supermarkets, entertainment center, schools, hospitals, and other large-scale public facilities. The community shuttle bus can run on new energy. At the same time, new energy vehicle rental points can be built in the community for short-distance driving for residents.

19 Improve the supporting infrastructure near the community. For example, community supermarket, school, hospital, and entertainment centers can be established, so that it has equal access to public services under the administrative

jurisdiction of Beijing. This can reduce long-distance trips for residents. In addition, the supporting charging piles in the community will promote the purchase of new energy vehicles. In designing community supporting facilities, it is necessary to encourage community residents to come up with ideas and opinions.

20 Green products and organic food in the community. Wangjing community residents have a high income, making them one of the target consumers of organic food. The community can take the lead in cooperating with organic food producers, so that manufacturers can promote green and organic products in the community. Activities such as organic food tasting and organic farm visits can be held to attract residents to buy organic products. It is also possible to operate organic food counters in shopping malls or to open exclusive stores of green and organic food at appropriate locations in the community.

## Notes

1 Ma Jing, Chen Jining. Concept of building of green community. *Ecological Economy* (Chinese Edition), 2003 (5): 24–27.
2 Guidelines for the building of green communities. http://www.docin.com/p-843753130.html.
3 Assessment standards for green community in Shenzhen. http://www.docin.com/p-1693945845.html.
4 Shenzhen ranks first in China in terms of the number of green communities for building a livable ecological city. *China Environment News*, May 7, 2012.
5 The government subsidizes the replacement of water-saving appliances in Beijing, priority for old communities. www.ce.cn, November 5, 2015.
6 Liu Xi, Li Hui'an, et al. Ideas and practice of water-saving management in Beijing. *City and Town Water Supply*, 2015 (5): 59–62.
7 Liang Lu. *The Effect of Tiered Household Electricity Pricing Policy in Beijing and Coping Strategies*. Beijing: North China Electric Power University, 2013.
8 Zhang Quanyou. Energy-efficient supermarkets lead green consumption. *Energy Conservation and Environmental Protection*, 2015 (4).
9 The data given above refer to data for 2015.

# 6 Outlook of the development of green consumption in China

## 6.1 Problems in China's policy on green consumption

### *6.1.1 Overall framework*

#### *6.1.1.1 Lack of legal and institutional support*

Judging from international experience, developed countries such as the United States, Japan, and Germany promote green consumption based on perfect relevant policies and regulations. In China, the 18th CPC National Congress and the 3rd, 4th, and 5th Plenary Sessions of the 18th CPC Central Committee successively put forward the concept of green development. The Chinese government also regards green consumption as a national strategy. Documents such as the *Opinions of the CPC Central Committee and the State Council on Accelerating the Promotion of Ecological Conservation*, the *Circular of the CPC Central Committee and the State Council on Issuing the "Overall Plan for the Reform of the Ecological Civilization System,"* and the *Guiding Opinions of the State Council on Leveraging the Leading Role of New Consumption and Accelerating the Cultivation of New Supply and New Sources of Growth* set forth the requirements for promoting green consumption, ecological conservation, and green economic and social development. To this end, other government departments including the National Development and Reform Commission jointly issued the *Guiding Opinions on Promoting Green Consumption.* However, green consumption is still in the early stage in China. Despite the system of laws, regulations, and policies governing green consumption, these are not properly enforced. For example, there is a lack of laws for green government procurement; due to a lack of supporting policies, the mandatory sorting of household waste is not effectively implemented; there is a lack of laws as well as inadequate mechanisms to supervise the production and sale of green products; China still lacks the laws, regulations or policy that promote and support green consumption in communities.

#### *6.1.1.2 The system on green government procurement needs to be improved*

Developed countries order or encourage green government procurement in the form of special laws or decrees and have achieved obvious results. In contrast, China

DOI: 10.4324/9781003433040-6

got off to a late start in green government procurement. It was not until 2008 that the *Opinions on the Implementation of Government Procurement of Environmental Label Products* and the *List of Environmental Label Products for Government Procurement* were implemented, which indicates the government's determination to promote green consumption through green procurement. However, the regulations and policies governing government procurement exist in a number of laws, such as the *Government Procurement Law* and the *Law on Promoting Cleaner Production*, and there are also local regulations and policies. Compared with Japan's *Green Procurement Promotion Law*, China still lacks complete and detailed laws on green procurement. Moreover, the list of green government procurement has a limited scope of energy-saving and eco-friendly products. Technical support capacity remains to be improved. Furthermore, the supervision and management mechanism as well as information release mechanism underpinning the green government procurement are imperfect. Regulations exist in paper only, and there is a lack of relevant rules. This undermines the role of green procurement in promoting green consumption.

#### *6.1.1.3 Economic means are not fully exploited*

In developed countries, the green industry is developing at a fast clip, the market share of green products is expanding, and the green concept enjoys popular support. The results are due in large measure to complete policies on green economy. In China, in contrast, economic policy instruments are not turned to good account, and the tax and fiscal policies shall play a greater role in guiding green consumption. At present, China's policies and regulations only stresses curbing illegal acts that damage the environment. It is necessary to tap the great potential of taxation and financial subsidies to regulate the market in order to promote green consumption. Immature green industrial policy, credit policy, product responsibility system, ecological tax policy, etc., slow down the progress of green consumption to a certain extent.

Green tax policies promote green consumption through the following ways: (1) In terms of consumers, tax incentives or tax relief encourage consumers to choose and use green products in the initial stage of promoting green consumption. (2) In terms of producers, the ecological tax is adjusted to reward, punish, or support producers so as to restrict and promote enterprises to engage in green production on their own initiative. Judging by the experience of developed countries, it requires more human, material, and financial resources to produce green products compared with similar ordinary products, because it is necessary to introduce technical personnel and increase funding for technological innovation and equipment upgrading. Accordingly, the state needs to give fiscal subsidies to producers of green products in support of their transformation and upgrading. Therefore, China must do more when it comes to tax policy for green production and green consumption.

#### *6.1.1.4 The role of information means needs to be enhanced*

Consumers are most concerned about the quality of products. In terms of the attention paid to green products, 45.2 percent of consumers value product quality, followed by price and services, which account for 27.1 percent and 16.3 percent, respectively. Only 11 percent of consumers are concerned about whether a product is eco-friendly. Consumer attention to whether a product is convenient ranks bottom. It can be seen that the public have a low level of awareness of green consumption. A survey on the green consumption awareness of community residents in Beijing reveals that Chinese residents have a low level of awareness of green consumption, indicating that the efforts to publicize green consumption are far from enough.

Moreover, according to polls conducted in developed countries, as consumers' environmental awareness increases, the majority of consumers are willing to pay at a premium for a clean environment, most of whom are willing to buy products with an ecolabel. A study entitled "Environmental Labeling and Product Management in Green Europe" conducted by the German Environmental News and Data Services (ENDS) in 2004 reveals that environmental labeling raises environmental awareness among consumers and prompts them to choose eco-friendly products. At present, Chinese consumers have a low level of perception and recognition of environmental labeling products and green foods, due to financial reasons and a lack of trust in quality and brand. Therefore, China needs to step up efforts to guide and supervise environmental labeling products and green foods, increase the market penetration and share of ecolabel products and green food, promote the supply-side reform through consumers, and bring about the upgrading and transformation of green production and green consumption.

In addition, leadership, management, supervision, and evaluation by specialized agencies are needed to effectively promote green consumption. Judging from the success stories of various countries in promoting green consumption, most developed countries have set up special agencies independently or under the environmental protection department to foster green consumption. In China, in contrast, only the Ministry of Ecology and Environment is an independent agency that enforces environmental law, and its overall capacity to manage environmental issues in an all-round way is inadequate. Green consumption is a key aspect of sustainable development and also an issue that involves multiple parties. If we rely on the work tasks and authority of the Ministry of Ecology and Environment alone, it is difficult to coordinate across ministries and departments and to ensure that green consumption policies yield good results.

### *6.1.2 Community level*

#### *6.1.2.1 Residents lack an awareness of green consumption*

Without a doubt, consumer awareness and consumption concept are key factors affecting consumer behavior, and even affect consumption expectations to a certain extent. Green consumption awareness primarily refers to the concept of green, rational, moderate, low-carbon, and culturally advanced consumption established in the process of consumption. At present, the deteriorating living environment has awakened residents to the hazards of the harsh environment. The rapidly developing new media provides information technology support for enhancing residents' environmental protection concept. As the questionnaire results show, most residents are aware of the drawbacks of the current consumption model and are in favor of establishing a green consumption model. However, the residents' perception of green consumption is not optimistic. Only half of the respondents heard of green consumption and have a low level of perception of green consumption behavior. The reasons for this are as follows: (1) Foreign consumerist ideas penetrate into China. Some residents define identity based on the grade of goods and services. As a result, the consumption pattern is gradually characterized by waste, which destroys the harmonious relationship between man and nature to a certain extent and leads to unsustainable economic development. (2) Being hardworking and thrifty are traditional virtues of the Chinese people, and contribute to a social culture of resource conservation. However, when productive forces are highly developed today, excessive economization will lead to insufficient consumption and slow down economic development. This is also a pattern of unsustainable consumption. The residents' lack of awareness of green consumption highlights the necessity and importance of promoting environmental education in China.

#### *6.1.2.2 Lack of public facilities and community management*

The Chinese government has not clearly defined the role and status of the communities as social governance units in implementing sustainable consumption policies at the social level and guiding and regulating residents' consumption behavior. Communities lack specialized agencies and personnel who can undertake this work. There is a lack of system and institutional guarantee to promote sustainable consumption in communities.

At present, community improvement is underway in Beijing. The community-based organization model not only brings convenience to residents but also offers a favorable platform for implementing public policies at the community level. However, when the community is the most basic unit of public administration, the management system and infrastructure are inadequate. Moreover, community workers are rarely aware of sustainable consumption. Raising awareness of sustainable consumption is crucial for putting sustainable consumption into practice in Chinese communities. This also shows the need for communities to mobilize community workers, members of residents' committees, etc., to implement capacity building for sustainable consumption in the field of sustainable consumption.

As far as the communities mentioned herein are concerned, there are obvious problems in waste recycling and disposal:

(1) The sorting signs of garbage cans are not clearly affixed. Most of these lack the sorting signs for kitchen waste. Even if residents classify waste into recyclable and non-recyclable waste, municipal sanitation department disposes of the sorted waste in a mixed way. Community waste sorting supervisors fail in their duty. (2) The communities lack recycling transfer stations for recycling large-scale waste such as waste electrical appliances, and there is a lack of facilities to guide residents' green consumption behavior. (3) Residents have no support because the

communities lack personnel who are responsible for waste sorting, and the management system is imperfect, reducing residents' enthusiasm for practicing green consumption. (4) Community and municipal waste removal and transportation are not linked to junk recycling and treatment enterprises. Residents perform waste sorting at home, but the municipal sanitation department transports waste in a mixed way. Residents are unable to engage recycling services for waste articles, while waste recycling and treatment enterprises cannot find customers.

## 6.2 Policy proposal for promoting green consumption in China

Given China's reality and the survey results of communities in Beijing, it requires the guidance of the government and the efforts of many parties to take combination measures to promote green consumption in China. The government makes overall and top-level planning and policy, establish sound laws, regulations, policies, and technical standards, and improve the green procurement system. Economic and information means in terms of resources and environment are integrated. Production enterprises and community residents work together to create a market-led green product market. At the same time, the community should promote the concept of green consumption among residents and promote residents to play a main role in making green consumption. Based on the above idea, this section makes policy proposal for promoting green consumption in terms of top-level planning and concerted efforts.

### *6.2.1 Top-level and overall planning*

#### *6.2.1.1 Formulate an overall strategy for green consumption*

Although the State Council proposes and advocates eco-friendly consumption pattern and the establishment of green consumption and production models, the concept of green consumption is not manifested in decision-making at all levels. There is also a lack of specific strategic goals and action plan for green consumption at the national level. The existing green consumption rules in Beijing are imperfect because of a lack of mandatory and operable nature, as well as a lack of articulation of policies.

Therefore, on the basis of the existing policies that promote green consumption, the Chinese government should construct an institutional framework for promoting green consumption, include green consumption into relevant laws, and make clear the legal binding nature of green consumption as well as the responsibilities and obligations of all stakeholders. While promoting the establishment of the green consumption policy, attention shall be paid to the following issues: (1) The concept of product life cycle is applied to the design of the policy system throughout. The relevant laws and regulations should take into account the resource and environmental problems that may occur in various stages of the product life cycle; (2) Specific and feasible management measures should be taken on the basis of drawing on the views of all stakeholders, such as governments, communities, and consumers;

(3) Equal emphasis is put on mandatory means and market instruments. Economic means and voluntary tools should play an important role in guiding consumption behavior in the process of resource and environmental management. In addition, China should establish a sound all-round management system for green products, tighten the supervision of green product production throughout, regulate the conduct of manufacturers at the production end, and create a good market environment for green products to provide consumers with reliable green products. Finally, top-level and overall planning are carried out through the formulation of a national strategic plan for promoting green consumption.

#### *6.2.1.2 Improve and implement the green government procurement system*

Green government procurement plays an increasingly important role in promoting green consumption and building a resource-conserving and environment-friendly society. The *Opinions on the Implementation of Government Procurement of Environmental Label Products* and the *List of Environmental Label Products for Government Procurement* were introduced and implemented in 2008, and China's green procurement website (cgpn.org.cn) was established simultaneously. However, green government procurement still faces problems such as flawed evaluation and supervision mechanism and a lack of relevant rules.

In order to improve and implement the green government procurement system, the Chinese government shall first promulgate the law on green government procurement at an appropriate time to define the government's mainstay role and responsibility in green procurement. At the same time, supporting policies should be adopted to ensure that green procurement standards and lists are issued or updated. Second, the government should use indicators of green procurement, green production, green marketing, and green consumption as key indicators for appraising the performance of government officials, disclose information on green procurement, improve the supervision mechanism, link it to the performance assessment system, and tighten management. Finally, while integrating the existing green procurement network, the government must establish a dedicated green consumption network, covering information on green procurement, green industry planning, downloads of text of laws and regulations, and publicity of green consumption. Of course, it is also highly necessary to step up technical support for the green government procurement. The relevant government departments should tighten the management of green labels, ensure the high caliber of certification, and carry out international certification of green labels; speed up the formulation and revision of standards on environmental labeling product certification; and extend the scope of procurement from goods to services and projects. In the field of certification of environmental labeling products, it is necessary to launch the certification of type II and III environmental labels. In the field of engineering, it is necessary to strengthen green planning and green design for government, manufacturers and design units, green manufacturing for material suppliers, and green construction for manufacturers. At the same time, a full range of economic means, including price subsidy, fiscal subsidies, and tax policies, are used to support green procurement and promote green consumption.

#### *6.2.1.3 Use a variety of economic means to encourage green consumption*

Given China's immature green consumption market, profit-oriented producers will not invest in the R&D and production of green products on a large scale. Moreover, in view of the current chaotic green consumption market, consumers will not extensively buy green products with higher prices. Therefore, the government should employ various economic means to improve the market and promote green consumption.

In the case of fiscal and taxation policy, green fiscal and taxation reform is implemented to raise the tax rate of major resource taxes. On the basis of levying environmental protection taxes, we can consider introducing carbon emission taxes, adjust taxes, and move faster to improve the system of compensation for use of resources and for damage caused to the ecological environment. The central and local governments should have a full, objective, and rational understanding of green consumption and implement fiscal and tax policies in due course to promote green consumption. In this regard, China can draw on the experience of Organisation for Economic Co-operation and Development (OECD) member states in levying environmental taxes and strengthening environmental protection through consumption taxes.

In terms of investment and financing in green consumption, policies are used to diversify investment entities, tap the potential market for green consumption, and make investment more effective, thereby promoting green consumption. A national green consumption fund is established under the management of the Ministry of Finance and the Ministry of Ecology and Environment. It is used for the formulation and revision of laws, regulations, policies, and technical standards governing green consumption, for the R&D of key green consumption projects, and for the promotion of demonstration circular economy and green consumption. In terms of financial credit, the limit, term, and even interest rate of loans to producers of green products can be appropriately relaxed. The fund can be used in the forms such as funding grants, low-interest loan, and loans with discounted interest, depending on the nature of projects.

#### *6.2.1.4 Explore the use of information means to promote green consumption*

Attention shall be paid to the use of modern media to publicize green consumption and raise the public awareness of green consumption. In order to raise the public awareness of environmental protection, develop a concept of green consumption, and promote green consumption, we should increase the content of environmental protection and green consumption in the national education system step by step, and spread the idea of green consumption.

While increasing publicity and education, we should do so in a targeted manner for better results. Attention should be paid to education for women about consumption, because women play a main role in household consumption and children's education on consumption. For farmers, information on ecological agriculture, green food, etc., should be publicized. For public servants, it is necessary to increase green government procurement, promote green office, etc. For middle-income people, we can make green consumption a fashion statement and encourage eco-friendly housing, cars, etc. For high-income groups, we should publicize rational consumption, encourage them to undertake the responsibility of leading the trend of green consumption, and reduce conspicuous consumption. The government can commend enterprises and individuals who perform well in promoting green consumption, create an exemplary image, and encourage more consumers and producers to learn from role models.

It is necessary to strengthen the position and role of the community in the publicity of environmental protection and green consumption. The survey on green consumption in communities in Beijing reveals that the community plays an irreplaceable role in raising residents' awareness of green consumption and guiding green consumption. Therefore, communities need to hold green consumption publicity and education of all descriptions, including community lectures, community bulletin boards, opening WeChat public account for green consumption publicity, and launching community demonstration projects. It is necessary to set up a social action system in which all people participate on their own initiative, promote ecological conservation, advocate green culture, and raise public awareness of green consumption. It is necessary to open up effective channels for information release, so that green consumption gradually becomes the cultural concept and the people's conscious action, providing an inexhaustible impetus for sustainable development.

In addition, it is necessary to establish specialized agencies or vest existing institutions with green consumption management responsibilities to manage, coordinate, and supervise the implementation of green consumption; enforce and supervise laws on green consumption, maintain the consistent policies on consumption, environment, society, etc., promote the intergovernmental synergy, and maximize the effectiveness of policy tools.

### *6.2.2 Concerted efforts*

#### *6.2.2.1 Improve the green product regulatory system and guide correct green production and consumption*

In view of the imperfect regulatory policy system for green products, the imbalance of demand and supply of green products, the shortage of some green products, high prices of products, and other problems, it is necessary to first comprehensively regulate the green product market and establish sound laws and regulations on the administration of green products. Second, it is necessary to perfect the standard system for green products and regulate the market access of green products. Third, it is necessary to give full play to the role of regulatory authorities and third-party supervision agencies to ensure the quality of green products. Finally, it is necessary to strictly control the issuance and use of energy conservation and green labels, prevent the abuse of labels, and improve the credibility of green products in the eyes of consumers. Regarding the issue of high prices, the government should provide green manufacturers with certain financial subsidies and technical support, encourage technological innovation, lower the production cost of green products by means of technology, motivate green manufacturers, and properly regulate products with inflated prices. Moreover, the government should utilize the price mechanism to restrict the production of energy-intensive and highly polluting products, and restrict the exploitation and utilization of non-renewable resources and scarce resources. The prices of disposable products can be increased through taxation and extra fees and the use of disposable products can be restricted.

Regarding the promotion of green products, green producers can cooperate with residents' committees in order to use community-related media to market green products, which is a highly effective method. Specific marketing model of green products can be taken into account: (1) Introduce green products to the community. Introduce green products to the community every month, set up special green product stalls in the community, and sell them in the form of trade-in. (2) Communities organize day trips to organic farms. Organizing day trips to organic farms by communities can increase residents' trust in suppliers. On day trips, residents can see and taste organic food on the spot, which is more effective than marketing means such as advertising. (3) Centralized distribution of green products in the community. Green product suppliers can directly cooperate with communities and distribute products in a centralized manner to cooperative communities, which solve the problems such as few sales outlets and the inconvenience to buy green products. (4) Launch community experience activities for green products, such as trial tasting of organic food and the use of green products. In terms of community publicity, communities where the target customers are concentrated are selected according to categories of communities. Compared with mass media such as television and the Internet, community marketing is more targeted.

#### *6.2.2.2 Highlight the responsibilities of all parties in waste sorting and establish a sound recycling system*

Promoting waste sorting and recycling is an important move to promote green consumption. Given the current problems in the field of waste sorting, such as lack of mandatory policy, slow updating of policies, and imperfect policy system, breakthroughs need to be made in the following areas: (1) Legislate for the source of waste sorting, amend relevant laws such as the *Circular Economy Promotion Law*, raise the responsibility of communities and residents to perform the sorting and disposal of household waste, and compel residents to sort waste; (2) Improve the waste sorting management system and set feasible waste sorting goals and management rules, including unified planning of community waste sorting and municipal waste cleaning system, and cooperation with waste recycling and treatment enterprises; (3) Strengthen the extended responsibility of producers, use plans and policies to guide the engagement of resource recycling enterprises for community waste sorting and recycling, and encourage all enterprises to launch trade-in, packaging recycling, and other businesses in the community.

A perfect management system for urban waste sorting, recycling, and removal should have the following characteristics: (1) The institutional arrangement of the front-end source reduction and sorting should better reflect the government's management capability and the mandatory policy; (2) The end-of-pipe treatment link should give institutional incentives to the venous industry; (3) The mid-end recycling system emphasizes the role of the community and establishes community sorting and recycling stations. Garbage cans for sorted waste should be set up in the community. The community management should designate personnel to be responsible for waste sorting affairs, so that waste sorting becomes one of the indicators of community appraisal. The leading role of the community in waste sorting and recycling should be strengthened. On the basis of waste sorting by community residents, detailed management rules and supporting regulations should be formulated to ensure the consistency of the community waste sorting methods and the municipal waste cleaning, transport, and recycling methods. This achieves the seamless connection between community waste sorting, municipal waste collection, and the resource recycling by enterprises.

#### *6.2.2.3 Improve the technology of new energy vehicles and supporting facilities*

The results of empirical analysis reveal that the few functions of new energy vehicles and a lack of supporting facilities are the principal reasons for sluggish demand. At present, China's promotion policy on new energy vehicles is mainly focused on consumers, and the subsidies are mainly targeted at consumers. The subsidies are high but the effects are poor. With the withdrawal of purchase subsidies, the role of economic incentives will gradually diminish. As a result, the policy should focus on vigorously developing new energy vehicle technology. Financial subsidies, establishment of scientific research funds, etc., are employed to encourage manufacturers to vigorously develop technologies of charging, battery duration, etc., and promote technological innovation, so as to make new energy vehicles more competitive. Although electric vehicles vigorously promoted in China are not at an advantage in terms of speed and convenience, the fact that the batteries are always connected to the internet make electric vehicles the best tool for realizing intelligent connected vehicles. Therefore, becoming intelligent cars and connected cars is another way forward for electric vehicles.

In order to increase charging facilities at the community level, the residents' committee can rationally increase the number of charging facilities according to the geographical location of the community, the layout of buildings, and the distribution of electric vehicle owners, and maintain and update the charging piles on a regular basis. Mobile Internet has played a tremendous role in easing traffic pressure and advocating green travel. Governments can issue "smart community" policies and build intelligent networks in the communities, such as: (1) Draw an electronic map of charging piles in communities, release information on the occupation and maintenance of charging piles, and facilitate charging for residents; (2) Release information on traffic around the community in real time, including road congestion, stations of public transport such as subway and bus as well as arrivals timetable; (3) Release information on community shuttle bus routes, departure time, departure frequency, etc., in real time and improve the utilization and user experience of shuttle bus.

#### *6.2.2.4 Leverage the role of community education and demonstration in green consumption*

China has been publicizing the concept and connotations of green consumption and its related knowledge, and information on waste sorting, energy-saving, and eco-friendly products, new energy vehicles, environmental labels, and so on through a variety of channels. However, community residents are rarely aware of these. It is urgent to increase publicity and education on green consumption policies. The survey results reveal that different groups of people learn about green consumption through different channels. Therefore, in its future publicity and education activities, Beijing should differentiate between different media and audiences, so that media publicity is more targeted. Publicity targeted at middle-aged and elderly people shall be held through television broadcasting, while online media is mainly used for young people.

It is essential to leverage the important role of the community in connecting residents and the government and to increase the publicity of green consumption in communities. The focus of community-level publicity of green consumption should be on the young and middle-aged groups, who have strong spending power and a high demand for creature comforts. They are the main users of WeChat and Weibo platforms. Therefore, communities can open dedicated WeChat public accounts and Weibo accounts to promote environmental protection activities in the community and spread the concept of green consumption. For elderly people, the community can organize colorful public welfare environmental protection activities, such as community lecture halls and community flea markets, etc. In addition, it is necessary to take into account the international experience in green consumption and the key knowledge about green consumption, such as Beijing local standards on waste sorting. Key publicity and education are carried out by means of the distribution of paper publicity materials, community blackboard newspapers, classroom education for primary and secondary school students, etc., so that green consumption becomes part of everyday life for consumers.

An evaluation index system of community green consumption model is established to foster the awareness and concept of green consumption at the community level, guide the establishment of green communities, explore models of green consumption in the community, and enable residents to realize and exercise their rights and responsibilities relating to environmental protection. As a result of cooperation between governments, NGOs, the public, and even enterprises, green consumption is incorporated into government decision-making and community management, and a community-level public participation mechanism is established. Green community and green consumption model in the community can be piloted in communities where conditions permit. The standards and evaluation index system for green communities and green consumption model can be improved through the pilot program. It is necessary to comprehensively promote the practice of green consumption among residents, advocate the building of livable and healthy green communities, and popularize green consumption in communities.

## 6.3 China's strategic planning framework for promoting green consumption

In conjunction with the international experience in green consumption and China's actual green consumption, and based on the aforesaid policy proposal, this section discusses the overall plan for promoting green consumption in China, form green consumption principles of "conservation, environmental protection and renewable nature," and establish a planning framework for green consumption led by China's administrative organs in light of actual needs. It mainly includes three areas: objectives, control measures, and mechanisms:

The first is the objective of green consumption. (1) Protect the health and safety of consumers. This is the primary requirement for promoting green consumption. Products produced meet the needs of people's working and living and also protect people's health and safety. (2) Ensure moderate production and consumption. This is required of sustainable development and the development of circular economy and is also the focus of green consumption. Green consumption mode is used to guide moderate consumption and affect the moderation of production, thereby achieving the purpose of resource conservation. (3) Ensure fairness and sustainability. Green consumption should lead to the rational allocation of social resources as well as the equal intergenerational enjoyment of resources.

The second is the control measures for green consumption. (1) Strengthen the principal responsibility of administrative organs. A comprehensive administrative assessment system of green consumption is established to evaluate the government's green consumption in regional economic development and promote the government's leading role in promoting green consumption. (2) The government should put in more energy, human resources, material, and financial resources to publicize green consumption, raise the awareness of green consumption among the public and enterprises, and boost green consumption in society as a whole. (3) Formulate standards for mandatory green consumption. Environmental protection authorities should draw up specific rules according to the green production and consumption standards in different industries, so that corporate production and individual consumption behavior are standardized and the green consumption objective is achieved.

The third is the formation of a mechanism for green consumption. Green consumption requires the sufficient support of the state. In terms of implementation, complete mechanisms should be put in place to ensure the realization of green consumption objective. (1) Establish a system of Chinese laws and regulations on green consumption. (2) Establish a special institution or vest existing institutions with functions for managing green consumption, which is responsible for managing and promoting green consumption from top to bottom. (3) Further regulate the green government procurement. The government should strictly follow the standards on green consumption and play an exemplary role. (4) Promote green consumption by means of industrial policies, fiscal and taxation and credit policies, and other favorable policies in resource allocation. (5) Use modern information technology to facilitate the transmission of information on green consumption and green products and enhance awareness and concept of green consumption among consumers. The public supervision of green products is enhanced through information disclosure, and the publicity and government oversight of green products are increased. (6) Strengthen the publicity of green consumption. The national competent education department incorporates environmental education (mainly ecological conservation and sustainable consumption-related education) into the quality education of primary and secondary schools as well as the quality education curriculum of higher education. At the same time, it is necessary to publicize green consumption in the community. Community education spreads green consumption in the community, so that the concept of green consumption is embraced by all households in the community. (7) The capacity building of green consumption. We can carry out international cooperation and draw on the international experience in sustainable consumption or establish special research centers for green consumption at universities and social groups with a research foundation to help government agencies undertake research into green consumption-related projects on a larger scale in the future, impart green consumption-related knowledge to community workers, and hold training on management capacity building. It is also possible to provide theoretical and technical support for the government to draw up policies on green consumption. Overall, it is necessary to take all-round, multi-tiered measures in all fields to promote green consumption, guide and drive the transformation and upgrading of supply-side green production, and then realize green development in all respects.

# References


All-China Environment Federation, Jin Min. Survey on Sustainable Consumption Awareness among Community Households in Beijing and Policy Advocacy Project (Green Community Sustainable Consumption Project, SSFA/2014/CPL-2788-3FEE-1161-), 2016.

Beijing Energy Conservation and Environmental Protection Center, China Household Electric Appliance Research Institute. 2016 Beijing Green Consumption Development Report, 2016.

Cao Mingdi. The 13th Five-Year Plan period: Let green development be a new driving force for economic growth. http://opinion.china.com.cn/opinion_71_145271.html.

Chen Yajun. Energy conservation and environmental protection: A realistic and eternal topic: Interpretation of the U.S. *Energy Policy Act of 2005. China Inspection and Quarantine*, 2006 (10): 39.

China Association for Science and Technology and People's Government of Henan Province. Proceedings of the 10th Annual Conference of China Association for Science and Technology (II), China Association for Science and Technology, 2008.

European Commission (EC). Sustainable public procurement in EU Member States: Overview of government initiatives and selected cases. Final Report to the EU High-level Group on CSR, 2007.

Ge Wangqi, Shao Dan, et al. The impact of short-time car leasing on the development of passenger cars in Shanghai. Proceedings of the 2017 China Urban Transport Planning Annual Conference, China Architecture & Building Press, 2017, 2962–2973.

Green Studio. *Green Consumption*. Beijing: The Ethnic Publishing House, 1999.

Guo Dandan. *Research on Green Consumption Issues in the Context of Scientific Outlook on Development*. Jinan: Qilu University of Technology, 2013.

Hu Ye. *Research on the German Environmental Labeling System*. Changsha: Hunan Normal University, 2010.

Jiang Hong. Green consumption: Drive green production through green demand. *Environmental Economy*, 2007 (1): 16–19.

Julia Hailes. *The New Green Consumer Guide*. New York: Simon & Schuster Ltd., 2007.

Li Shiyan, Lu Jiayin. The history of Chinese ecological philosophy theory. *Journal of Nanjing Forestry University (Humanities and Social Sciences Edition)*, 2016 (1): 32–42.

Li Wenying, Wang Guohong, Wu Chunyou. Research on the obstacles to and countermeasures for the promotion of green consumption in China. *Journal of Liaoning Normal University (Social Science Edition)*, 2004 (1): 31–34.

Li Ying, Liu Ben. A review of ecological consumption studies in China. *Commercial Times*, 2010 (8): 23–24.

Liang Lu. *The Effect of Tiered Household Electricity Pricing Policy in Beijing and Coping Strategies*. Beijing: North China Electric Power University, 2013.
Liu Xi, Li Hui'an, et al. Ideas and practice of water-saving management in Beijing. *City and Town Water Supply*, 2015 (5).
Ma Zhong, Lan Hong. Performance analysis of environmental taxes imposed on consumers under poverty constraints. *Fudan Journal (Social Sciences Edition)*, 2005 (2): 53–59.
Su Hang, Sun Jian. The role of fiscal policy in Japan's low-carbon economic development. *Journal of Dongbei University of Finance and Economics*, 2010 (6): 61–65.
The government subsidizes the replacement of water-saving appliances in Beijing, priority for old communities. www.ce.cn, November 5, 2015.
UNEP. Global outlook on sustainable consumption and production policies: Taking action together, 2012.
UNEP. SCP Indicator for developing countries: A guidance framework, 2008.
Wang Conghu, Wang Xiaopeng. Government procurement should play a part in the full implementation of supply-side reform. www.ccgp.gov.cn, April 08, 2016.
Wu Hongyan. *Research on Green Consumption Issues in China*. Changchun: Northeast Normal University, 2008.
Wu Min. *Research on the Ecology of Industrial Structure in Wuhan Urban Circle*. Wu Han: Wuhan University of Technology, 2009.
Yang Yan. Foreign ecolabels. *China Environmental Protection Industry*, 2003 (8): 37–39.
Yin Xiaoliang, Ping Liqun. What can we learn from Japan's "Environmental Protection Points System"? *Environmental Protection*, 2009 (17): 75–76.
Zhang Lu, Shuai Chuanmin, Liu Yang. Analysis of psychological attribution of consumers' green consumption behavior and intervention strategy: An empirical study based on theory of planned behavior and situational experimental data. *Journal of China University of Geosciences (Social Sciences Edition)*, 2013, 13 (5): 49–55 + 139.
Zhang Quanyou. Energy-efficient supermarkets lead green consumption. *Energy Conservation and Environmental Protection*, 2015 (4): 38.
Zhou Huawei, Shen Weixiong. Exploring the origins of community engagement theory. *Value Engineering*, 2013 (30): 326–328.
Zhou Meihua, *Research on Sustainable Consumption Theory*. Xuzhou: China University of Mining and Technology Press, 2003.
Zhu Qinghua, Guo Yaru. An empirical study on the influencing factors and behavior of sustainable consumption. *China Population Resources and Environment*, 2011 (S2). 6,000 pure electric passenger cars for short-time leasing in 2016. www.news.cn, December 17, 2015.

# Index

FSC
www.fsc.org
MIX
Papier | Fördert gute Waldnutzung
FSC® C083411

Kolibri 360 GmbH
Ferdinand-Jühlke-Straße 7
99095 Erfurt, Deutschland
produktsicherheit@kolibri360.de